GENDER, EXPERIENCE, AND KNOWLEDGE IN ADULT LEARNING

In this wide-ranging book, Elana Michelson invites us to revisit basic understandings of the 'experiential learner'. How does experience come to be seen as the basis of knowledge? How do gender, class, and race enter into the ways in which knowledge is valued? What political and cultural belief systems underlie such practices as the assessment of prior learning and the writing of life narratives?

Drawing on a range of disciplines, from feminist theory and the politics of knowledge to literary criticism, Michelson argues that particular understandings of 'experiential learning' have been central to modern Western cultures and the power relationships that underlie them. Presented in four parts, this challenging and lively book asks educators of adults to think in new ways about their assumptions, theories, and practices:

- **Part I** provides readers with a short history of the notion of experiential learning.
- **Part II** brings the insights and concerns of feminist theory to bear on mainstream theories of experiential learning.
- **Part III** examines the assessment of prior experiential learning for academic credit and/or professional credentials.
- **Part IV** addresses a second pedagogical practice that is ubiquitous in adult learning, namely, the assigning of life narratives.

Gender, Experience, and Knowledge in Adult Learning will be of value to scholars and graduate students exploring adult and experiential learning, as well as academics wishing to introduce students to a broad range of feminist, critical-race, materialist and postmodernist thinking in the field.

Elana Michelson is Professor of Liberal Studies and Adult Learning at Empire State College, University of New York.

First published 2015
by Routledge
2 Park Square, Milton Park, Abingdon, Oxon OX14 4RN

and by Routledge
711 Third Avenue, New York, NY 10017

Routledge is an imprint of the Taylor & Francis Group, an informa business

British Library Cataloguing in Publication Data
A catalogue record for this book is available from the British Library

Library of Congress Cataloging in Publication Data
Michelson, Elana, 1949-
Gender, experience, and knowledge in adult learning : Alisoun's daughters / Elana Michelson.
pages cm
Includes bibliographical references and index.
ISBN 978-1-138-89216-3 (hardback) -- ISBN 978-1-138-89217-0 (pbk.) -- ISBN 978-1-315-70929-1 (ebook) 1. Experiential learning--Social aspects. 2. Adult learning--Social aspects. 3. Feminist theory. I. Title.
BF318.5.M54 2015
153.1'5--dc23
2014042659

ISBN: 978-1-138-89216-3 (hbk)
ISBN: 978-1-138-89217-0 (pbk)
ISBN: 978-1-315-70929-1 (ebk)

Typeset in Bembo
by Saxon Graphics Ltd, Derby

To Penny, beloved pilgrim

CONTENTS

LIST OF FIGURES

ACKNOWLEDGEMENTS

This book is the product of many years of writing, thinking, reading, and talking, and I am profoundly indebted to the friends and colleagues who have added to my knowledge, critiqued my work, and challenged me to think differently and more deeply. They constitute a long list, and there is no naming them all. Special thanks, however, are due for many long, rich conversations with Judy Harris, Diane Hill, Banakonda Kennedy-Kish Bell, Cathy Leaker, Alan Mandell, Helen Peters, David Starr-Glass, Alan Tait, and Jane Thompson. Their intelligence and wisdom are reflected on every page, though the errors are surely mine. I am equally indebted to my South African friends and comrades, Mignonne Breier, Linda Cooper, Daryl MacLean, Kessie Moodley, Enver Motala, Ruksana Osman, Lynn Slonimsky, Alan Ralphs, and Shirley Walters, whose struggles to honor experiential learning in the service of social justice have taught me so much.

Many thanks to Philip Mudd, Natasha Ellis-Knight and Natalie Larkin at Routledge for their support, responsiveness, and warm professionalism. And a special thanks to Tara Fenwick and Richard Edwards for reminding me to get this book done already and to Clive Millar for being such a gentle sceptic.

A mere 'thank you' does not suffice for what I owe my partner, Penny Coleman, whose loving heart made this book possible and whose exacting eye made it better. And a final thanks for their love and enthusiasm to the three young people in my life, Charlie Wittenberg, Sophie Wittenberg, and Yaelle Stempfelet. The world is a more hopeful place because they are in it.

Chapter five was originally published as "The Body in Question," *All About Mentoring* (43), 2013.

An early version of the example of Mary in Chapter six was published in "Remembering: The Return of the Body to Experiential Learning." *Studies in Continuing Education*, Vol. 20, No. 2, 1998.

Sections of Chapter seven were originally published in the Introduction to Michelson and Mandell, *Portfolio Development and the Assessment of Prior Learning*. Sterling, VA: Stylus, 2004.

Chapter eight was originally published as "Inside/Out: A Meditation on Cross-Dressing and Prior Learning Assessment." *Prior Learning Assessment Inside Out* Vol. 1, No. 1 2012.

Chapter ten was originally published as "Autobiography and Selfhood in the Practice of Adult Learning." *Adult Education Quarterly*. Vol. 6, No. 1, 2011.

Chapter eleven was originally published as "If the Self is a Text, What Genre Is It?: Structure and ideology in narratives of adult learning. *Adult Education Quarterly* Vol. 63, No. 3, 2013.

INTRODUCTION

Experience, though noon auctoritee
Were in this world, is right ynogh for me
To speke. …

[Experience, though no authority were in this world,
is sufficient grounds for me to speak.]

Geoffrey Chaucer, *The Canterbury Tales*, III 1–3[1]

Wanderynge by the weye

The Tabard Inn in Southwark, England, may seem an odd place from which to begin a book on experiential learning. It is the spot from which, in the final years of the fourteenth century, Geoffrey Chaucer conjured a "compaignye of sondry folk" (I 24–25) and sent them on a pilgrimage to Canterbury Cathedral. To be sure, *The Canterbury Tales* are filled with very un-adult-learning-type pilgrims: self-important magistrates and scholars, hypocritical clerics, and bawdy yeomen. Yet this book is named for one of those pilgrims, a middle-aged cloth manufacturer named Alisoun whose favorite activities are sex, gossip, travel, and self-justification.

From the point of view of medieval Christian doctrine, Alisoun, better known as the Wife of Bath, is utterly outrageous. She has been married five times and grown wealthy trading marital favors for control over her husbands' businesses. She lies when it suits her, treats pilgrimages as a pleasant form of packaged tourism, and happily excuses her sexuality on the grounds that "Venus me yaf [gave] my lust" (III 611). Yet she has no hesitation in challenging venerable textual authorities on the grounds that her life has taught her to know better than such preeminent authorities as St. Paul and St. Jerome.

As a medieval set piece, Dame Alisoun is the incarnation of the long tradition of patristic and clerical denunciations of women: garrulous, greedy, scolding, hungry for both money and pleasure, and happy to fight the war between the sexes using either seductiveness or talk. At the same time, as a member of the new middle-classes, she has rights of property, ownership, and contracts that had become commonplace among the bourgeoisie, but that were denied to women in medieval common and canon law (Carruthers, 1979). As a woman claiming agency in a highly gendered game of power, as a commodities manufacturer among the feudal estates, and as a loudly opinionated layperson in an environment still dominated by the Church, Alisoun of Bath is a transitional figure. She is both a medieval cliché and, in effect, English literature's first modern. And the first word she utters in *The Canterbury Tales* is "experience."

One of the things this book is about is the invention of 'experience' as a foundational move in the emergence of the modern subject. That is, it is about how the claim that we can 'learn from experience' has played out historically within the material and discursive structures through which knowledge and power have been adjudicated in the modern world. In what follows, I will take the position that how we 'learn from experience' is not simply a question of cognitive theory or theories of adult learning. Rather, it is a question of understanding the forms of personhood enabled and required by liberal capitalist societies and thus a question of culture and politics. Experiential learning, to use Foucault's helpful phrase, is a technology of the self. That is, it is a way both of constructing a particular kind of selfhood and of deploying that self in the world.

In calling experience an invention, I do not mean to deny that human beings have always and everywhere received information from the senses, processed that information in a variety of ways, and solved problems and made choices on that basis. Nor do I wish to deny that human societies have long told stories about the interaction between the person and the world. But 'experience' as such is the product of a particular social and intellectual moment that is personified by Alisoun of Bath. In contrasting experience and "auctoritee," that is, in insisting that her own life provides an alternative and corrective to the authoritative texts of Christian doctrine, Alisoun represents a particular historical moment in which forms of traditional textual authority are being met with a crisis of legitimacy. Alisoun is speaking – or, rather, Chaucer is writing – during a period that was marked by rebellions against both religious and civil authorities: the Wycliffe movement, Lollardy, the Great Schism, the Peasants' Revolt, and the depositions of Edward II and Richard II.

Most notably, Alisoun's invective against patristic authority comes at a time in which the Church's monopoly on doctrinal interpretation was already being threatened by increasing lay literacy, fed in part by the Wycliffe movement for vernacular translation of the Bible. It was, Wycliffe claimed, no longer "inowgth to the to beleuen as holychurche techeth the and lat the clerkes alone with the arguments" [enough for you to believe as Holy Church teaches you and leave the clerics to debate among themselves] (as cited in Grudin, 2000, p. 211).

Rather, common sense, plain speaking, and the use of the senses would keep people from a too-gullible acceptance of official beliefs. By translating the Bible into English, the Wycliffites opened the gates of interpretation to unauthorized – or, rather, self-authorized – laypeople whose previous function had been only to obey (Knapp, 1990). As knowledge moved out of the closed interpretive community of the Church to a public marketplace of ideas, it became possible to insist, as Alisoun does, that the production, dissemination, and uses of knowledge are the result of human, not divine, agency (Galloway, 1997; Robertson, 2000).

The radical significance of the claim to have learned from experience is clear if we contrast two long-standing interpretations of Chaucer's pilgrimage to Canterbury. If we interpret it allegorically, as the soul's journey to the New Jerusalem, then the pilgrims must be judged according to the eternal truths of revelation. Each pilgrim represents a fixed point in both the feudal social hierarchy and Christian typology. Each is characterized through association with Christian virtues and vices, "parfit charitee" (I 532), for example, versus "wantownesse" (I 264). Even the time of their journey fixes them within a Christian medieval framework; it is the time of Easter and salvation, and the pilgrims' destination is less Canterbury than the City of God.[2]

Experience, as the interaction of a fallen creature with a profane, ephemeral world, cannot, according to this interpretation, be the basis of knowledge. Alisoun's unlicensed experiences – and her unlicensed opinions about that experience – are only so many instances of damnable folly. Vigorous and vivacious as her account may be, her experience is that of "a worldly woman whose vivacity and laughter hide the soul of a lost and wandering pilgrim," and her claims are only instances of "the delusion which makes her life an empty lie" (Huppe, 1964, pp. 135, 108). Seen in these terms, experience and, indeed, history can have no epistemological value. Eternity is the true home of the soul and the repository of true knowledge. Only mistakes take time.

According to an alternative tradition of Chaucerian scholarship, however, the pilgrimage is no allegorical journey. Having met by "adventure" [coincidence], the pilgrims wend their way down from London across Kent at a time that is less the Easter of the liturgy than the April of the calendar (Bowers, 2000). Far from being eternal and absolute, the claims of "auctoritee" must be understood as ideological and institutional power moves, in this case an aspect of the Church's long-standing war on women, and Alisoun is right to resent being judged according to standards that claim to be otherworldly, but that are very much a part of earthly power relationships. It is "the clerk whan he is oold" and impotent who writes denunciations of women. "By God! If wommen hadde writen stories," the stories would tell of the "wiikkednesse" of men (III 706–10, 692–696).[3]

Seen in these terms, Alisoun is laying claim to experience as both a corrective to received truth and an alternative authority. Churchly dogma can say what it likes – that the sole proper use of the genitals is "for purgacioun of uryne," for example – but experience "woot [knows] wel it is noght so" (III 120–124). This not only changes the nature of evidence, but also the site from which knowledge can be generated; knowledge is available from the tangible, material world rather than from the received truths of an eternal realm. Truth can be produced by the human mind based on the accumulating evidence of observation and social interaction. What is at stake is a new kind of epistemological indeterminacy based, not on a prior schema, but on what we would call experiential learning. The point is not so much that Alisoun – or Chaucer, for that matter – holds this or that heterodox opinion;[4] rather, what is being reflected here is a new relationship between personal experience, credibility, and time. The Wife of Bath's raucously autobiographical prologue is the prototype of a new form of personal narrative in which the lessons of an individual life emerge gradually.

The Canterbury Tales are the product of an historical moment in which the world that people experience can no longer be adequately held by the hegemonic ideology that is supposed to explain it. It is a time marked, in Peggy Knapp's (1990) words, by "the discontinuities, the consciously articulated struggles and the unconscious, inarticulate unease engendered when a set of ideologies no longer adequately accounts for people's experienced lives" (p. 1). H. Marshall Leicester's (1990) term for such an historical moment is "disenchantment," which he defines as "the suspicion, or even the conviction, that the category of transcendence itself is a human construction" and the tendency "to see experience and social existence as an encounter between conflicting interpretations rather than the passive reception of preexisting meanings" (p. 27). *The Canterbury Tales* represent a variety of individuals holding loud and boisterous opinions in contradiction to each other, and the meaning of their tales, like the pilgrims themselves, can no longer be prevented from "wanderynge by the weye" (I 467).

In this book, I will be using Alisoun as a node around which a new epistemological dispensation emerges, personifying a world in which the meaning of experience is fluid, socially situated, and subject to debate. I want to take a moment, therefore, to lay out a number of trends in the society of late fourteenth-century England that form the basis for the experiential learner that Alisoun, as both religious upstart and commodities manufacturer, represents.

First, as a cloth manufacturer, Alisoun is a participant in the most highly developed capitalist industry of the day, the one that, by the late fourteenth century, has moved furthest in the direction of wage labor and a monied economy (Carruthers, 1979). She thus represents both an economic independence and a geographic mobility outside the traditional feudal estates. What emerges is a subjectivity less 'fixed' in and by the medieval social hierarchy: intellectual contestation matched by mobility of social status, individual agency, the fluidity of money, and freer forms of trade. The more fluid marketplace of ideas, as it were, is both cause and effect of the fluidity of the marketplace itself. Alisoun herself is no mean interpreter of Biblical texts, and the connection between personal experience and the market is embedded in her narrative; one key text in her commentary, Paul's first Epistle to Timothy, blames women's sexual license on the economic independence that allows them to purchase immodest clothing, thus imperiling their "chastitee" (Tinkle, 2010). This is a charge to which Alisoun, as a cloth manufacturer, is understandably sensitive. In this sense,

Alisoun is championing, not only the rights of her gender, but also those of her class (Patterson, 1983).

At the same time, it matters that Alisoun is a woman. In placing the claim that one can learn from experience in the mouth of a female character, Chaucer inscribes "auctoritee" and "experience" as another set of the highly gendered Western dualisms in terms of which knowledge has traditionally been authorized: like mind and body, reason and emotion, objectivity and subjectivity, and in this case, eternity and history, the terms associate men with the abstract and universal and women with the partial and concrete. What Lee Patterson (1983) calls Alisoun's "verbal licentiousness" (p. 662) combines a number of the characteristics that patristic writers traditionally attributed to women such as sexual license and garrulousness, but it also associates experience with the body and experiential learning with unauthorized speech. Bawdy and sexualized as she is, Alisoun's instrument of ideological and social transgression is less her "bele chose" [pretty thing, i.e. her genitals] (III 447) than her mouth (Root, 1994).

In making his experiential learner one of St. Jerome's "unruly women," Chaucer casts experience as a site of fluid and unsanctioned meanings, bringing together the variety of emergent discourses that converge in the figure of Alisoun of Bath: the body as a source of knowledge, speech as an act of self-authorization, and knowledge claims based on individual subjectivity and belief. The textualized body of male authority gives way to the sexualized body of female experience, and we still live in a world boundaried, in part, by the questions thus produced. How can the traditionally unsanctioned body be the instrument of sanctioned knowledge? How can the (male) authorized knower claim experience and still retain authority? The contentious relationship between experience and knowledge has characterized modernity since Chaucer's time. Viewed with hindsight, Alisoun both won her point and lost it. This book is about how and why.

I wot as wel as ye

Historically, the use of experience as an alternative authority must be understood as both an epistemological and a political innovation. That is, Alisoun's insistence that "I woot [know] as wel as ye" (III 63) is a claim for the capacity of human beings to produce valid and usable knowledge on their own. In her substitution of ancient texts with the authority of her own experience, Alisoun is insisting that subjectivity itself entitles one to a certain say.

This implied relationship between knowledge and democracy, however, is predicated on a certain kind of selfhood that emerged in the centuries following Chaucer's death. It is a product of the period in which the individual was being born as an autonomous, rational subject and in which the modern relationships among experience, reason, knowledge, and individual liberty were being formulated in the course of the Enlightenment. First, Descartes' (1637/1960) foundational postulate, "never to accept anything as true which I did not clearly know to be such" (p. 51) considers that the individual conscious mind is both the origin of and the validating mechanism for knowledge. This tenet, often referred to as epistemological individualism, holds that human beings gain knowledge of the world as autonomous, contemplative beings rather than as members of active and historically evolving communities (Jaggar and Bordo, 1989). Second, the right to claim epistemological independence is seen, not only in terms of truth and falsehood, but in terms of tyranny and liberty. The epistemological agent and the democratic subject not only emerge simultaneously, but are in many ways creations of each other. The right to argue for individual truths becomes foundational to claims for the full range of bourgeois democratic freedoms, from the right to private property to the right to overthrow the king. In breaking with the received opinions of others, Galileo, Descartes, Locke, and many others were announcing both the modern knower and the modern political subject simultaneously or, rather, they were fashioning a world in which the two were one and the same.

It is in this context that Alisoun both wins and loses the argument. On the one hand, with the rise of both empiricism and the scientific method, experientially based, widely accessible forms of information become the sanctioned forms of knowledge. We can hold some truths to be self-evident – the formulation is originally Locke's – because the raw materials of reality, the use of the senses, and the organizing framework of reason are universally available. Alisoun's claim that "experience woot [knows] well" (III 124) is echoed, for example, in Galileo's claim that anyone can look through his telescope to solve the problems that have bothered the honored scholars of the ages:

> By the aid of the telescope anyone may behold this in a manner which so directly appeals to the senses that all the disputes which have tormented philosophers through so many ages are exploded at once by the irrefragable evidence of our eyes.
>
> *(as cited in Toulmin and Goodfield, 1999, pp. 193–4)*

On the other hand, however, as experience does indeed become a new form of authority, the insurgent, counterhegemonic voice that Alisoun represents becomes subject to new constraints and regulation; Galileo's statement sounds democratic, but when he and his contemporaries said "anyone," they did not mean the likes of her. The new epistemological agent, the experiential learner, in effect, was constructed as a particular kind of human being who claimed a place in the new world order by vanquishing the irrational and disorderly. The emotional, corporeal, and sensate parts of the self – everything Alisoun of Bath represented – were projected onto groups of people who were then denied economic and political rights based on their supposed inability to interpret their own experience rationally.

Specifically, the denial of political rights – the withholding of the franchise from women and workers, for example, and the appropriation of the non-European world – was justified by the claim that not everyone could learn from experience. Women's greater emotionality, it was claimed, precluded a reasoned understanding of the world and would play havoc with the deliberations of public life.

Members of the working-classes were children in need of instruction, not adults who could learn from their mistakes. Africans could not make inferences based on causality, experience, and observation and thus were incapable of governing themselves. Arabs were too backward to conduct their own affairs, or else too degenerate and lazy to try. A system of social practices arose for the study and management of the unruly experience of the Other: colonialist anthropology for the natives, scientific management and sociology for the working-class, and medicine and psychiatry for the three closely related categories of women, homosexuals, and lunatics.

In one sense, then, the claims of experience that were once foundational to a democratizing world have come to serve to opposite function. Where once Alisoun's insistence that experience was "right ynogh" [right enough] was an act of epistemo-logical insurgency, the iconoclastic has become a conservative force for justifying entrenched social institutions and norms. We still claim the rational management of experience through science, self-reflection, rational dialogue, and consensus-building as the basis for both legitimate knowledge and the practice of democracy. One might characterize the Enlightenment project as first stealing Alisoun's best lines and then creating a world in which it was again possible to shut her up.

By God! If wommen hadde writen stories ...

Alisoun, however, is not so easily silenced. If the insistence that we can learn from experience is at the heart of the world the Enlightenment made, it is also at the heart of the ways in which the meanings of that world are being contested. The claims of experiential learning have again become central to the struggle for a redistribution of social and economic power and epistemological authority. Contending views of what and how we "learn from experience;" the re-examination of the relationship between "reason" and the body; and the rehistoricizing of the relationships between politics and knowledge suggest that the meaning of "experience" is again at the center of a widespread and deeply felt debate.

First, greater attention to experience has been claimed both by women and by a variety of non-Eurocentric cultures as foundational to their particular 'ways of knowing' (Gilligan, 1982; Belinki *et al.*, 1986; Collins, 1991; Asante, 1987). In opposition to masculinist and European-normed epistemologies that value abstract observation and technocratic potency, alternative epistemologies also acknowledge the emotional and embodied qualities of knowledge, hold personal testimony and shared experience as epistemologically valuable, and thus challenge the Enlightenment claim that knowledge is ever value-free.

Second, the experience of disenfranchised groups has again been used as a corrective to forms of knowledge produced within the social institutions of the powerful. One important aspect of second-wave feminism, for example, was the repudiation of the scientific authority of medicine and the reclaiming of knowledge available from "our bodies, ourselves" (Boston Women's Health Book Collective,

1971, title), to use the title of one representative text. Similarly, post-colonialist and critical race theory has challenged the anthropological construction of 'primitives' and 'savages' in which "for too long our experiences have been told by others . . . , our reality has been claimed by 'foreign' authorship, and our thoughts have been re-presented by those who stand outside of our existential location, personal desire, or social perspectives" (Jansen, 1991, p. 5). By making the claim for people in oppressed social categories as "agents of knowledge, as actors on the stage of history, as humans whose lives provide a grounding for knowledge claims that are different from, and in some respects preferable to, knowledge claims grounded in the lives of men in the dominant groups" (Harding, 1991, p. 47), scholars from multiple communities have been highlighting knowledge born of experience to challenge relations of social power and hegemonic versions of the world.

Finally, these new approaches have named the power relationships within which knowledge is constructed and deployed and questioned the too-easy association between experiential learning and democracy. Galileo's insistence that anyone could look through his telescope, after all, has only ever been partially true. One needs access to a telescope, for one thing, and knowledge-production participates in the social division of labor in which differential access to resources is the norm and in which the interests of specific professions, classes, and social groups are advanced. If Alisoun is right, if our learning takes place within human time and space, then all knowledge is produced within the politics of human relationships, and knowledge-practices that fail to understand themselves in those terms will arguably always do us more harm than good.

Thus, in the past generation, investigations into the historical and social embeddedness of knowledge have both reintroduced experience as a topic for academic inquiry and historicized the ways in which 'experience' has been used in the past. In the process, it has challenged Enlightenment assumptions concerning knowledge and the knowing self, problemized a narrow understanding of 'reason' as the sole legitimate faculty through which knowledge can be constructed, and rewritten experiential learning as a mesh of historically specific, politically loaded practices through which human activity is delineated and given meaning and which are sometimes shared and sometimes contested among people and social groups. The understandings of experience that emerge in these approaches allow for experiential learning practices that take both the specificity and the contingency of knowledge into account and make experiential learning a site for articulating outlaw knowledges and counter-hegemonic experience.

As the coming chapters will attest, however, none of these understandings of experience is uncontested. Questions abound. Is there any such thing as direct 'experience' unmediated by culturally received understandings of the world? Is it liberatory to claim that women know through their bodies, or is that simply another iteration of a highly gendered stereotype? Does the celebration of intuitive knowledge come perilously close to permission for dangerous, deeply bigoted irrationalities? These and similar questions suggest that what we call 'experiential learning' is neither epistemologically obvious nor innocent of culture and history.

Part I of this book is, in effect, a short history of the experiential learner. Or, rather, it is a history of the *notion* of experience, not as a cognitive category or a philosophical concept, but, perhaps more nebulously, as an idea within Enlightenment and post-Enlightenment Western cultures that has been central to the construction of a particular kind of human 'self.' Part I traces the emergence of the experiential learner as the bourgeois, liberal humanist subject and explores the power relationships that enabled and were enabled by that particular kind of personhood. More specifically, the first three chapters explore the ways in which assumptions about the nature of knowledge combine with assumptions about the individual to construct a particular kind of experiential learner. That learner, I argue, is characterized by two related forms of detachment, each of which contradicts – and compromises – the presumed groundedness of experiential learning itself. Chapter one focuses on the historical emergence of a stable self whose identity is fixed and who is understood as fundamentally separate from other people. Chapter two then traces the valorization of reason detached from emotions and the body, a detachment that plays out both in theories of knowledge and, more broadly, across historical justifications for domination and inequality. Chapter three extends this analysis both historically and conceptually by exploring the emergence in the nineteenth century of the disciplines of sociology and anthropology and the use of the claim to have learned from experience in the context of middle-class hegemony and colonialist expansion. These three chapters delineate a type of authorized knower who understands 'learning from experience' as an exercise in self-mastery and for whom the right to make judgments about the experience of others is an emblem of authority. The relationship of learning to self-management, I argue, is importantly tied to the rise of the bourgeois, bureaucratic state in which the ability to manage oneself justifies one's management of others and in which the professional, the intellectual, the physician, and the social scientist embody the claims to the rational ascendancy of the middle-class as a whole.

Each of these chapters draws broadly on a generation of scholarship that, in my view, is insufficiently utilized by scholars in adult learning: the critique of the Enlightenment, materialist and postmodernist treatments of the humanities and social sciences, and theories of Otherness that come out of contemporary feminist, critical-race, and queer theory. As my use of *The Canterbury Tales* suggests, I also draw on my original training in literary criticism, a homecoming that has been both a personal joy and a way of broadening and problematizing the more typical discourse of adult learning. Each chapter also engages the relationship of broader historical and cultural patterns to theories of adult learning, connecting them to specific adult learning theorists such as Malcolm Knowles, David Kolb, Jack Mezirow, and Paulo Freire.

Part II brings the insights of feminist theory to bear on mainstream theories of experiential learning. Chapter four explores the contentious debates within feminist theory concerning experience and knowledge. I then focus on a particular theme within feminism, namely, the body as an agent of knowing and as a bearer of culture and history. Chapters five and six continue that discussion by looking carefully at specific writings in adult learning. Chapter five focuses on a single text, a recent issue of *New Directions for Adult and Continuing Education* (Lawrence, 2012a), in which a variety of adult learning practitioners explore their understandings of the role of the body in adult learning. I use that rich but problematic text both to point to the important and nuanced work of feminist theorists of adult learning and note the ways in which other treatments of embodied learning rest, often in spite of ourselves, on unexamined conceptual foundations.

Chapter six brings two famous names in experiential learning, John Dewey and David Kolb, together with feminist theorists of knowledge whose own work draws on Dewey. One main point of the chapter is to challenge Kolb's claim that his work continues that of Dewey and to delineate the fundamental differences in their approach. I argue that Dewey is an important precursor to theories of experience that do not separate mind and body, experience and learning, or similar dualisms and explore the ways in which Kolb's learning cycle is directly contrary to Dewey's ideas.

In Part III, I examine one experiential learning practice, the assessment of prior experiential learning (APEL)[5] for academic credit and/or professional credentials. APEL is the site in which my own practice of adult learning has largely been located, and I use it here as a way of exploring the continued political and social situatedness of adult learning practices. APEL's quantification of knowledge provides an explicit meeting point for philosophical premises, institutional policies, and social relations of power and therefore offers a uniquely fruitful site for exploring how practices of experiential learning both enact and contest hierarchies of epistemological authority. As a technique for naming and rewarding particular kinds of knowledge and not others, APEL is inevitably embedded in how a society apportions status and visibility. It thus can't help but be a site in which the social order is mediated, in which differently powerful groups and institutions struggle towards contending visions of human society.

Chapter seven explores APEL as it has evolved, initially as a North American practice, and traces the social and educational contexts surrounding its emergence. I map the ways in which APEL is consistent with feminist and other post-positivist theories of knowledge and their emancipatory impulses, but attend as well to the complex value- and power-laden nature of APEL. Chapters eight and nine revisit APEL through two alternative theoretical lenses. In Chapter eight, I use what has come to be known as "queer theory," that is, the theoretical perspectives available from lives that do not conform to binary categories of gender and sexuality, to explore the non-neutrality of the categories to which APEL currently conforms, the power-effects of those categories, and the 'in'-sider and 'out'-sider hierarchies of epistemological prestige. In Chapter nine, I ask what APEL might look like we were not required to take academic organizations of knowledge as the norm. Drawing on the work scholars of workplace learning, I explore the complexities of knowledge that adheres in a deep and nuanced understanding of context, interpersonal relationships, and the imperatives of work.

Part IV of this book addresses a second pedagogical practice that is ubiquitous in adult learning, namely, the assigning of life narratives. Chapter ten explores the central role played by autobiographical writing by students and suggests that, however much we intend these narratives to be authentic accounts of students' coming into identity, they are, in important senses, fictions. Citing the extensive literature on life writing among adult learning theorists, I tease out the ideological suppositions in the practice and argue that our expectations concerning plot, characterization, and narrative voice are based on a narrow range of allowable experience.

It is in Chapter eleven that my academic origins in literary theory are most visible. Using the tools of literary analysis to unpack the life writing most privileged in adult learning, I ask a very literary question: if the self is a text, what genre is it? I argue that expectations for students' life narratives conform to a quite specific literary genre, the *Bildungsroman*, or novel of individual maturation. I then use an alternative genre, magical realism, to suggest that our narrative expectations of students do not fully account for the complex lives that many of our students have led, lives that cannot be 'captured' in a narrative of growing self-awareness, surety, and individual development. Chapter twelve begins with a discussion of the ways in which the narrative psychology currently in use in adult learning interacts with our more traditional roots in humanistic psychology. It then focuses on the ways in which our expected narratives impact a particular group of adult learners, namely, veterans. Using both the scholarship on adult learning and life writing by veterans, the chapter asks for a revisiting of both our assumptions and our practices. I use the example of Ryan Smithson, a student at my own institution who began his memoir of his experience in Iraq in the classroom and has now published that memoir, *Ghosts of War*.

Finally, the concluding chapter, Chapter thirteen, is an attempt to connect the multiple themes that run through the book: the relationship between the individual and the collective, knowledge and the body, life writing, experiential learning, and the expectation that we can find a coherent narrative of selfhood in an often-incoherent world. I ask what experiential learning looks like when taken out of the tradition of the detached, abstract knower, how knowledge resides in the experience of the body in history, and how alternative narrative forms can reflect the complexities of experiential learning. That final chapter, in part, is a way of returning to Alisoun of Bath's insistence that "I am expert in al myn age" (III 174) and asking how the unauthorized knower – female, irreverent, rooted in her body, and threatening to the status quo – can stake her claim for the "auctoritee" of experience.

Much of this book was written initially as a series of articles published between 1996 and 2013. As I began revising these articles as chapters, I often found that there was more to say and that, in response to the recent scholarship of others, some of my ideas had changed. The current volume is thus an amalgam of old and new thinking and writing, and I have tried to make it a relatively seamless one.

What may appear less seamless at times is my attempt to bring the scholarship of multiple fields – from literary theory to critical anthropology to the history of seventeenth-century science – into dialogue with the more conventional disciplinary foundations of adult learning. My goal in so doing is to broaden the scholarly dimensions of adult learning theory, to identify new lenses and tools, and to give a sense of how such lenses and tools might contribute to our understanding of what we do as the educators of adults. In the process, I have also sought to bring adult learning theory more fully into line with contemporary academic discourses and concerns. As I suggest at various times in the book, adult learning remains a marginalized field within the academy. This is in part because adult students are themselves devalued, but it is also because those who serve adults in higher education are rarely positioned, or rewarded, for a life of scholarship.

In many ways, that is a very good thing. We are paid to teach, to advise, and to create and staff adult-friendly programs and courses, and that is profoundly important work. That said, our intellectual, if not institutional, marginalization is both a vicious circle and a self-fulfilling prophesy. As Tara Fenwick (2003) has pointed out, the literature on adult learning draws very little on the rich philosophical literature on experience that has characterized the past generation of scholarship (p. viii). This concern was echoed by Arthur Wilson and Elizabeth Hayes (2002) in an editorial in *Adult Education Quarterly*: "learning and experience are central ideas in the thinking and practice of adult education. Yet we have never really asked ourselves what these things might, may, should mean" (p. 173). Thus, our focus on the labor-intensive work of serving students is not an unmixed blessing, and one of the prices we pay is that we are not always challenged to think deeply and rigorously about our assumptions and our practices, to read outside of a narrow range of sources, or to keep our own intellectual imaginations alive.

Alisoun has been with me in multiple ways on this journey. She has jostled my thinking, kept me company, and sent me back to my old love of medieval literature and its resplendent oddities. But she has also reminded me of the graduate student I used to be who could think of no better career than one spent in a conventional university, teaching the same works of literature every year to students who stayed the same young age while only I kept getting older. Instead, I have been privileged to teach Alisoun's twentieth and twenty-first-century progeny, adults who, like her, are experienced, outrageous, knowing, weather-weary, and still, through all the sundry complications of adulthood, on a pilgrimage.

Notes

1   All quotations are from F. N. Robinson, ed. (1957) *The Works of Geoffrey Chaucer*, 2nd ed. Cambridge, MA: Houghton Mifflin.
2   For the classic statements of this school of Chaucerian criticism, see Huppe (1964) and Robertson (1962).
3   For examples of this school of Chaucer criticism, see Knapp (1990), Patterson (1983), and Leicester (1990).
4   Chaucer's own view of the Wife of Bath has long been debated by critics, with her various characteristics and assertions read as so much evidence of his view. While I agree with those who argue that she should be read as an aspect of the contentious social realm of the fourteenth century and not as a sinner within Christian typology,

I am less concerned with taking a position than I am with using the terms on which it rests. As Peggy Knapp (1990) argues, "The issue at stake is not what Chaucer intended, but how texts interact with the social formations within which they function" (p. 17). The critical debate itself is itself the mirror image of the *Tales* as what Knapp calls a "boundary text,... one whose environment holds more than one configuration of power contending for preeminence as the fundamental way for its society to see life" (p. 8).

5   The practice of assessing experiential learning for formal academic or vocational recognition has multiple names and acronyms, among them prior learning assessment (PLA) in the US, prior learning assessment and recognition (PLAR) in Canada, assessment of prior experiential learning (APEL) in the UK, and the recognition of prior learning (RPL) in Australia and South Africa.

1

PURGING THE TRANSGRESSIVE FROM EXPERIENTIAL LEARNING

The children of Mercurie and Venus
Been in hir wirkyng ful contrarius;
Mercurie loveth wysdam and science,
And Venus loveth ryot and dispence.

[The children of Mercury and Venus
Are in their workings opposed.
Mercury loves wisdom and learning,
And Venus loves riot and free expenditure.]

Geoffrey Chaucer, *The Canterbury Tales*, III 697–700

In her invective against the misogyny of the clergy, the Wife of Bath first questions why "no wommaan of no clerk is preysed [praised]" (III 706) and then proceeds to offer a simple explanation. An elderly churchman, she says, will lash out at women when, owing to dotage and impotence, he cannot "do of Venus werkes worth his olde sho [shoe]" (III 708). As the above epigraph attests, however, Alisoun also understands the tension between women and clerics to be the result of dissimilar astrological natures. Clerics are from Mercury; women are from Venus, as it were.

In associating the battle between churchmen and laywomen with the contrary natures of Mercury and Venus, Alisoun is appropriating – and using to her advantage – a gendered dualism that associates men with order and learning and women with disorder and lack of discipline. That dualism, deeply ingrained in Western culture, will be the subject of Chapter two, but for the moment, I want to explore Alisoun's own side of the dualism, that is, the association of the female-normed experiential learner with the chaotic and the irreverent. In what follows, I trace the ways in which 'experiential learning' became constrained within the normalizing structures and ideologies of the emerging economic and political order. Many of the values most associated with the adult learner – self-direction, independence of mind, and critical self-reflection, for example – are a direct product of the gradual disassociation of experience from the "ryot and dispence" that Alisoun here associates with Venus.

Carnivals and the taming of experience

The story begins, not with a pilgrimage, but with a carnival, another customary feature of the medieval landscape. Both a symbol for and an enactment of the world beyond imposed ideologies, the carnival has come to represent the communal nature of medieval life and has been used by scholars to explore modes of being that were gradually erased from public view in the course of the Enlightenment.

In his classic study, *Rabaleis and His World* (1984), Mikhail Bakhtin explored the medieval and Renaissance carnival as a space within which the common people could breach the rigidities of a class- and Church-bound society. In opposition to, and in parodic relationship with, the ideological and social hierarchies of official culture, the periodic fairs of pre-capitalist Europe offered a transgressive realm in which sententiousness and ideological certitude were suspended in favor of sensuousness, mutability, and play. As described by Bakhtin, the carnival took its energy from "the material bodily principle, that is, images of the human body with its food, drink, defecation, and sexual life" (p. 18). If the body is the site of worldliness and sin, it is also the site of energy, irreverence, and the transgression of boundaries. In the carnival, the body is celebrated for its capacity to express joy and audaciousness; it overflows its own limits, refuses confinement and order, and functions as a site of excess and extravagance.

Bakhtin's work focuses on Rabaleis' *Gargantua* and *Pantagruel*, written a century and a half after Chaucer, but it just as easily could have focused on *The Canterbury Tales*. The *Tales* are famously filled with images of bodily functions and pleasures – adulterous escapades, raised skirts and naked buttocks, flatulence – and while the pilgrims have a variety of responses to this imagery, it does not seem remarkable to any of Chaucer's characters that they be spoken of in very mixed company. Christian virtue may claim the upper hand, but greed, lust, ridicule, and bawdy laughter all have a public face. The pilgrims' outing itself is a kind of moving carnival; the longing "to goon [go] on pilgrimages" is stimulated less by a wish to honor "the hooly blisful martir" St. Thomas Becket than by the fact that "Aprill with his shoures soote" [fragrant showers] is a nice time to be out of doors (I 1–18).

Bakhtin makes the important point that the carnival body is a communal body. It is contained "not in the biological individual, not in the bourgeois ego" (p. 19), but in the collective mass of the people, for whom the carnival represents a breathing space and an alternative sociality. Within that space, the body is valuable precisely because it "is not a closed, completed unity; it is unfinished, outgrows itself" (p. 26). It violates the boundaries between self and other, self and world. Bakhtin notes that Rabaleis' imagery, which in this regard is quite close to that of Chaucer, accentuates those parts of the body that are open to the outside world. The emphasis is placed on the parts through which the world enters the body or emerges from it, or through which the body opens itself to or goes out to meet the world: the mouth, the genitals, the breasts, the anus, the potbelly, the nose.

This emphasis is of a piece with the role of the carnival as a site of experiences that we would now call border-crossings, that is, the "interchange" (p. 317) between entities whose separateness from each other is inherently unstable. Carnival experience, like the carnival body, is transgressive both in the literal and figurative sense. One aspect of this is a form of symbolic inversion, a parodic relationship to hierarchical authority and fixed social identities. The peasant is crowned king; the fool is promoted over the priest and the magistrate. Dualities are turned upon themselves in what is at once licensed release, a ritual of resistance, and a form of serious play (Stallybrass and White, 1986). In Alisoun's terms, carnival is the site for privileging Venus over Mercury and, with it, the embodied over the cerebral. Stewart Justman (1994), who views Alisoun as a negative figure because of her association with the uncontrolled and disorderly, uses a word from Chaucer's "Parson's Tale" to identify this quality of reversal: "Like carnival or sin, she turns the world 'up-sodoun' [upside-down]" (p. 345).

The notion of interchange, however, does more than reverse the hierarchy of social and intellectual status; the "monstrueux assemblage" – monstrous jumble – of the carnival (Bakhtin, 1984, p. 109) also enacts the breakdown of any such dualities. That is, the fluidity of embodied experience in the carnival not only turns dualities on their heads, but undermines duality as such. The presiding spirit is neither Mercury nor Venus – in Greek, Hermes and Aphrodite – but rather the Hermaphrodite. Carnival represents a hybridization, a commingling of incompatible elements (Stallybrass and White, 1986). It makes possible impossible identities, unstable boundaries, unauthorized truths.

In such a world, experience is transgressive precisely because it *cannot* be made into a form of authority. It slips out from under the confines of official culture and insists on the human love of "ryot and dispense." It is embodied, communal, and fruitfully incoherent; its very excess is what allows it to undermine hegemony. Experience, in other words, is liberatory precisely because it is unstable and provisional, because it is collective and not individual, because it always contains a chaotic element that resists categorization and management. In a world in which authority is a celibate male by definition, experience is the sexual woman who simply refuses – in all senses of the word – to mind.

Clearly, the form of experience I am calling carnival will never be serviceable as authority. It will first have to be tamed. Experiential learning as a legitimated social practice is a product of the time in which that taming happened, in which experience became situated within the modern relationships among reason, individualism, and self-mastery. First, the communal body of the carnival was privatized; new norms of social behavior privileged bodily autonomy and inviolability, and the ability to maintain distance from the bodies of others came to signify the management of society as a whole. Secondly, the emerging economic and political rights were predicated on individualized mental processes and a stable, self-regulating subjectivity. Thirdly, as I will explore in Chapter two, the terms of the mind/body duality shifted so that the body was to be controlled, not by virtue, but by reason. These three shifts – the privatization of the body, the fixing of internalized subjectivity, and the rule of reason – each rested on the rejection of the embodied, communal aspects of experience. In the process, 'experiential learning' became an algorithm for purging experience of its transgressive qualities, asserting a coherent, rights-bearing selfhood, and claiming its accompanying economic and political prerogatives. The 'self' thus circumscribed within carefully crafted, socially governable norms both defined the limits of acceptability through a series of outcast Others and restrained the transgressive and creative possibilities of experience.

The privatization of experience

In *The Politics and Poetics of Transgression* (1986), Stallybrass and White use a Bakhtinian analysis to explore the growing attack on carnivals and public rituals that took place in the seventeenth and eighteenth centuries. They argue, first, that the decline of the carnival in Europe was part of a larger social transformation in which the life of the body was becoming ever more privatized as the autonomous, self-regulating economic 'man' of capitalism and the Enlightenment became the new social ideal. Rather than serving as a joyous point of exchange between the individual and the world, the newly isolated body came to represent what the poet and playwright Ben Jonson (1572–1637) called a "gathered" self, a self that is closed to the world, impenetrable, and "untouch'd" (as cited in Fish, 1984, p. 39). Henceforth, the body was to be valorized as "the border of a closed individuality that does not merge with other bodies and with the world" (Bakhtin, 1984, p. 320).

There is no place in this new social formulation for the "mobile, split, multiple self" of the carnival, "a subject of pleasure in processes of exchange" (Stallybrass and White, 1986, p. 22). Central to both the formulation of bourgeois public space and the construction of the gathered bourgeois self was a change in manners to refine those bodily behaviors – yawning, spitting, and passing wind, for example – that exist at the boundaries of self and world. Simultaneously, moral rectitude became associated with civil crowd behavior. One established a unitary, autonomous bourgeois identity through disciplined public behavior, while the rabble that Wordsworth called "this Parliament of Monsters" (as cited in Stallybrass and White, 1986, p. 120) demonstrated their inferiority through vulgar behavior in public spaces such as theaters and fairs.

Contagion[1] by others in the form of epidemic disease had long been associated in the Middle Ages with both socially marginalized populations and socially unsanctioned activities; leprosy, for example, was seen as evidence of sexual licentiousness, and bubonic plague was blamed on the Jews. In the centuries following the Enlightenment, a discourse concerning dirt and cleanliness, licentiousness and self-control was joined to the new distaste for bodily contact as official attention became more and more focused on the threats of invasion and permeability. As Catherine Gallagher (1987) describes it,

> the body came to occupy the center of a social discourse obsessed with sanitation, with minimizing bodily contact and preventing the now alarmingly traversable boundaries of individual bodies from being penetrated by a host of foreign elements, above all the products of other bodies
>
> *(Gallagher, 1987, p. 90; see also Poovey, 1988)*

The autonomy of the individual was thus represented in the first instance by an exactitude of bodily separateness that would have been impossible at a carnival or, for that matter, on a pilgrimage.

As an index of changing notions of selfhood, the privatization of the body as the sign of the gathered self has enormous implications for the emergence of the 'experiential learner.' The forms of identity both required for and enabled by the rise of bourgeois individualism rest on a symbolic order of borders, margins, and limits (Fuss, 1991, p. 1). Bodily surfaces demarcate social and personal boundaries, and what Stallybrass and White call the "logic of identity formation" (p. 25) develops within an experience of self that is unitary, closed, and self-possessed. The modern notion of identity itself originated when Locke applied the philosophical term for sameness to the fixed medium of the body, whose stability over time then forms the basis for political and economic personhood under the terms of the Enlightenment social contract. Resting on a concept of possessive individualism that grants rights to individuals as owners of themselves, this discourse sees the body as the delimiting grounds for human individuality (Cohen, 1991). In the process, the fruitful instability of experience, the transgressive meanings and unsanctioned subjectivity celebrated by Alisoun, are constrained within narrow rules for setting the newly privatized body within the socially recognizable parameters of economic and judicial personhood.

Judith Butler (1999) has noted that categories of personal identity are themselves a part of internalized regulatory regimes. That is, they are how we come to understand who we are, what – and whom – we desire, how we should feel, and how we must behave. The privatization of experience behind the closed, proprietary boundaries of the self is thus not only an aspect of the privatization of society, but also an aspect of a growing emphasis on self-regulation. As the body came to represent the unitary identity of the (male) bourgeois individual, one asserted one's entitlement to economic and political rights by controlling one's own bodily behavior and by projecting lack of self-control onto a series of despised Others who were portrayed as 'low' and disorderly. With the emergence of what we would now call medical and sociological discourse, the association of disease and vice became focused on the notion of self-control: disease was seen as caused by those whose own bodily imprudence, now redefined as pathological, threatened to invade the social body as a whole.

"a process of learning in which people take the primary initiative for planning, carrying out, and evaluating their own learning experiences" (Merriam *et al.*, 2007, p. 110). Variously treated as a description of a learning process, a teaching strategy, and a personal attribute, self-directed learning has achieved what Candy referred to as a "cult status" in adult learning (as cited in Kerka, 1994, p. 3). Originally seen as a descriptor of what adult learners were like – Knowles, for example, posited that adults get more self-directed as they mature – and increasingly treated as an attribute that could be measured,[4] the self-directed learner serves for many practitioners as the ideal toward which both learners and educators should aim.

The qualities variously attributed to the self-directed learner are of a piece with those claimed for the autonomous 'man' of the Enlightenment, the socially unconstrained Romantic hero, and, as Stephen Brookfield (2000b) has noted, the self-made rugged individualist that is the American version of those ideals. "The image of self-direction is of a self-contained, internally driven, capable adult learner" who functions in "splendid isolation," a "free-floating, autonomous, volitional agent able to make rational, authentic, and internally coherent choices about learning while remaining detached from social, cultural and political formations" (pp. 10–11). The characteristics attributed to the self-directed learner include "personal autonomy" and "self-management" (Candy, as cited in Kerka, 1994, p. 4) and the exercise of "free choice," "rational reflection," "willpower," self-restraint," and "self-discipline" (Merriam *et al.*, 2007, p. 122).[5] In what may or may not be a nod to Rousseau's Emile, Moore refers to this autonomous learner as an "intellectual Robinson Crusoe" (as cited in Kerka, 1994, p. 4), dependent on no one and claiming the right of freedom from the importunate needs of others. The self-directed learner is the product of what Deci and Ryan (2000) approvingly call "introjected regulation" (p. 86), autonomous to the degree that socialization has been internalized" so that "the regulation is self-determined" (p. 84).

In recent years, notions of self-directed learning have been challenged both for a lack of attention to the ways in which social structures shape the goals and learning opportunities of adult learners and for cultural narrowness (Merriam *et al.*, 2007; Brookfield, 2000a; Kerka, 1994). At the same time, however, the notion of the autonomous learner battling the expectations of others continues to serve as the implicit ideal.

Indeed, many theorists of experiential learning view experience as liberating only insofar as it frees us from the influence of others. Underneath the avowal that community is indispensable is a longing for a unitary, authentic self untouched by the demands of human mutuality. Malcolm Knowles' use of humanistic psychology is a case in point. Experiential learning encourages psychic growth by freeing us from the oppression of other people's choices. Knowles (1990) quotes Carl Rogers to the effect that "I have yet to find the individual who, when he [*sic*] examines his situation deeply, and feels that he perceives it clearly, deliberately chooses dependence, deliberately chooses to have the integrated direction of himself undertaken by another" (pp. 42–3). According to this formulation, *all* influence is undue.[6]

More recently, theories of experiential learning have been influenced by the materialist and postmodernist insistence that experience is neither unmediated nor wholly individual. It is now a commonplace that we experience according to received meanings that evolve within material structures and cultural and discursive norms. While this insight has corrected a number of false assumptions concerning the autonomy of the experiencing self, it has also reproduced the Cartesian insistence that experience is unreliable. The question, as posed by Boud *et al.* (1993), has become "How can we recognize how our own experience can be a trap which limits learning?" (p. 127). The general answer is that we must interrogate our experience, free it from potentially misleading preconceptions, and overcome sociocultural and psychic distortions. Adult learning is transformative to the degree that it frees us from "libidinal, linguistic, epistemic, institutional, or environmental forces that limit our options and our rational control over our lives" (Mezirow, 1991, p. 87).

Defining the authentic self in terms of freedom, first, from the imposition of the will of others and, second, from the distortions bred of socialization both constructs and sustains the isolated knower. While both freedom of choice and the critique of received opinion are arguably important educational goals, they are also part of a dream – a myth – of self that is, ultimately, a dream of escape from sociality. They are ways of denying that we will always need others, that only some truths are ever available, that, far from being "the weakness of our nature" (Descartes 1637[1960], p. 175), the historical and interpersonal quality of our experience is the enabling structure within which we can know anything at all. Thus, many theories of experiential learning have yet to recover from Descartes' determination to accept nothing as true that he has not personally tested and its dream of freedom from contamination by the Otherness lurking both within and without.

In later chapters, I will return to the question of asociality and the isolated knower and explore experience as historical and social rather than individual. Before doing that, however, I want to take up a further form of detachment that characterizes the Western epistemological tradition, namely, valorization of reason and the concomitant devaluing of other paths to knowledge. Specifically, Chapter two will explore how the discourse of experiential learning replicates the traditional Western binary between mind and body and reproduces the assumptions and power relationships that are maintained by that divide.

Notes

1   For the classic study of the body as a metaphor for boundaries, boundedless, and threat, see Douglas (1966).
2   For a classic treatment of this tradition of autobiography, see Weintraub (1978). For feminist critiques of this form of autobiography, see, in addition to Gilmore, Benstock (1988), Friedman (1988), and Baena (2005).
3   Like most of his contemporaries, when Rousseau said "man," he meant it. Rousseau's proposed education for girls is an education in dependency rather than independence, docility and obedience rather than autonomy, conformity to received opinion rather than indifference and contempt. For the classic eighteenth-century feminist response

to Rousseau, see Mary Wollstonecraft's *A Vindication of the Rights of Woman with Strictures on Political and Moral Subjects*. For a discussion of the sexism of the Enlightenment view of selfhood, see Gatens (1988).

4 According to Hiemstra (2003), tools for measuring self-direction in learners include the Self-Directed Learning Readiness Scale, the Oddi Continuing Learning Inventory, the PRO-SDLS, and the Learner Autonomy Profile.

5 For an example of this kind of description, see Hiemstra (2000).

6 Wildemeersch and Jansen (1992), among others, have pointed out that the critical pedagogy of Paulo Freire also holds autonomy as a normative value, albeit a collectivist one. Within the liberal humanist perspective of Knowles and Kolb, autonomy requires us to recapture an inner core of authentic self. Freire's collectivist version of this sees the social existence of oppressed people as leading to false consciousness and mystification. If they are to have a truer, more authentic vision of their own knowledge and interests, they must be freed from the blinders imposed by sociality.

2

GENDER, REASON, AND THE UNIVERSAL KNOWER

I was beten for a book, pardee!
[I was beaten on account of a book, by God.]

Geoffrey Chaucer, *The Canterbury Tales*, III 712

Experience is arguably *the* major theme of contemporary discussions of adult learning. Beginning with Eduard Lindeman's foundational statement that "experience is the adult learner's living textbook" (as cited in Knowles, 1990, p. 29), adult learning has been understood as the process through which "learners become aware of significant experience" (Knowles, 1990, p. 30). "Learning," according to David Kolb (1984), "is the process whereby knowledge is created through the transformation of experience" (p. 38). Jack Mezirow (1991) argues in a similar vein: "to the extent that adult education strives to foster reflective learning, its goal becomes one of either confirmation or transformation of ways of interpreting experience" (p. 6).

As this last quotation suggests, however, a substantial amount of discussion has centered on precisely *how* experience can and should be analyzed. As the means for "turning experience into learning" (Boud *et al.*, 1985, title), what is typically referred to as "reflection" has been especially valorized. Reflection, according to Boud *et al.* (1985), "is a generic term for those intellectual and affective activities in which individuals engage to explore their experiences in order to lead to new understandings and appreciations"(p. 19). Such activities matter, according to various theorists, because the experiences adults have had in the world can give rise to intellectually limiting suppositions. Adult education must therefore help adults to "examine their habits and biases and open their minds to new approaches" (Knowles, 1990, p. 60). Reflective forms of thinking allow adults to analyze their own experience, identify their characteristic assumptions and belief systems, and scrutinize the origins, validity, and consequences of their ideas.

Twentieth-century traditions of adult learning posited at least two versions of this self-reflective probing of experience. In the liberal humanist tradition, experience is understood as the shapeless, prelinguistic product of unmediated sensory input; we only come to understand "the meaning of our concrete immediate experiences by internally reflecting on their presymbolic impact ..." (Kolb, 1984, p. 52). More radical, emancipatory schools see experience as socially constructed rather than as unmediated; the first step toward true consciousness, therefore, is the process through which "individuals analyzing their own reality become aware of their prior, distorted perceptions and thereby come to have a new perception of that reality" (Freire, 1974, p. 107). While these two versions offer quite different understandings of experience, the relationships posited between experience and reflection are more alike than different. In each case, experience happens first, while reflection is the "processing phase" (Boud *et al.* 1985, p. 18), the subsequent period of self-exploration through which the mind transforms experience into learning. Experience, whether pre-rational or ideologically over-determined, is seen as insufficient in its own terms; both schools assume, and, to a certain degree, construct, specific algorithms for how reflection transforms experience into something beyond itself.

Specifically, the distinction between experience and reflection imposes both a hierarchy of value and a chronology of increasing detachment. Experience is immediate but messy; it comes with all the human frailty still attached – impressionistic sensory input according to one view; socially imposed distortion and bias according to the other. That messiness can be transcended only through the application of sustained and self-conscious rational thought that, by encouraging distance and objectivity, will allow us to identify our prior assumptions, use our minds to critique them for validity and serviceability, and reconstruct them to make them more accurate, inclusive, and empowering. Reflection is thus both ordered and ordering; it bestows meaning where there was none or else greater clarity where there was lesser. Through reflection, we are always getting better. Through reflection, we partake of the dream of reason, the Western tale of progress through rationality.

In Chapter one, I focused on one aspect of this model of experiential learning, specifically the privatization of the self and the imperative to detach from others. The suspicion of others articulated by Descartes is deeply anti-social, an epistemological version of rugged individualism that, in effect, raises paranoia to a virtue. In this chapter, I want to address a second form of detachment that again continues to weave through treatments of experiential learning, namely a particular form of the mind/body dualism that emerges in the course of the Enlightenment. That dualism, which posits an active, rational, male-coded mind whose task is to regulate the passive, experiential, female-coded body, underlies assumptions concerning experiential learning that are much in effect today. In brief, my argument will be that the emphasis on rationality at the expense of the non-"rational," the devaluing of embodied forms of experience and learning, and the accent on (self)-observation and (self)-interrogation all play out within a particular social and epistemological history. That history has produced a version of the experiential learner in which learning from experience is understood as an exercise in self-mastery. This not only traps us within power differentials that have historically played out across gender, class, and race, but entangles us in a worrisome relationship to ourselves in which the emotions and the body are seen as unreliable and dangerous and in which reason's task is to internalize matrices of sovereignty and control.

In what follows, I focus on specific Enlightenment figures to trace the emergence of an exemplary 'experiential learner' who gains status as an authorized knower by detaching from the elements of experience itself: its emotional and sensate qualities, its embodiment, its locatedness in the ongoing stream of social life. The result is a curiously abstract, faceless knower whose human specificity has been erased but who occupies a very real social location, one that grants privilege in a new intellectual order in which Alisoun as the epistemological rebel has again been marginalized.

Reason, control, and the mind/body dualism

From Plato onward, Western epistemology has seen reason as the key to knowledge. Associated with form as opposed to matter and the mind in opposition to emotion and desire, the human faculty for producing reliable knowledge has been located at the furthest possible remove from human corporeality. The human body itself, notoriously demanding and implacably material, has traditionally been seen as the enemy of reason, and the search for truth has been represented as a chronology of detachment from the specificity that adheres to human bodies and human histories. Knowledge based on everyday, lived experience is seen as partial and subjective; knowledge is authorized in the Western tradition through a discourse that feminist scholars have called 'abstract masculinity,' the claim that, through the right exercise of reason, all interestedness, corporeality, and subjectivity can be excised (Flax, 1993; Nead, 1992).

Feminist scholars have argued that the taxonomy of dualisms allied to mind versus body – thought/feeling, objectivity/subjectivity, abstract/concrete, and culture/nature – is always a gendered construct. The male stands for order, civilization, form; the female, associated with nature, experience, and the body, represents the very categories that must come under the domination of the mind. While the Western tradition posits rationality as universal and therefore sexually neutral, knowledge is seen as power over unreason and disorder, and the failure to detach from the emotional and sensual is traditionally associated with the formlessness and disarray of the female body itself (Gatens, 1988).

As Susan Bordo (1986) has pointed out, the 'masculine' in abstract masculinity names "not a biological category but a cognitive style, an epistemological stance" (p. 451). Its key term is *detachment*, not only from others but from one's own emotional life, from the particularities of time and place, from personal quirks, prejudices, and interests, and from the objects of one's inquiry. More specifically, the claims to detachment focus on the capacity to transcend two specific sites in which human beings are always located: their bodies and their position within the human matrix. The claim discussed in Chapter one, that one can disassociate from a life within social, economic, and political relationships, is matched by the claim that one can rise above one's own corporeal existence and detach simultaneously from one's own body, from the body of the cosmos and of nature, and from those – i.e. women – whose being is seen as too enmeshed in corporality to make the same claim.

Again, Chaucer's Wife of Bath represents both the medieval view of mind and body and the ways in which their relationship is seen to change in the course of the Enlightenment. Alisoun's identification with Venus is, as we have seen, an identification with the life of the world, but it is also an identification with the "sely [happy] instrument(s)" (III 132) and "jolitee" (III 470) of the body that, in medieval terms, could be condemned as the site of sin but that are none the less part of the cosmic unity of God. The medieval division of the cosmos into matter and spirit associated the female with both *mater* and *materia*, the inferior but nonetheless necessary stuff out of which the temporal world was made. Thus, however despised by the dominant discourse, the body placed human beings within nature as surely as the soul connected them to the cosmos within mutually determining structures of meaning (Bordo, 1986). The body was the mundane world writ small.

In replacing the medieval presumption of cosmic unity with the ideal of detached, autonomous consciousness, the Enlightenment initiated a new relationship between reason, corporality, and self-mastery. The primary terms of the mind/body dualism shift from sacred/profane to reason/unreason. In the process, the medieval *psychomachia*, the war of the soul between the vices and the virtues, becomes an internalized exercise in self-control in which reason rather than virtue authors the emergence of the bourgeois individual (Falk, 1994).

This change has implications that are political as much as they are religious. Rather than a soul fit for entrance into heaven, the new ideal is a rational and self-interested consciousness that is compatible with the franchise and the social contract. It becomes reason's task to fit the corporeal 'man' into the economic and political Order, "which is nothing else than a regimen that bodies pass through; the reduction of randomness, impulse, forgetfulness; the domestication of an animal, as Nietzsche claimed, to the point where it can make, and hold to, a promise" (Welbery, as cited in Falk, 1994, p. 5). The mind/body relationship, in effect, is a political relationship in which the mind must subjugate and govern the unruly body and in which the ability of reason to exercise such control mirrors political authority (Gatens, 1988). The birth of the human subject who can exercise self-government through reason thus parallels the birth of the body politic, the artificial body of the state that enables an ordered society. As Moira Gatens points out, the two births presuppose each other; the body politic both supports and requires a human subject capable of self-government.

The centrality of reason and its managerial relationship to embodied and sensate experience explains the close connection in Locke's thinking between epistemological and political agency and between empiricism and liberalism; the positing of the individual as autonomous and rational justified the resistance to absolute monarchy and enabled political and economic agency to adhere in the individual. That is, individual rights of liberty and property are a function of the ability to make reasoned choices that further the rational management of society (Lawson, 1991). Thus, the ability to rise above contingent self-interest forms the basis of moral and political no less than epistemological authority; having rights is a function of the ability to make rational choices that prevail over the waywardness of embodied desire and thus contribute to maintaining the social order and the social good.

The erasure of human specificity

There are enormous implications for the theories of experiential learning in the emerging paradigm. Before turning to them directly, however, it will be helpful to explore an odd paradox in the 'experiential learner' who emerges in the Enlightenment, specifically the seemingly democratic claim, on the one hand, that all knowers are interchangeable and, on the other, the use of that claim to justify the exclusion of many, including women, from the ranks of those who can claim to learn from experience. While Descartes may be typical of the period in his insistence that "even those who have the feeblest souls can acquire a very absolute dominion over all their passions if sufficient industry is applied in training and guiding them" (as cited Bordo, 1986, p. 452), it appears that only a very specific group of people are seen to have such "industry."

The democratization of knowledge that emerges with the Enlightenment is based on the supposition that, all things being equal, all have access to the same world, the same rules of evidence, and the same ability to utilize reason to decide what is true. Access to vernacular texts through translations from the Latin, the overturning of ancient verities in favor of empirical observation, and claims such as Galileo's that anyone applying the rules of observation and analysis will reach the same conclusions all promote a new empirical reality in which old forms of *auctoritee* [authority] have been overthrown.

At the same time, the "anyone" who looks through Galileo's telescope is an oddly faceless figure, curiously devoid of human specificities. The ideal knower is interchangeable with all others; able to rise above the human contingencies of emotion, historicity, and social position, the rationale, knowledge-making self is disembodied and universalized. Who we are and what our experience has been doesn't ultimately matter; the same knowledge is available to everyone because, no matter where we are situated, everyone will see the same thing.

Donna Haraway (1991a) has named this claim "the god-trick of seeing everything from nowhere" (p. 189). Whatever ties the knower to a contextualized human life must be purged of all of its specificity so that one can achieve a "view from nowhere" (Nagel, as cited in Bordo, 1990, p. 137), detached equally from body, feelings, values, cultural and economic interests, and sociality. Thus, however much the new epistemological paradigm recognizes concrete experience, the goal is to use the evidence of the senses to derive objective and universal knowledge that is always and everywhere the same.

No concrete embodied human life, of course, can actually gain purchase on this view from nowhere. The claim to have transcended a specific social location requires the rejection of the body in several interrelated ways that both undergird relations of real social power and limit the ability to create knowledge to a specific social location: that of European upper-class men. Now that it is laudatory for men to learn from experience, not only they can, but they are the *only ones* who can; women, whose ties to the body cannot, according to this view, be transcended are newly dismissed on the grounds that they are unable to construct knowledge from experience.

Drawing on important work by Steven Shapin and Simon Schaffer, Haraway (1997) has used Robert Boyle's experiments on the air pump in the mid-seventeenth-century as paradigmatic of forms of knowledge production that deny the social locatedness of the universalized knower while simultaneously limiting the ranks of experiential learners to a small demographic elite. Historically, Boyle's use of the air pump to prove the existence of a vacuum was deeply embedded in material and social conditions. The experiments took place in the presence of other leisured gentlemen like himself and required laboring men to work the bellows of the air pump. Since the existence of a vacuum was established through the asphyxiation of mice, it was argued that the experiments would upset the ladies, and experiments were therefore purposefully performed late at night so that women could not attend. Yet neither the absence of women nor the presence of working-class men is mentioned in Boyle's own accounts of his experiments. The historical and social moment disappears, not only the gender and class relationships, but the air pump as technological apparatus, rapidly changing cultural standards for evidence and proof, and a shift in the culture/nature dualism that allowed animals to be tortured in the name of science. Rather, Boyle presents his findings as the universalized, transparent, socially neutral effects of measurement, experiment, and reason.

Contemporary theorists have argued that this "seventeenth century English disappearing act" (Haraway, 1997, p. 113) is less a matter of transcending social location than of rendering one's location invisible. That is, the abstract masculinist knower is not detached from historicity and social location as such, but is able to frame his relationship to them in such a way that its social character disappears. This erasure is itself an effect of social relations; because life maintenance activities are performed for him by others and because the prosperous, white, heterosexual, male body constitutes the "unmarked" category, his knowledge can be portrayed as a function of abstract measurement, technology, and reason rather than the result of historically specific, socially located practices and relationships.

Specifically, the claim to have transcended the body is based on a relationship to the body that is doubly materially located, first in the concrete life experience of men of the dominant social group and, secondly, in the power to render those social relationships invisible. Those activities most associated with the sustaining of bodily life – preparing food, maintaining the living environment, caring for the young and old, tending the sick, etc. – are performed by women and by lower class men who carry out their tasks figuratively and often literally outside the view of elite males. Dorothy Smith (1987), among others, has argued that the abstract, conceptual mode of producing knowledge "exists in and depends upon a world known immediately and directly in the bodily mode" and on the

> actual work and organization of work by others who make the concrete, the particular, the bodily. ... It is taken for granted in the organization of work that such matters are provided for in a way that will not interfere with action and participation in the conceptual mode.
>
> *(Smith, 1987, p. 81)*[1]

[handwritten margin note: does this cnx to theory about men never understanding women?]

Thus, Boyle can claim this kind of disembodied knowledge because he and his fellow researchers are all of a social class – Protestant gentlemen of independent means – who alone among the population are sufficiently "diligent and judicious" to attest to the truth of an observation. Trustworthiness required the freedom, disinterestedness, and independence that only gentlemen could claim. Those who were by definition dependent, such as servants and women, did not have the independence and disinterestedness to be credible witnesses, while merchants were too self-interested and Catholics too crafty to be relied on to tell the truth (Shapin, 1994). Boyle himself, son of the wealthy and powerful Earl of Cork, personifies what he himself called a "modesty" that was understood by his contemporaries to be a new form of absolute authority. In separating fact from causal explanations, Boyle could display modesty concerning the latter while at the same time claiming that his "matters of fact" were unassailable mirrors of reality, not open to debate or interrogation. It was nature itself that forced acceptance of one's facts while one stood modestly by.

Modesty, of course, is itself a gendered concept. The Royal Society to which Boyle and his colleagues belonged has been characterized as a continuation of a medieval clerical culture that was both ascetic and exclusively male (Noble 1992, as cited in Haraway, 1997, p. 27). Boyle, a lifelong celibate, describes mathematics as contributing to the "Practice of Vertu" and maintains that he uses "Geometricall Speculations" to control his "raving tendencies." The use of mathematics in the emerging world of scientific experimentation, moreover, becomes a way to distance science from the very experiential foundations that form its core. Boyle held to the Aristotelian distinction between representing the world in symbolic form and the world of material particulars, and he valued mathematics as a means of verifying knowledge without recourse to direct experience. Thus, mathematics is sacred precisely because of the dropping away of the metaphoric content of mundane reality. As a practice owing nothing to experience, it carries the promise of protection from the defilement of the everyday.

Old wives and authorized knowledge

Thus, Alisoun and her sister old wives have again been relegated to the margins of knowledge. With the rise of experimental science, Alisoun, the cloth manufacturer proclaiming the right to her own experiential learning, is reabsorbed into the trope of the illiterate, superstitious old woman who gossips as she spins (Reeves, 1999). By 1570, a "Canterbury tale" had become synonymous with an old wives' tale to mean a silly superstition with no experiential foundation or evidence. Galileo invokes Alisoun's old nemesis, St. Jerome, to dismiss "the chatty old women" (as cited in Reeves, 1999, p. 326) whom he associates with all that impedes scientific progress: ignorance, garrulousness, oral tradition, and literal-mindedness. Sir Francis Bacon portrays nature as an enigmatic female who must be undressed, squeezed, penetrated, and, by some accounts, tortured so that her secrets can be revealed (Merchant, 1980; Merchant, 2008). The case of Johnannes Kepler is perhaps the most ironic. Kepler claims that "untutored experience … is the mother who gives birth to Science as her offspring" (as cited in Reeves, 1999, p. 347) while defending his own mother from the charge of witchcraft by calling her a silly and ineffectual old woman who is much too powerless to be a witch.

Indeed, even knowledge-practices such as healing and midwifery that had traditionally been practiced by women became subject to the new claims for disembodiment and objectivity. The usurping of the role of female midwives by male obstetricians took place at a time in which the competence of midwives was demonstrably greater than that of physicians (the mortality rate for puerile fever, for example, was far higher for physician-assisted births), yet the rise of a male-only cadre of obstetricians was hailed as a victory for knowledge, culture, and science over superstition and ignorance. A number of qualities allowed midwifery to be thus disparaged: it was an oral tradition passed on through family and community networks, for example, not a text-based curriculum taught in formal centers such as universities (Dalmiya and Alcoff, 1993). But the significance extends further into new formulations based on the traditional gendered dualisms associated with male/female, with midwifery inescapably coded within the despised second terms: embodied, practical, experiential, particular, emotional, and concrete.

First, the denunciation of midwifery rested on the dismissal of the body as a site of experiential knowledge. The term 'old wives' tale' originally referred to the lore of midwives; because midwives were older women (old wives) who had themselves been through childbirth, their knowledge could not be separated either from their own experience of life in a sexual and gendered body, and it could not be considered objective because of their ability to empathize with what the birthing mother experienced. The lack of empathy, indeed the utter ignorance, of the female experience of childbearing was construed as an epistemic advantage rather than a limitation for male physicians; their greater distance from the physicality of birthing made their knowledge more, not less, legitimate (Dalmiya and Alcoff, 1993).

It is interesting to note how, in this process, only female knowledge is seen as gendered. The midwives' femaleness, that is, their experience of life in a body that can carry, bear, and nurse children, is central to the way their knowledge is represented. Male physicians, of course, are also implicitly defined in terms of gendered physicality – in this case, the inability to bear a child – but that is portrayed as an absence of gendered experience and a detachment from physicality rather than an equally gendered relationship to the processes of birth. As was the case with the claims of gentleman scientists such as Robert Boyle, it is only the marked body of the marginalized that is considered to have social and biological embodiment, with the privileged given the status of the universal knower unmarked by human particularity.

Further, as Dalmiya and Alcoff have argued, the victory of obstetrics rested on the specific distinction between theory and practice, that is, between propositional knowledge, defined as science, and the practical knowledge of pregnancy and birth. Medicine, it was argued, offered systematic axioms that could be abstracted from specific cases and contexts. Midwifery, on the other hand, could not be detached from the situatedness of experience and practice: it was performative rather than conative, it focused on individual cases rather than on universal laws, and it was based on intervention and interaction rather than disinterested contemplation and research. In opposition to the Cartesian rejection of labor, desire, and materiality, midwifery thus remained implicated in all three, ineffably social, rooted in family- and community-based women's knowledge, and undetachable from all the corporeal messiness of pain, fear, blood, sexuality, endurance, life and death, and love.

The gendered relationship to birth, moreover, takes on additional meanings in a period that early seventeenth-century scientist and jurist Sir Francis Bacon called "a truly masculine birth of time." Taken literally, the science of the period denied the role of women in human reproduction. No longer seen even as the nurturing raw material for life, as had been the case in earlier periods, the female was believed merely to incubate the generations of fully formed human beings, or homunculi, whom God had placed in Adam's semen (Bordo, 1986). Taken metaphorically, this fantasy of male auto-procreation played out as the 'birth' of the self-governing male political subject. While Enlightenment liberalism and eighteenth-century political philosophy questioned the power of father over son and king over society, it refused to question the power of man over woman, whose body was specifically excluded from membership in the artificial body of the state. As the not-I of a newly alien universe, allied to nature as "an unruly and malevolent virago" (Bordo, 1986, p. 454), the female body is the disruptive Other in need of on-going, and often violent, control. According to Aman, representative of the French revolutionary Committee for General Security, "Women by their constitution are open to an exaltation which could be ominous in public life. The interests of the state would soon be sacrificed to all kinds of disruption and disorder that hysteria can produce" (as cited in Gatens, 1988, p. 65).

As Carole Pateman (1988) has pointed out, the sons who challenged the father-king created, not democracy, but fraternity. Like its prototype, Athens, the body politic of the Enlightenment was founded on male-only political rights whose patron was a masculinized, motherless goddess born directly from the head of Zeus (Gatens, 1988). The severity of the attack against revolution-era feminism was

Kolb, it would seem, does not intend to replicate the universalized, rationalistic Enlightenment knower. He explicitly argues that adults construct knowledge differently depending on gender, class, and ethnicity. Yet the "learning cycle" described above, which is by far the most influential part of his work, replicates Enlightenment epistemology quite closely. The sides of his cycle are the methods of science – observation, experimentation, and reason – through which, according to Locke, the mind transforms experience into knowledge. Top and bottom, in turn, replicate the Lockean dichotomy between immediately available data and ideas constructed within the mind. Reality is seen as "simply there, grasped through a mode of knowing here called apprehension" (Dewey, as cited in Kolb, 1984, p. 39); comprehension is a second-order activity, the product of applied rationality through which "we impose order into what would otherwise be a seamless, unpredictable flow" (Ibid., p. 43).[2] The knowledge thus abstracted is the product of an individual mind; at the same time, it takes the form of universalized concepts that are at significant spatial and temporal remove from the original experience. The theme of shaping and control, moreover, is matched later in Kolb's text by a gendering of epistemological values. Apprehension is both highly personal and lovingly communal; it is a "process of affirmation … based on belief, trust, and conviction" and is tied to subjectivity, like-minded community, and silence. Comprehension, on the other hand, is both autonomous and public. Its critical edge offers "tremendous powers of communication, prediction, and control" (Ibid., p. 44).

I have used Kolb as an example because he is at once representative and influential, but these same elements of Enlightenment epistemology – knowledge as a transformation of experience, reason as the sanctioned path to knowledge, and the universal knower – undermine treatments of adult learning that are otherwise quite disparate. Theorists such as Jack Mezirow, for example, whose approaches to both reason and democracy owe a great deal to the work of Jürgen Habermas, question the ideal of abstract knowledge, contending that all knowledge is constructed within power-laden social process. At the same time, Mezirow follows Habermas in what feminists have critiqued as a falsely universalizing approach to consensus and truth claims (Benhabib, 1996; Hart, 1990a), maintaining that we arrive at our best knowledge through the exercise of reason and that, freed from bigotry through dialogue and self-reflection, all knowers can arrive at congruent truths.

The same gendering of experience and reflection, I would argue, characterizes the work of Paulo Freire. Freire's male-normed language is notorious, as is his failure to treat gender as a category of difference (Weiler, 1991; Luke, 1992), but his treatment of the colonized mentality of the oppressed raises issues of its own. The masses are described in his work as self-deprecating, emotionally dependent, and passive – in other words, as womanly – and Freire sees their intellectual disempowerment as acts of "domestication" (1974: see, for example, p. 36), thus metaphorically equating male-dominated systems of class and national oppression with the subjugation of men within a female-dominated sphere.

Secondly, education itself is seen by Freire (1993) as an act of intellectual ordering. Freire quotes Mao to the effect that we must "teach the masses clearly what we have learned from them confusedly" (p. 74, note 7). This capacity for order and clarity is not seen as arising from the experience of the masses themselves, whose view is seen as partial and subjective. Rather, clarity arrives with the educator who, as authorized knower, is assumed to have access to objective knowledge; like Boyle's gentlemen, but unlike the peasants, the educator is able to detach from the distortions of social location. The oppressed cannot do so and therefore have no coherent analytical framework or self-authorizing capacity of their own.

In Freire's work, of course, gender is subsumed under an explicit attention to class and nationality, and the school of adult learning with which his work is aligned reminds us that gender is not the only category of difference through which people are denied epistemological authority. In Chapter three, I will add class, race, and nationality to the meld of the dualisms through which experiential learning is or isn't acknowledged and the social practices through which knowledge is or isn't recognized. In so doing, I will also complete this short history of the 'experiential learner' by moving from the emergence of experimental science and political citizenship in the seventeenth and eighteenth centuries to the development of the social sciences in the nineteenth century and the rise of the bureaucratic state.

In some ways, the following chapter can be seen simply as expanding the terms of dualisms already explored: mind/body, male/female, and experience/reflection. Certainly, a number of patterns continue: Locke's notion of experience as raw material, the pretense of detachment from social location, the notion of the mind as something to be explored. At the same time, I want to mark a number of additions and changes that will be central to what follows. First, the relationship between knowledge and detachment we have seen in the natural sciences of the seventeenth century are both transferred onto and changed by the human sciences that emerge in the nineteenth and twentieth centuries. With the rise of the professions, the human sciences, and modern bureaucratic state, the appropriation of the experience of others and the privileging of mind at the expense of body become explicit material power moves within which knowledge is coded as power. The erasure of non-rational sites of knowledge-production such as emotion, the body, and material labor is re-enacted in the draining of knowledge from the shop floor, the home, and the colonial village in favor of professionalized expertise. The knowledge so constructed is a form of social power co-determinous with the rise of middle-class society, and the ability to control irrational elements of the self becomes the justification for the right to control new proletarian and subaltern classes created by colonialism and industrial society.

Notes

1   Abstract masculinity depends on the paradox that what is most socially privileged is at the same time least socially visible to itself. The ability to see one's own experience as universally valid is easier if it is cast in terms of the representatively and even universally human. As typically white, higher class, and male, the universal knower is not seen, and is not encouraged to see himself, as marked by social specificities of race, class, and gender. Unlike women, whose gender is always visible, for example,

'man' is at one and the same time a gendered being *and* a figure of representative humanity. Similarly, unlike people of color, whites in a white, racist society are not invariably seen as members of a race. Many who occupy one or another unmarked category may find ourselves wishing this were not the case, but social inequality makes this subject to something other than our own (good) will. Consider the following two sentences: Tony Morrison, the African American woman novelist, won the Nobel Prize for Literature in 1993. William Wordsworth, the white male poet, was appointed Poet Laureate in 1843. That the second but not the first sentence appears odd is not the result of explicit sexist and racist bias on the part of the individual reader, but the effect of "white" and "male" as unmarked social categories.

2 The quotations from John Dewey that I have used in this chapter are taken from the writings of David Kolb and Peter Jarvis. My own view, which I discuss extensively in Chapter six, is that such quotations by Dewey are misleading and often taken out of context and that both the separation of experience and reflection and the mind/ body dualism are foreign to Dewey's thought.

3

"OTHERING" RATIONALITY

the Other is denied full human status

Who peyntede the leon, tel me who?
By god! if wommen hadde writen stories,
As clerkes han withinne hire oratories,
They wolde han writen of men moore wikkednesse
Than al the mark of adam may redresse.

[Who painted the lion, tell me? Who?[1]
By God, if women had written stories
As clergy do in their oratories,
They would have written about more wickedness by men
Than all of Adam's sex could correct.]

Geoffrey Chaucer, *The Canterbury Tales*, III 692–6

In the preceding chapters, I approached the changing understandings of experience and reason almost exclusively in terms of gender. In this chapter, I want to expand the discussion to include the ways in which epistemological hierarchies are also embedded in discourses of class and race. Within modern societies administered by industrial and governmental bureaucracies, gender continues to function as a category of differential power but must be understood as part of a broader taxonomy that serves to justify multiple forms of inequity. Specifically, the claim to be able to learn from experience, and the parallel claim that other people cannot, are central to the class identities and class relations of capitalism, the rise of the bureaucratic state, the emergence of the professions, and the European appropriation of the non-Western world. As Donna Haraway (1989) has argued, "the marked bodies of race, class, and sex have been at the center, not the margins, of knowledge in modern conditions" (p. 289). While the 'Other' is denied full human status, the anxiety *about* the Other is the focus of attention. It is *the* topic of politics, of epistemology, of epistemology *as* politics.

Irrationality and the 'Other'

In what follows, I will pay a good deal of attention to the emerging discourses of sociology and anthropology, but I want to start with another genre of the period, namely the industrial novel that sought to communicate the misery of working-class conditions to a middle-class readership. Written in the city of Manchester in the middle of the nineteenth century, Elizabeth Gaskell's *Mary Barton* tells the story of the class turmoil existing between factory owners and workers. Gaskell's stated goal for writing the novel was to encourage acts of compassion on the part of the more fortunate and to argue that class strife might be averted if "masters" and "men" understood each other's common humanity.

In comments concerning the novel in the year following its publication, Gaskell describes the impulse behind the novel.

> I bethought me how deep might be the romance in the lives of some of those who elbowed me daily in the busy streets of the town in which I resided. I had always felt a deep sympathy with the care-worn men, who looked as if doomed to struggle through their lives. ... A little manifestation of this sympathy and a little attention to the expression of feelings on the part of some of the work-people with whom I was acquainted, had laid open to me the hearts of one or two of the more thoughtful among them; I saw that they were sore and irritable against the rich, the even tenor of whose seemingly happy lives appeared to increase the anguish caused by the lottery-like nature of their own. Whether the bitter complaints made by them, of the neglect which they experienced from the prosperous – especially from the masters whose fortunes they had helped to build up – were well-founded or no, it is not for me to judge. It is enough to say, that this belief of the injustice and unkindness which they endure from their fellow-creatures, taints what might be resignation to God's will, and turns it to revenge in too many of the poor uneducated factory-workers of Manchester.
>
> The more I reflected on this unhappy state of things between those so bound to each other by common interests, as the employers and the employed must ever be, the more anxious I became to give some utterance to the agony which, from time to time, convulses this dumb people; the agony of suffering without the sympathy of the happy, or of erroneously believing that such is the case. ...
>
> I can remember now that the prevailing thought in my mind at the time ... was the seeming injustice of the inequalities of fortune. Now, if they occasionally appeared unjust to the more fortunate, they must bewilder an ignorant man full of rude, illogical thought, and full also of sympathy for

suffering which appealed to him through his senses. I fancied I saw how all this might lead to a course of action which might appear right for a time to the bewildered mind of such a one.

(Gaskell, 1997, p.74)

In terms of the politics of experience, this statement is noteworthy in several ways. First, the experience of the working-class themselves is represented in terms of "the expression of feeling" rather than of thought: the poor are made "sore," "irritable," and "bitter" by the neglect and injustice they experience and the sympathy they feel for others; as they "endure" and "struggle," what might be resignation changes to the desire for revenge. Second, while Gaskell represents herself as taking no position as to whether or not working-class perceptions are correct, she repeatedly qualifies the truth of those perceptions in phrases such as "looked as if," "seemingly happy," "appeared to increase," "erroneously believing," "seeming injustice," and "might appear right." Thus, experience does not serve the poor as the basis for knowledge; as "uneducated" and "ignorant" people "full of rude, illogical thought," even their feelings of sympathy can only lead them astray. Gaskell twice uses the verb "bewilder" to describe the mental processes through which workers attempt to make sense of their experience. Even the few "more thoughtful among them" are not seen as being able to construct an understanding of their own based on their experience. Nor are members of the working-class seen as being able to speak for themselves. They are "dumb" and need Gaskell to "give utterance" to what they themselves cannot express.

There is a particular irony about this last point, in that *Mary Barton* depicts, albeit in a distorted fashion, the contemporaneous Chartist movement for working-class rights, a movement notable for its printed material, literacy classes, and networks of working-class self-education (Vicinus, 1974). As elsewhere in mainstream discourse, *Mary Barton* characterizes working-class political speech in terms of its opposite, an animal-like *in*ability to make or articulate meaning, a trope that was conventionally used in this period to justify the denial of the very political rights to which workers laid claim.[2] Thomas Carlyle's influential "Chartism," for example, justifies the refusal to extend the franchise by characterizing working-class speech as mindless and suggesting that what workers really want is to be governed by others.

What are all the popular commotions and maddest bellowings, from Peterloo to the Place-de-Greve itself? Bellowings, inarticulate cries as of a dumb creature in rage and pain; to the ear of wisdom they are inarticulate prayers: 'Guide me, govern me! I am mad and miserable, and cannot guide myself!'

(as cited in Cottom, 1987, p. 60)

Rationality, power, and the rise of the social sciences

As recent theories of representation have demonstrated, any construction of an 'Other' is of necessity also a construction of a 'self.' Carlyle's description of working-class protest and Gaskell's comments about her novel implicitly construct a middle-class reader no less than a working-class object of discussion, a reader who, unlike the working-class, has the intellectual capacity to make reasoned sense of experience. The experience of the poor can be made into meaning, but it requires the analytical capacity of those who, as bell hooks (1990) has written, claim "to know us better than we can know ourselves" (p. 22; see also Jansen, 1991). The association of the white middle-class with sagacity and conscious awareness meant that knowledge could be used to justify power; as John Stuart Mill, among others, argued, the educated members of society could better judge the interests of the uneducated than they were able to do themselves. Two closely related chronologies of detachment interact within this formulation. First, direct social experience is insufficient to understand the 'true' workings of society, so that insight into society comes to characterize a (not only) epistemological elite. Second, intellectuals and professional experts are seen as being above class and national interests, so that privileged access to knowledge and to the right to render meaning can be reformulated as objective, disinterested schemes for influence and control (Fabian, 1983).

It is in that context that the rise of the social sciences in the nineteenth century must be understood, not only as the emergence of new disciplines and knowledge-practices, but as part of the self-definition of the middle-class as what Carlyle here calls the "ear of wisdom." By promoting the middle-class identification with professionalized and bureaucratized expertise, the social sciences served as a justification for middle-class power and hegemony. The emerging discourses of sociology, anthropology, and public health held ignorance, sexuality, and lack of self-awareness to be indicative of lower human status; the capacity for rational self-management came to be associated with middle-class modes of being, while irrationality was seen to characterize a series of largely interchangeable Others that included 'savages' abroad and, as we have seen, the working-class at home (Torgovnick, 1990; Cottom, 1987).

Indeed, the anthropological discourse on native peoples ran in parallel fashion to that concerning the working-class; as with the poor of Europe, the inability of colonials to rule themselves was considered to derive from a lack of ordered rationality and coherent speech. The Enlightenment may have stressed the universality of reason, yet such key figures as Voltaire in France, Hume in Scotland, and Jefferson in America denied literary and cognitive capacity to Africans and other 'natives', and nineteenth-century philosophy and social science continued in this discourse. Even in the twentieth century, anthropological discourse consistently characterized Africans as lacking the intellectual organization to construct knowledge from experience. In *The Primitive Mentality* (1922), Levy-Bruhl distinguishes the pre-logical thought of 'primitives' from rational understanding of causal determination and relationships (as cited in Mudimbe, 1988, pp. 135–6; see also Masolo, 1994). As Edward Said (1994) has said, imperialism and colonialism "are supported and perhaps even impelled by ... notions that certain territories and people *require* and beseech domination, as well as forms of knowledge affiliated with domination" (p. 9; italics in original). Since natives could not describe their lands using the language of deeds and land claims, they could not be said to own them (Davis, 1987).

The politics of vision

With the rise of the social sciences, professionals, bureaucrats, philanthropists, reformers, commissioners, doctors, and what we would now call social workers were among the groups of middle-class intellectuals who would become involved with the health, living conditions, schooling, sexual practices, and diet of the poor. As the nineteenth century progressed, various categories of "lesser" beings became subject to interventions by practitioners of the emerging disciplines of economics, sociology, anthropology, psychiatry, pedagogy, and sexology (Levy, 1991).

One feature of the emerging social sciences that is of particular relevance to adult learning theory is a growing emphasis on sight, that is, on the act of observation, and the development of social practices that allow the authorized knower to observe others unobserved. Detailed, intimate knowledge of the Other came to be understood as itself a kind of power, and the professional and bureaucratic elites of the nineteenth century justified their existence by citing a penchant for inspection and research. When, for example, the Aboriginal Society of Britain changed its name to the Ethnographic Society in 1842, the change was taken by participants as the transformation of charity into science and was marked by a resolution to the effect that the best way to help the natives was to study them (Stocking, as cited in Levy, 1991, p. 53).

In English, as in other Indo-European languages, the language of thought is the language of inspection and penetration: we contemplate, speculate, regard, explore, measure, survey, and probe. It is only with the rise of medical and social sciences, however, that the metaphorics of inspection become concretized in practices for the investigation of human beings. In nineteenth-century sociology, the ability to rationalize society – to clean up the slums; to solve the inter-related problems of disease, urban crowding, sanitation, and the uncontrolled, sexualized working-class body – was seen as the power to observe unobserved, to render working-class neighborhoods visible through a series of interventions that ranged from house-to-house surveys and statistical compilations to the substituting of narrow streets for open boulevards (Levy, 1991; Poovey 1988). In *Dombey and Son*, published at the same time as *Mary Barton*, Charles Dickens (1848 [1950]) refers to a host of urban ills ranging from air pollution to drunkenness and expresses the wish for "a good spirit who would take the house-tops off," the better to peer inside and "show a Christian people ... where Vice and Fever propagate together" (p. 616). The discourse of anthropology was similarly marked by what Marianna Torgovnick (1990) calls a "keyhole vocabulary, the vocabulary of voyeurism" (p. 4): Tyler began his classic text, *Anthropology*, by asking readers to imagine themselves in the position of the observer, standing on the dock examining people of different races (as cited in Levy, 1991, p. 51), while a generation later, in *The Sexual Life of Savages*, Malinowski bespoke the need to "follow several [of the villagers] in their love affairs, and in their marriage arrangements" and "pry into their domestic scandals" (as cited in Torgovnick, 1990, p. 3).

Jeremy Bentham's Panopticon is perhaps the clearest example of how the right to observe and the need to study code new forms of national and class power. Defined by Bentham as "a mill for grinding rogues honest and idle men industrious" (as cited in Stephan, 2011[1900], p. 201), the Panopticon was offered in 1791 as an architectural solution for prison and, later, workhouse reform. Designed and built in such a way as to permit continual one-way observation by wardens who could not themselves be seen, panopticonic structures would both allow for constant study and inspection and impose self-regulation on inmates who would never know whether or not they were being observed at any given time. The Panopticon itself was never built; after being debated through the 1790s and the first decade of the 1800s, it was never funded and ultimately, to Bentham's distress, abandoned as a scheme. The influence of the Panopticon remained, however, if only as a metaphor for observation as social technology.

Originally meant as an edifice of glass and stone, the Panopticon functioned as a metaphor for the social relations it was meant to further, unidirectional observation in which the position of the privileged knower is that of the observer outside the frame, looking down on those cast as lesser human agents (Pratt, 1986), and whose right to observe and interpret signals the ability to order and control. The same power relationships are coded in the discourses of the emerging human sciences, in which metaphors of vision and positionality produce the sociological gaze as a form of power linked to the relationships and apparatus of ruling.

> The 'sectioning off' is an effect of framing the moment of observation, the moment of 'looking at.' It is the outsider's point of entry into a living process. … The relations that underlie it organize the account over and above the observer's privileged interpretations of what was there and what happened. That very privileging is itself an 'expression' of those relations.
>
> *(as cited in Smith, 1987, pp. 115–6)*

Like the Enlightenment claim to the God's-eye view, this framing of the moment of observation is both a denial and re-inscription of social relationships. On the one hand is the assumption that the observer is detached from subjective self-interests or motives. The data collected can be separated from contaminating social contexts such as patriarchy, class friction, or colonial domination, with power re-conceived as a natural outgrowth of disinterested reason rather than the property of any individual or class (Cottom, 1987). On the other hand, quite specific social relationships are of course produced by and through that moment of vision. Those who are being studied have no input into what is being seen, what questions are being asked, what values are being forwarded, or whose interests are being served.

There is an interesting example of these same dynamics in experiential learning theory. David Kolb (1984) traces the development of his learning cycle to the insights provided by Kurt Lewin's T-groups. According to Kolb, the lesson of the

T-groups is that people learn best through a "dialectic tension and conflict between immediate, concrete experience and analytic detachment." What is interesting about this genealogy is that the knowledge base of two social groups with differential levels of authority was represented in the original encounter; the T-groups brought together the "immediate experience" of trainees and "conceptual models" of professional staff (p. 10). Kolb's grafting of this interaction onto the individual experiential learner suppresses the original power relationship between professionals and clients, but that relationship survives Kolb's internalization of the experience/reflection dualism, and the story connects experience/reflection to the hierarchies constructed by the professionalization of expertise. According to Kolb's rendition of the event, the professional staff are somehow removed from the experience itself; their understanding is in no way circumscribed by their own social roles, and their view is above and detached from any personal feelings and professional interests in the event.

I want to anticipate discussions later in this text to point to the ways in which panopticonic power relationships infuse what we tend to treat as acts of personal self-reflection. Betty Bergland (1994) argues that the self that is constructed in narratives of life and experience is never "an essential individual" who is "the originator of her own meaning." Rather, we must read that self "as socially and historically constructed and multiply positioned in complex worlds and discourses" that are themselves value- and power-laden (pp. 134, 131). Reflection on experience thus changes according to shifts in the religious, psychological, and philosophical formations, the sociocultural milieu, and the institutional power relationships within which particular stories are told and heard.

In this context, it is worth noting that the tradition of self-narrative in the West begins with the late-fourth-century *Confessions of St. Augustine* and, more generally, with the Catholic ritual of confession, a lineage that carries several implications for life narratives more generally. First, confession, as Gilmore (1994a) argues, is built around a power relationship in which the audience for the confession is both the person who mandates and judges the confession and the speaker's subsequent punisher or rewarder. Second, the speaker is prompted by what Foucault calls an "institutional incitement to speak" (as cited in Alcoff and Gray, 1993, p. 271), but in the process of speaking is stripped of authority over the meaning of what she says (Alcoff and Gray, 1993). Both the meaning and the status of the speaker's words are determined by the expert listener, in this case the confessor. That same power relationship is recreated when confession moves out from theological contexts and into clinical and judicial structures.[3] In other words, self-narrative fostered first through Catholic confession and then through psychotherapy and criminology require an expert who can make judgments and reinterpret what is said according to the dominant discourse. While, as I argued in Chapter one, adult learning theory tends to emphasize the self-assertion of meaning that characterized Rousseau's confessions rather than Augustine's, the practice of self-reflection on experience plays out within a contentious field in which the right to assert meaning is neither innocent nor simple.

Experience, reflection, and self-management

Indeed, the concept of reflection itself represents the most important grafting onto theories of adult learning of the politics of inspection that I have been tracing. The split in the self between experience and thought, the view of experience as the raw material for the subsequent making of meaning, and the emphasis on self-observation and self-interrogation make 'critical self-reflection' panopticonic to the core. Our conventional notion of experiential learning, in effect, reproduces the power relationship between observer and observed, internalizing that relationship and denying cognitive agency to those embodied and emotional parts of the self that, like 'savages', proletarians, and women, must be investigated, organized, and managed.[4]

Before exploring this further, it will be helpful to examine the etymology of 'reflection.' Our use of the word to mean a second-order processing phase casts reflection in chronological terms, but etymologically, reflection is part of a vocabulary of bodies, angles, and surfaces. It is a metaphor of space, not time. It means to 'turn back, to bend in a certain direction,' and in Renaissance usages it often refers to mirrors and the refraction of light. In optics, the reflection (in a mirror, for example) is the thing itself freed from its original concreteness. Disembodied, in some senses portable, it is an image from the physical world whose materiality has been excised.

According to the *Oxford English Dictionary* (1971), reflection takes on its modern, cognitive meaning only in the Enlightenment: "Let thine eyes Reflect upon thy soul," wrote playwright Fletcher (1579–1625), "and there behold How loathed black it is (XIII, 471)." Locke's definition of reflection as "that notice which the Mind takes of its own Operations" (1964[1689]: II,i,4) is consistent with this usage, as it is with the new Enlightenment belief in the autonomy and interiority of the mind. Francis Bacon combined the old optical and new cognitive meaning in describing the mind as a glass or mirror. Like a mirror distorted by uneven glass, the mind can be made rough both by the emotions and by the received errors of tradition. The new methods of observation and reason, however, can correct these distortions and allow the mind to be like "a clear and equal glass, wherein the beams of things should reflect according to their true incidence" (as cited in Park, 1984, p. 290).

But this etymology raises important questions; if reflection is a spatial metaphor, by definition it involves positionality and point of view. The angle of reflection, whether physical or optical, concretely determines how an object rebounds or what can be seen in the mirror. Thus, while the reflected image may appear to be objective, as undistorted as the smoothness of the surface can make it and the product of universal scientific laws, reflection always participates in the social relations of its making. What politics of inspection are being enacted in a given act of reflection? How does relative positionality determine what is and isn't visible? Who is looking? Who is being looked at? Who is standing where?

The implications of this can be seen most readily in the development of modern aesthetics. The Platonic traditions of both knowledge and virtue have customarily distinguished between the lower and higher senses based on degrees of physical distance; touch, smell, and taste, which require proximity, are lower than hearing and sight (Falk, 1994). As aesthetics developed out of moral philosophy, the contemplation of the beautiful was seen to require distance in two related senses: physical separation and erotic dispassion. At the same time that the female nude was becoming *the* subject of Western art (Nead, 1992), the distant senses, especially sight, came to be seen as a means of achieving virtue through disinterested contemplation. Kant's privileging of meditative over sensual pleasures required that desire be held in abeyance in favor of detached reflection, with disinterestedness the basis for aesthetic judgments no less than political and moral ones (Falk, 1994).

As is clear from its implicit coding of the art object as female and both the artist and the viewer as male, this formulation reproduces a number of gendered dualisms. First, the female body, as undifferentiated matter, is regulated and contained through the mediation of art, a process that the iconic mainstream art critic Sir Kenneth Clark viewed as "the most complete example of the transformation of matter into form" (as cited in Nead, 1992, p. 14). Secondly, and importantly for our discussion, the gender-based alliance between artist and viewer constructs the male gaze as an assertion of power, an act of epistemological mastery in itself.

At the same time, however, the discourse of aesthetics discriminates *among* male viewers; the right to gaze is measured by the ability to observe without desire, which is associated with the elite. The distinction between pornography and art, for example, hinges less on the content of the image itself than on the response of the viewer: sexual arousal versus the 'pure' aesthetic gaze. Anti-pornography legislation arose historically in response to the unregulated access made possible by new photographic and mass-production technologies, lest erotic images be seen by those, such as the poor, with insufficient self-control and a propensity for depravity (Nead, 1992).

This means, as the terms of this legislation suggest, that the right to contemplate – to see – from a distance is not only a function of virtue; it is also a function of power that becomes more and more explicit in the rise of the bureaucratic state. Self-control, the ability to discipline one's own self, is once again matched by a politics of vision that legitimates authority over other selves, other bodies. Thus, the internalization of reflection in the constitution of the (white male) bourgeois subject is matched by an increasingly public and bureaucratic discourse on managing the non-white, the non-male, the non-bourgeois. Mastering the disruptive aspects of the self signals the right to mastery over others who represent those same disruptive forces and signals membership in those social groups empowered to administer society in the name of order and objectivity.

I would suggest that current notions of reflection reproduce a similar politics of inspection, making it as much an internalization of social control as it is a practice of freedom (O'Reilly, 1989). The freedom of experience as an individual attribute ensuring individual worth is belied by its dependence on normalizing structures that define the relationships among internalized subjectivity, sanctioned behavior, and the legitimation of social identity. More specifically, current notions concerning experience and reflection encourage an identification with the social norms of disengagement from immediate experience through which the white middle-class has historically claimed epistemological sovereignty. 'Experiential learning' thus becomes an algorithm for purging experience of its unmanageable qualities, walling off one's own emotional and sensate existence, and partaking of the claim to superior disinterestedness and reason.

> Subcultures that try to get away from tactics of linguistic control over others include academic, scientific, legal, diplomatic, ecclesiastic, and journalistic worlds, in which people make a sustained and deliberate attempt to bar their use. These tactics can still creep in, but the prevailing norms in these dialogic communities disapprove of them because each of these communities in its own fashion is consciously committed to validating contested meaning claims in a rational way.
>
> *(Mezirow, 1991, p. 134)*

To recap, I have argued that, in the post-Enlightenment West, the notion of experience is contradicted, that while experience is lauded as the realm of individual freedom, 'experiential learning' must also be understood to be a mechanism within which social control is internalized. As experiential learning has been drained of association with the communal and libidinous life of the carnival, it has lost its connection to the transgressive insistence that there is always something to be said apart from received authority. Instead, the claims of experience have been brought to conform to normalizing structures of modern capitalist societies, and the management of experience has become a way of regulating how people define themselves and construct an identity.

More specifically, I have sought to tie 'reflection' on 'experience' to the series of gendered dualisms around which privileged Western knowledge-practices have long been structured: mind/body, culture/nature, universal/particular, objectivity/ subjectivity, and abstract/concrete. Through 'reflection,' we distance ourselves from what is seen as chaotic and distorted within the self, thus replicating within ourselves a power move shared in different ways by fourteenth-century clerics, seventeenth-century scientists, and nineteenth-century sociologists and anthropo- logists. Yet is worth reminding ourselves, as I have noted, that reflection is a spatial metaphor. Where, precisely, are we standing when we "reflect" on experience, and what kind of self is constructed in the process? Does reflection require that we stand outside ourselves, and, if so, with what organ, and what angle, of vision? How do we frame our own experience? What theory of mind – and what social history – positions us outside the frame?

At the heart of the notion of reflection is the question: what kinds of people and which parts of ourselves are we to trust? The dream of reason is a dream of power, or, more precisely, a dream of power *over:* over messiness, ignorance, violence, partiality. But it has also been a dream of power over those places where such qualities have been seen to fester: the disorderly bodies of women, the disarray of working-class neighborhoods, the steamy swamps of the colonial world.

In Part II, I will have more to say concerning the ways in which experience and reflection must be understood, not as two separate entities enacting a chronology of detachment from embodied sociality, but as mutually determined within it. In the following chapter, I will use a broadly feminist critique to revisit the relationship between experience and the body, the claims of situated rather than universal knowledge, and the deeply social nature of individual experience. I will explore the ways in which women's experience in particular has again been used as a corrective to the received truths of authorized knowledge and as an attempt, to use Chaucer's words, to turn the world "up-sodoun".

Notes

1   Alisoun's rhetorical question, "who painted the lion?" refers to a fable of Aesop's in which a man and a lion are arguing over relative strength. As evidence for his greater strength, the man shows the lion a tombstone on which a man is depicted strangling a lion. The lion responds by pointing out that it was a man who painted the picture and that, had a lion painted it, the situation would be reversed.

2   There is a good deal of historical evidence that the nineteenth-century middle-class feared the ability of workers to articulate their own point of view. Many middle-class social reformers in Victorian England, for example, wished to teach the working-classes to read but not to write. Through reading they might be educated in proper values, but, as writer and philanthropist Hannah More expressed it at the time, the knowledge of writing would only encourage and facilitate rebelliousness (Cottom, 1987).

3   How this plays out in judicial settings is arguably obvious – confessions are elicited under specific power-laden procedures that, if followed, make them legally binding, and the prisoner is the last person who can decide what they mean or how they will be used. The narrative model instituted by early psychoanalysis, however, is troublingly similar. Indeed, Freud's case studies are famous for the ways in which the physician replaces the patient as both meaning-maker and protagonist. The patient herself, as Freud (1989 [1905]) relates in his classic case study of Dora, fights against both the act of confession and the discovery of meaning: she is "obliged to admit" (p. 192). Drawing self-consciously on the steps of a detective investigation – Freud was an enthusiastic fan of Sir Arthur Conan Doyle – he recounts Dora doing "something which I could not help regarding as a further step toward the confession" (p. 215). What we read is Freud's narrative, not Dora's; it begins with the role the confession plays in his life, not in hers, and it is structured according to the steps though which Freud pieces together a meaning that explains the facts of the case.

4   This occasionally translates into an explicit insensitivity to the implications of class and racial stereotypes: Mezirow (1991) cites Bruno to the effect that some cultures like the Wolof of Senegal and the Anchorage Eskimo cannot be fully self-reflective because they "suppress expression of individualism" and reports that lower-class children were found far less capable than middle-class children of critical reflection, a distinction he surmises would be greater "between an (adult) English barrister and a dock worker" (p. 147). Indeed, it is rare to find mention of reflective thinking that is indigenous to working-class communities. As in nineteenth-century middle-class discourse, workers are seen as people who must be brought along with the help of those like 'ourselves.' Knowles (1990) suggests, for example, that "if a group in a factory is resisting a new work procedure, it may be because they don't understand how it will work, in which case a demonstration or trial experience will be superior to exhortation or pressure" (p. 105). That workers might have used their own critical reflection to identify reasons for resisting such a change – the loss of jobs the new procedure may make possible, for example – is never considered by Knowles.

PART II

Gender, experience, and the body

4

BODY, CULTURE, AND THE FEMINIST CLAIMS FOR EXPERIENCE

Yis, dame, quod he, tel forth and I wol heere.
[Yes, Madame, said he, tell a story and I will hear.]
Geoffrey Chaucer, *The Canterbury Tales*, III 856

Alisoun would be pleased. If there is any academic field that has devoted as much time as has adult learning to questions of experience, that field is feminist theory. Over the course of the past forty years, Alisoun's daughters in both academic and activist settings have privileged the concept of experience in their research, writing, and advocacy. Indeed, in an importantly defining essay, "Feminist Studies/Critical Studies: Issues, Terms, and Contexts," Teresa de Lauretis (1986) defined feminism itself as a "politics of experience of everyday life" (p. 10).

According to de Lauretis, the centrality of the concept to feminism rests on both the relationship of experience to "the major issues that have emerged from the women's movement – subjectivity, sexuality, the body, and feminist political practice" and the "epistemological priority which feminism has located in the personal, the subjective, the body, the symptomatic, the quotidian, as the very site of material inscription of the ideological" (1984, p. 159; 1986, p. 11). The feminist scholarship that began emerging in the 1970s and 1980s supports de Lauretis' observation, typically celebrating the everyday and the relational as categories within which women have traditionally constructed meaning and from which women's knowledge has traditionally derived.

That this is so is at least partly a product of the history of the contemporary women's movement, one that played out variously in the quite different political and intellectual contexts of societies around the world. In North America, two features especially contributed to the foregrounding of experience – the practice of consciousness raising and the repudiation of male expertise. In both cases, claims for women's knowledge began in the discovery of shared experience and in the perceived gap between that experience and normative assumptions concerning 'womanhood' (MacKinnon 1989; de Lauretis, 1986).[1] Within the women's movement as a whole, this gave rise to self-help and self-authorizing practices that challenged the hegemonic discourses and material institutions of psychiatry and medicine, while what came to be known as women's studies sought a language and methodology from which to show "that the perspectives provided by our devalued identities [could] be epistemologically powerful" (Harding, 1991, p. 273) and which allowed for "a different kind of philosophical space, for an ordering of women's experience as knowledge, for an emancipatory vision rooted in our own grounds" (Aptheker, 1989, p. 15).

> It is this essential return to the experience we ourselves have directly in our everyday worlds that has been the distinctive mode of working in the women's movement – the repudiation of the professional, the expert, the already authoritative tones of the discipline, the science, the formal tradition, and the return to the seriously engaged and very difficult enterprise of discovering how to begin from ourselves.
>
> *(Smith, 1987, p. 58)*

The titles of the books I have been citing here, Sandra Harding's *Whose Science? Whose Knowledge? Thinking from Women's Lives*, Bettina Aptheker's *Tapestries of Life: Women's Work, Women's Consciousness, and the Meaning of Daily Experience*, and Dorothy E. Smith's *The Everyday World as Problematic: A Feminist Sociology*, are themselves claims about the origins of knowledge in the experiential, arguing for women's epistemic status

> as agents of knowledge, as actors on the stage of history, as humans whose lives provide a grounding for knowledge claims that are different from and in some respects preferable to knowledge claims grounded in the lives of men in the dominant groups.
>
> *(Harding, 1991, p. 47)*

Feminist theory has challenged the "God's eye view" both by validating knowledge derived from women's social positionality and arguing for the social and historical contingency of all sites from which knowledge is produced. As Sandra Harding has put it,

> In societies where power is organized hierarchically – for example, by class or race or gender – there is no possibility of an Archimedean perspective, one that is disinterested, impartial, value-free, or detached from the particular, historical social relations in which everyone participates. ... The subject of belief and of knowledge is never simply an individual, let alone an abstract one capable of transcending its own historical location. It is always an individual in a particular social situation.
>
> *(Harding, 1991, p. 59)*

In its insistence that all knowledge is rooted in concrete, historical subject positions, feminist theory, in effect, has feminized the human knower, re-grounding authority in experience and positing partiality and locatedness rather than abstract universality as the basis for credible knowledge claims. It has re-engaged the despised second terms of the dualisms explored in Part I, focusing inquiry on the body rather than the mind, the particular rather than the universal, and the concrete rather than the abstract. Finally, it has challenged the idea of detachment – from the body and the emotions, from social location, and from the influence of others – as an epistemological virtue, asking us to re-locate our thoughts within the felt lives of our bodies, to see humanity and its cultures as a part of nature and vice versa, and to understand that there is no fixed point at which the experience of the individual stops and the life of the world begins.

Feminist theories of experience are complex and often contentious, more a question of family resemblances, as Nancy Tuana (2001) puts it, than consistencies.[2] The debates are worth reviewing, however, because of the insights they provide for critiquing what we call experiential learning. In what follows, I trace a number of specific debates across a generation of feminist scholarship concerning the status of experience; these include the charge that some feminist theories of experience reinstate the very dualisms that feminism purports to challenge, the felt erasure by mainstream white Western feminism of differences among women, the assumed immediacy of unfiltered experience, and the debate concerning the claim that the experience of marginalized groups provides an epistemic advantage. These debates raise important questions. If there is no Archimedean point, but only a series of socially located experiential standpoints, on what do we base our knowledge claims? What does it mean to claim that the body "knows"? What does the experience of and in such categories as gender have to do with knowledge? Are our bodies part of 'nature' or 'culture'? What is the relationship of experience to the languages and conceptual frameworks we use?

"Ain't I a woman?": The experiential body as nature or culture

The body, with its sensate, emotionally saturated life, has been an important focus of feminist inquiry for a number of reasons. First, there has been a felt need to confront the traditional gendering of the body as female in the taxonomy of Western dualities. Secondly, many issues of importance to feminism – contraception and abortion, sexual preference, and violence against women, to name a few – are focused on the body, and this has encouraged the recognition that experience, knowledge, and power are both sexually specific and corporeally inscribed (Grosz, 1994). As with experience, feminist theory has had to account for the body in several contending senses: claiming the body as a traditional female realm, recovering it for humans generally as a site of knowledge, and at the same time deconstructing the very dualisms that code the body as female, as nature as opposed to culture, and mark it as the despised antipode of mind.

Figuratively, as we have seen, the knowledge practices that have characterized modernity began on the day that René Descartes severed his head from his body. The attempt he records in the *Meditations* to create reliable procedures for creating knowledge was founded on the assumption that "I [that is, my mind, by which I am what I am] is entirely and truly distinct from my body" and that "body, figure, extension, motion, and place are merely fictions of my mind" (Descartes, 1637 [1960], pp. 165, 181). In performing that act of willed self-dismemberment, Descartes bequeathed to modernity a knowing subject for whom epistemological agency requires the rejection of the physicality of the self. Saved from emotion by the clear light of reason, able to separate moral judgments from personal desires and loyalties, and undisturbed by the implacable demands of the body, the knowing subject is, "precisely speaking, only a thinking thing" (Ibid., p. 121).

> For when I consider the mind, that is, when I consider myself in so far only as I am a thinking thing, I can distinguish in myself no parts ... yet when a foot, an arm, or any other part is cut off, I am conscious that nothing has been taken from my mind.
>
> *(Descartes, 1637 [1960], pp. 171–2)*

One of the issues raised by this formulation is whether the non-rational might ever be a form of knowledge or, stated differently, how emotion, the body, intuition, and personal history might be seen *as* knowledge rather than as its source. Feminist theorists have argued that, however much the abstract masculinist knower might wish otherwise, experience is continually reworked within bodily processes that include emotion, desire, pain and pleasure, needs, and physical abilities and disabilities in addition to cognitive thought. Rather than being a block to learning, our emotional, sensory, and physical being informs our knowledge of both self and others and makes accounts of the world available that are *less*, not more, distorted than those that mime an impossible dismemberment (Flax, 1993; Gallop, 1988; Grosz, 1993).

Other feminist theorists, however, have raised objections to this formulation. First, it has been argued that, in some of its forms, the valorization of female embodiment that characterized feminist theory in the 1970s and 1980s reproduced the gendered dualisms of mind/body and reason/emotion that had traditionally been used to justify gender inequality and disparage women's knowledge. That is, some schools of thought, such as eco-feminism, embraced the association of the earth with the female and valorized the superiority of the body over the intellect, the natural over the cultural, and the emotional over the rational, in effect keeping the gendered dualisms intact and simply turning them on their heads. Traditionally female-coded elements such as feeling and nurturing were seen as producing a world of more peaceful, loving human relationships and a more responsible, organic relationship with non-human life, and women's greater capacity for what Sara Ruddick (1989) called maternal thinking was seen as rooted in women's deep connection with the body and the earth.

Within feminism, such approaches have been challenged on a number of bases. First, many feminist thinkers have seen "maternal thinking" and similar notions as forms of essentialism, that is, the belief that particular categories of people and things have and behave according to underlying, inherent properties. 'Nature,' 'the body,' 'feeling,' and, indeed, 'male' and 'female' are treated by writers such as Ruddick as if they exist as timeless entities outside of history, each characterized by essentialized inborn qualities. Rather, many have argued, those very concepts are what we must account for if we are going to grapple with what it means to experience 'as' a woman or, indeed, as anything else.

Secondly, and related to the above, a variety of feminist theorists have argued that bodily experience is culturally, not simply biologically, constituted. Indeed, the refusal to draw a clear line between the body as a natural phenomenon and as a cultural artifact is one of the key moves made both by various versions of feminism and by the multiple schools of twentieth-century thought on which feminism has drawn. According to these theorists, feelings, sexuality, gender identity, and our relationship with our physical selves are no more natural or universal than thought; nature/culture, sex/gender, and similar dualities are themselves products of discursive and social history.[3] Key feminist texts from the 1970s and 1980s such as Carole Gilligan's *In a Different Voice* (1982) and Nancy Chodorow's *The Reproduction of Mothering* (1978) located the origins of gender differences, not in biology, but in what is, in effect, experiential learning, that is, in gender-specific matrices of social interaction, learned ways of thinking and behaving, and resonant activities.

There is a complex but, I think, ultimately fruitful tension between understanding the role of the body in learning and relocating the body in history. On the one hand, as we have seen, the body is seen as the site of lived experience; feminists have argued that "thinking through the body" (Rich, as cited in Gallop, 1988, p. 1) and reuniting the life of the mind with the sensate and emotional life of the body are important gestures of healing for all of us variously gendered human beings. On the other hand, many feminists accept the view most closely associated with Michel Foucault that the body is subject to political and juridical interventions. Bodies 'speak,' not only as the grounds of subjectivity, but as texts that carry psychic and cultural meanings. Bodily decorations, exercise regimens, corporal punishments, health-care practices, dieting, and eating disorders all write on the surface of the body deeply felt technologies of social control. Thus, the body, far from being a 'natural' realm, is the site of struggle among contending meanings that are enacted within culture and history. "Bodies are traversed and infiltrated by knowledges, meanings, and power" and can, at the same time, under the right circumstances, become "sites of struggle and resistance, actively inscribing themselves on social practices" (Grosz, 1993, p. 199).

An iconic line from an earlier moment in the struggle for women's equality has been particularly resonant in this ongoing discussion, specifically Sojourner Truth's famous rhetorical question, "Ain't I a woman?" The exact words of Truth's statement, which was delivered to the women's rights convention in Akron, Ohio in 1851, are themselves a topic of historical debate,[4] but the most regularly cited version is as follows:

> That man over there says that women need to be helped into carriages and lifted over ditches and to have the best place everywhere. Nobody ever helps me into carriages or over mud-puddles or gives me any best place. And ain't I a woman? Look at me! Look at my arm.... I have ploughed and planted and gathered into barns, and no man could head me! And ain't I a woman? .... I have borne five children and seen most of them sold into slavery, and when I cried out with a mother's grief, none but Jesus heard me. And ain't I a woman?
>
> *(Downloaded from* http://sojournertruthmemorial.org/her-words/
> *December 9, 2014)*

As Donna Haraway (2004c) points out, Truth's statement simultaneously both claims and deconstructs 'woman' as a biological category. On the one hand, it demands the recognition that there is a biological category, womanhood, of which Truth is a part. On the other hand, by drawing on her experience to undermine the characterization of woman as 'naturally' frail, privileged, and, by implication, white, Truth uses her own embodied specificity to demand that the category 'Woman' be seen as produced by cultural assumptions and social relationships.

Haraway notes that, according to witnesses, a white male doctor present demanded that Truth show her breasts to the women in the audience to prove that she was indeed a woman. This, in effect, raises the stakes of the question even further: where does 'womanhood' reside, exactly? In the breasts created naturally through chromosomal femaleness or in the arm muscles created culturally through the historical specificity of life in a Black, female, enslaved, rural, laboring body? Truth's declaration concerning her mother's grief undermines the distinction between nature and culture even further, taking the experience of motherhood out of gendered anatomy and into the horrific contingencies of history.

The insistence that gender differences are not fixed but, rather, historically produced has also been helpful in responding to another problem identified in the early years of second-wave feminist theory, namely, the unexamined assumption by mainstream feminism that the experience of women generally was more alike than different. The same feminists who challenged the false positing of male experience as the universal human norm were often seen as guilty of creating a new false universal by treating the experience of some (white, Western, middle-class, educated, heterosexual) women as that of Woman in the aggregate. This new universalizing ignored the ways in which various social positionalities across class, race, nationality, sexual preference, and other factors interface in the shaping of both individual and collective experience.

Many schools of feminism have engaged this issue, but in part because of their greater awareness of the ways in which gender interacts with other categories of difference, this critique has been most sharply articulated by feminists of color.

Ain't I a Woman?, bell hooks' (1981) ground-breaking updating of Truth's question, explored racism within the contemporary women's movement, sexism within the Black community, and the ways in which the experience of Black women in the US had been formed within the dual oppressions of gender and race. Similarly, feminists writing from non-Western perspectives such as Gayatri Spivak (1985, 1988a), and Chandra Talpade Mohanty (1992) challenged the universalizing of women's experience and questioned the uses to which appeals to experience were being put. By insisting such appeals are irreducibly political, inevitably implicated in discourses that are themselves constituted through class and race inequality, they asked in whose name 'we' claim the truth of experience. Whose experience gets appropriated in the process? Whose interests are being masked in the name of authenticity? In "Under Western Eyes," her classic essay on this issue, Mohanty (1988) delineates the ways in which some feminist scholarship of the period constructed a version of the "'Third World Woman' as a monolithic subject" (p. 61), failed to engage women as the "real, material subjects of their collective histories" (p. 62), and produced an ethnocentric universalism that took white, Western women as the norm. Parallel protests were lodged by lesbians, working-class women, and others whose lives could not be represented accurately within the categories set by mainstream Western feminism.[5] While these battles among feminists were often bitter and painful, the result has been a greater understanding of both the hierarchies of epistemic authority implicit in any claim for experience and the danger of claiming to represent the experience of the Other in ways that colonize and erase.

Thus, the attention paid by feminist scholarship to the historically located body has resulted in three moves that contribute to a more nuanced understanding of experiential learning. By attending to the body as a site of knowledge-production, it has problematized knowledge claims that are, in effect, acts of dismemberment, that deny the connectedness of mind to body and thus lose sight of knowledge as the product of corporeally and emotionally grounded human life. At the same time, however, it has problematized any notion of the body, or of experience, as immediate and pre-symbolic or as separable from historical conditions and power relationships. Finally, it has marked the relationship of the individual body as the bearer of knowledge to the other knowing, history-laden bodies that make up the world. Tara Fenwick (2006b) has put this in terms of "nested webs of interaction at many levels (molecular, emotional, libidinal, social, political). These webs dissolve mind-body, self-other, subject-object dualities, and allow a conception of fluidity among bodies – of human beings, objects, knowledge and nature" (p. 42). This fluidity, Fenwick argues, allows us to explore experience and meaning as contingent on interaction among people, their actions, and the surrounding environment and to understand knowledge as emerging, not in intellectual isolation, but as a product of those interactions.

Taken together, these three moves bring us a fair way toward problematizing a number of troubling assumptions in theories of experiential learning, most notably the separation of the experiential body and the reflective mind and the positing of an isolated knower detached from society and history. But this, in turn, raises other questions. If, as Fenwick claims, we are enmeshed in webs of interaction whose meanings are contingent on environmental interaction, then how do we claim that experiential learning makes us "free ... to chart the course of our own destiny" (Kolb, 1984, p. 109)? If our very bodies are the products of culture as well as nature, how do we ever access experiences that aren't filtered through "prior, distorted perceptions" (Freire, 1974, p. 107)? If experience is always culturally determined, how do we free ourselves from "libidinal, linguistic, epistemic, institutional, or environmental forces" framing our lives (Mezirow, 1991:87)? The short answer to those questions is: we don't.

Experience and language

A penchant for treating experience as straightforward and self-evident is one shared by feminist theory and adult learning theory. The important central insight that the two have in common, namely, the need to reground learning in daily life, has encouraged what Harding calls "experiential foundationalism," the insistence that "the spontaneous consciousness of individual experience" provides uniquely legitimating epistemic grounds (1991, p. 269). By assuming that experience provides unmediated access to reality, this view neglects the complex cultural, discursive, and psychological matrix within which 'experience' happens. Dorothy Smith's evocation in the beginning of this chapter of "the experience we ourselves have directly in our everyday worlds" (1987, p. 56), for example, begs a number of important questions. Who is the experiencing "we"? What does it mean (and is it possible ever) to experience "directly"? How do "everyday worlds" differ from worlds that are not "everyday"? Smith, of course, is affirming a knowledge unfiltered through abstract masculinist theoretics, but at the least her statement fails to ask whether experience is ever transparent and avoids attending to the social and semiotic practices through which experience is shaped.

The recognition that experience is shaped by structures of perception and interpretation is a part of what has been called the 'linguistic turn' in the humanities and social sciences. This renewed attention to language, which has its origins in twentieth-century philosophy, has played out over several decades and across national philosophical and psychoanalytic traditions, but a key strain has focused on the degree to which language is seen as *representing* reality or as *producing* it. Specifically, the postmodernist view that language constructs the very phenomena it purports to explain seriously undermines any claim that experience exists outside of the mental and linguistic forms that enable meaning. Thus experience cannot be understood, as adult learning theory has conventionally claimed, as preverbal or unmediated by culturally structured discourses and categories. Experience, in other words, is as much the product of thinking as it is its foundation. There is no experience outside of the ordering mechanisms of expectation and language; our experience arrives in our consciousness already structured by what we think we know.

Historian Joan Scott's controversial 1991 essay, "The Evidence of Experience," is a key text in this regard. It is not enough, Scott argues, to claim that we 'learn from experience;' we need, rather, to challenge our understanding of how something comes to be experienced in the first place by critically examining the system of ideology that structures it historically and discursively. Scott's argument is that explorations of experience cannot be separated from explorations of the discourses we use to talk about it because "language is the site of history's enactment and where we confront alternative ways of interpreting what we already knew, which is what learning from experience means" (p. 778). Thus,

> experience is at once always already an interpretation *and* something that needs to be interpreted. What counts as experience is neither self-evident nor straightforward. … Experience is, in this approach, not the origin of our explanation, but that which we want to explain.
>
> *(Scott, 1991, p. 797)*

Other feminists, however, are not willing to abandon the primacy of experience. Scholars working with the life stories of oppressed women, for example, have responded to Scott's challenge by reemphasizing the need to draw attention to the "micropolitics" of women's lives (Mohanty, 2003, p. 508). Narratives of experience are important, "not because they present an unmediated version of the 'truth' but because they can destabilize received truths and locate debate in the complexities and contradictions of historical life" (p. 524). Such scholars argue that, rather than taking such terms as 'everyday experience' as an unproblematized given, the focus on experience within the context of a shared social life reminds us to ask how 'everyday life' is constituted, what the relationships are between macro- and micro-politics, how people understand their own lives, and what difference it makes.

Indeed, the idea that experience is mediated by both language and history is at the heart of approaches to autobiography that take issue with the narrative of unitary selfhood I touched on briefly in Chapter one. Beginning in the 1980s, scholars have argued that the autobiographical writings of women, immigrants, and oppressed communities evidence a clear understanding of how language and culture mediate selfhood, both understanding the self as "fragmented, provisional, multiple, in process" and collectivizing their own experience. [6] Many life narratives by women, immigrants, and members of oppressed groups are less auto*biographies* than "auto*ethnographies*," both in the sense of speaking more for the collective than the individual and in Mary Louise Pratt's (1991) sense of self-conscious uses of the narrative forms of the powerful (p. 35). The result is the portrayal, not of an atomized self whose claims to authenticity rest on the immediacy of experience, but rather on the subject's self-location in the broader world, what Baena calls "a willful positioning of oneself in history and culture" (2005, p. 212).

The question of autobiography, however, is subject to the same debate within feminism as the experience it purports to narrate. On one side of this question is the insistence on the right to personal voice by women whose lives include social marginalization. "I write to record what others erase when I speak, to rewrite the stories others have miswritten about me, about you" says Chicana writer Gloria Anzaldua (as cited in Langellier, 1999, p. 126). Similarly, working-class lesbian writer Dorothy Allison (1994) describes the impulse behind her writing as wanting "to be seen for who I am and still appreciated – not denied, not simplified, not lied about or refused or minimized" (p. 182). Seen in these terms, autobiography becomes "a performative struggle for agency" (Langellier, 1999, p.126), a way to resist forms of discursive colonization rather than a claim to experience as foundational and unmediated. Rather than treating language as the direct reflection of the unfiltered experience of the autonomous individual, such writers "appropriate and subvert" conventional autobiographical forms in order to resist rather than incorporate hegemonic interpretations of experience (Baena, 2005, pp. 211–12). Such narratives, as Shari Stone-Mediatore (1998) argues, are important sources of knowledge; if we devalue renditions of experience as necessarily reproducing the very categories they should problematize, we leave marginalized women no way of representing their own lives.

Others, however, are not so sure. Linda Kaufman argues that "writing about yourself does not liberate you, it just shows how engrained the ideology of freedom through self-expression is in our thinking" (as cited in Langellier, 1999, p. 135). Alcoff and Gray (1993), in turn, argue that telling one's story makes one subject to hegemonic reinterpretations even when one's experiences have been deeply Other. As I will explore at greater length in Part IV, it is virtually impossible to write outside of culturally determined narrative forms that are themselves value- and power-laden, so that narratives on experience inevitably walk a fine line between "recuperation and transgression" (p. 260), that is, between returning one's story to comfortably familiar hegemonic cultural patterns and turning those forms against themselves.

In an interesting discussion that attempts to reconcile these two points of view, Shari Stone-Mediatore (1998) suggests that we do not need to choose between the imperatives of experience and the recognition that experience is constituted within language. If we begin with the "complexities and contradictions" of individual lives located within specific social arrangements, then experience can be seen as the matrix of material conditions, social ideologies, and the discursive structures through which individuals and collectivities make meaning. In other words, if renditions of experience are seen as "emerging from and engaging historical and ideological processes and exploring contradiction" (p. 117), then we can account for the shape of experience without treating it as a transparent confrontation with the real on the one hand or, on the other, as a mere artifact of language. Rather, we can see it as enacting the ways in which individual consciousness sustains, challenges, exceeds, and trips up on the language we use to explain things.

Destabilizing the universal knower: feminist standpoint theory

The importance of engaging the experiences of women in marginalized communities points, in turn, to a third debate within feminist theory concerning the efficacy of experience, specifically the relationship between perspective, knowledge, and social location in the experience of those communities. As we have seen, theories of adult learning have also engaged with this issue; the school of critical pedagogy associated with Paulo Freire has been especially attentive to the experience of the oppressed as a source of knowledge, and the school of transformational learning associated with Jack Mezirow and Stephen Brookfield has posited reflection on experience as enabling a critique of ideological presuppositions and received social roles. Most theories of adult learning, however, have not engaged fully with the notion that different knowledges are produced through different experiences or that what are generally known as 'Outsider knowledges' have a particular potency.

The relationship between the particularities of human experience and the role of social location is the focus of a branch of feminist theory known as standpoint theory. Drawing on both Hegelian and Marxist formulations, feminist standpoint theory attempts to replace the universal knower with a specific being whose knowledge is particular to a given place in human society. Its proponents make a point of asking whose knowledge and whose point of view are erased in hegemonic accounts of the world, what the same phenomena look like from the perspective of the Other, and how Outsider knowledges might enrich and often correct hegemonic accounts. In opposition to Galileo's claim that anyone looking through his telescope will see the same thing, standpoint theorists point out that differing views of an object in space are one of the reasons we trust our perceptions of it; the way we know something is real and not a hologram is that it looks different from different vantage points (Tuana, 2001).

As it developed in the 1980s and 1990s, feminist standpoint theory challenged one of the pillars of abstract masculinity by suggesting that relocating knowledge in socially situated perspectives allows for more, not less, objectivity.[7] The problem with knowledge practices that deny their own social locatedness is not that they try to be objective, Sandra Harding (1993) argued, but that they cannot be rigorous or objective *enough* (p. 51). Without what Harding calls the "strong objectivity" to understand their own embeddedness in culturally and socially specific points of view, there is no way for scholars to gain perspective on the blind spots and biases shared by an entire community; moreover, because they have been taught to think of their own knowledge as unproblematically universal, such communities of inquiry are disinclined to inquire what alternative information or perspectives might be available from other points of view. As Donna Haraway (1997) has articulated the general point: "working uncritically from the viewpoint of the 'standard' groups is the best way to come up with a particularly parochial and limited analysis ..., which then masks as a general account that stands a good chance of reinforcing unequal privilege" (p. 197).

In part because of their greater awareness of the ill effects of ignoring social location, feminists of color have been important spokeswomen for recognizing the epistemic advantage of particular standpoints. In her influential essay, "Learning from the Outsider Within," Patricia Hill Collins (1991) argued that the experience of Black women provides an epistemic advantage, using the example of the domestic worker as an 'outsider on the inside' whose unique point of view is productive of important insights. A sociologist by training, Collins suggests that Black and female sociologists have a similar advantage in maintaining perspective on the ruling assumptions and practices of their field because of the often-greater tension among their various social roles and the often-greater distance between the assumptions of sociology and their actual life experiences.[8] The insistence that one's social location matters has also been forwarded by women adult educators of color, as represented in the work of Juanita Johnson-Bailey, Mary Alfred, and others (Johnson-Bailey and Alfred, 2006; see also Brown, 2001 and Alicea et al., 2004).

Not all feminist epistemologists have been convinced by the arguments of standpoint theorists, however. While aware of the misuses to which empiricism has been put in the perpetuation of unjust knowledge-practices, feminists have also attempted to salvage empiricism and, with it, more conventional beliefs concerning objectivity, reason, and method. Feminist empiricists argue that standpoint theory, in effect, throws the baby out with the bathwater; the world is real, the methods of science are suited to the solving of multiple problems, and with due care to filter out bias and self-interest, empirical methods can further many vital goals, including those of marginalized groups (Intemann, 2010). Such theorists have pointed to the apparent contradiction in standpoint theory that is known as the bias paradox; as Louise Antony asked in 1993, "if we don't think it's good to be *im*partial, then how can we object to men's being *partial*?" (as cited in Tuana, 2001, p. 13; emphasis in original). If feminist epistemology takes as a given that all views are limited and that the only way to approach objectivity is to bring together multiple unavoidably biased perspectives, then what are the methods through which we can distinguish the good biases from the bad ones (Ibid.)?

As feminist standpoint theorists have learned, it is easy enough to trivialize the idea that social location influences knowledge. Of course golfers know how to swing a golf club in ways that non-golfers do not know. Of course most New Yorkers know the subway system better than most tourists, and of course mothers understand the pain of giving birth in a way that nobody else ever will. Nor is it at all self-evident that marginalized social locations necessarily yield epistemological advantage. Internalized oppression, self-doubt, and similar psychic processes can limit epistemological clarity, and the experience of oppression does not give epistemological advantage in a field such as theoretical physics, or at least not in any simplistic sense (Intemann, 2010).

This critique, and a generation of debate, have rendered the claims of feminist standpoint theory more rigorous and more nuanced. As currently understood, standpoint theory focuses less on how things look from a given social location and more on the impact of inequitable social arrangements on how problems are understood, priorities determined, research methods chosen, and interpretations made. It is not that one knows the world better as a woman, or a person of color, or a person whose life does not fit the norms of heterosexuality. Rather, those whose experience does not reflect the social norm are more likely to notice biases and problematic assumptions, so that perspectives available from those social positions are of value to epistemic communities. Similarly, knowledge communities that tend to take their own interests as the interests of the planet generally – and standpoint theorists would argue that is the understandable tendency of all knowledge communities – need the engagement of those who have a specific, but different, relationship to that which is under study: cancer patients, for example, will have a different investment in cancer research than oncologists, or pharmaceutical companies.

Thus, a 'standpoint' is not a claim for unmediated experiential access to a truer reality, but rather a way of entering into practices of inquiry that can provide less distorted knowledge of many kinds. One does not have to experience the world as a woman to have insight into patriarchy or as a person of color to investigate racism, but a fuller account is made possible if we start from the point of view of women's or Black people's experiences.

> Starting off from these lives provides fresh and more critical questions about how the social order works than does starting off thought from the unexamined lives of members of dominant groups … (who) receive a disproportionate share of the benefits of that very nature and social order that they are trying to explain.
>
> *(Harding, 1993, pp. 62–63)*

In a recent discussion of the relationship between experience and material location, Nancy Tuana (2001) proposes what she calls an "interactionist" approach that attempts to break down the dichotomy between empiricism on the one hand and standpoint theory on the other through a careful appraisal of the complexity of materiality. Empiricism, like realism, positivism, and related epistemologies, rests on the common-sense understanding that there is a world out there that is not dependent on our perceptions or our theories. Standpoint theory and other forms of social construction hold that there is no knowledge of the world outside of socially determined meanings and that those meanings do not adhere in the objects themselves. Tuana rejects both of these accounts as oversimplified. Some things, racism or sexism, for example, are the direct result of how we as humans have constructed the world and what we continue to tell ourselves about it. In that sense, the world is literally constructed by human interactions: treating people as gendered creates gendered human beings; racially inequitable social structures produce both oppressed races and racists. Other things, asteroids, for example, exist independently of what human beings say about them, but they become part of the world that humans engage through interactions among the structures of the material world, human actions and practices, sensory and technological ways of accessing information, and modes of interpretation that together give a meaning and coherence to experience. There is a world independent of what we think, and nobody really denies that, but our sense of 'what is' is also the product of particular kinds of historically embedded possibilities. Knowledge of the world depends on interactions among the technologies of knowing, the questions asked, the structures of social life, and other things that depend on what we do as human beings. Something becomes part of what we call 'experience' as a *result* of that interaction, not a cause.[9]

Thus, feminist theory reveals an ambivalent relationship to the claims of experience, deconstructing the notion of experience even while privileging it as a woman's realm. Feminists have both validated authority claims made in the name of experience and challenged the transparency of those claims; both valorized 'woman' as the experiencing subject and problematized the discourses through which that subjectivity is constructed and maintained. The body both as nature and culture, the experience of 'everyday life,' the modes of intelligibility through which experience is given meaning, and the situating of experience within material and/or discursive practices have been among feminism's most contested terrains.

A more nuanced understanding has emerged from debates among contending feminisms, specifically from the development of a feminism that acknowledges the relationship between material, corporeal, and discursive structures in the development of subjectivity. This view insists neither on a directly accessible reality nor on one that retreats endlessly into discursivity and ideology. It both restores the body as a site of experiential learning and understands the body itself as a product of culture and history. It sees the construction of subjectivity in language and the formation of a material human world as equally the products of the same social history and posits experience as the product of their mutual determination, as the historically located but always provisional point of contact between what we are taught to think of as 'inner' and 'outer' worlds.

In the following two chapters, I will bring these issues to bear on specific treatments of experience in the literature of adult learning, focusing both on the relationship of mind to body and on the embeddedness of individual experience in the social world. In so doing, I want to make the case that any version of 'experiential learning' necessarily stakes out a position within the debates I have been exploring in this chapter. The claims we make about experiential learning, that is, rest on beliefs concerning the individual or social nature of experience, the existence or not of unfiltered experience, the role of the body in learning, and the relationship of 'reality' to language. Those beliefs are unavoidable, if not always conscious, and are inevitably ideological. The assumptions behind them, I will suggest, are something about which scholars and practitioners of adult learning must be both more accountable and more self-aware.

Notes

1   On the importance of the practice of consciousness-raising, see MacKinnon (1989, pp. 83–105) and de Lauretis (1984, p. 185). On the gap between women's experience and the norms of male "experts," see, for example, Rich (1986). On the importance of such realizations as those of Rich to the rise of the North American women's

movement, see Smith (1987, pp. 51–60). For a now-classic example of the critique of masculinist knowledge claims and practices concerning women, see Ehrenreich and English (1978). On the relationship between consciousness-raising and transformative practices of adult learning, see Hart (1990b).

2   For an excellent overview of similarities and differences among feminist epistemologies, see Tuana (2001). For a related summary, see also Longino (2010).

3   Jaggar (1989), for example, argues that emotions are the product of culturally specific assumptions and relationships and of linguistic and social preconditions, not instincts and innate responses.

4   With the exception of the word "ain't," I have rendered Truth's speech in standard English rather than using any of the typical dialect in which it is usually quoted. Drawing on the work of Edith Blicksilver, Donna Haraway (2004c) has noted that Truth, who was born in Ulster County, NY to a Dutch slave owner, would have spoken the Afro-Dutch English of the former New Amsterdam and that the conventional rendering of her speech into Black Southern English is an unfortunate and inaccurate stereotyping. Indeed, the very question, ain't I a woman, by which the speech is known is probably inaccurate. The Afro-Dutch of the period would have been ar'n't, not ain't.

5   See, for example, Stanley (1992) and Ferre (1980).

6   While there is no doing justice in a short discussion to this rich literature, three themes are of particular relevance to the question of life writing in adult learning: the existence of forms of life narrative that do not enshrine the individual self as a coherent, accomplished unity; the location of the self in history; and the possibility of structural forms that allow for more fragmented and troubling experience. Specifically, students of autobiography since the 1980s have noted that the individualist view of autobiography, like the coherent self it both constructs and presupposes, is class-, race-, and gender-specific, typical of the masculine, European tradition of autobiography. Very different patterns characterize the autobiographical writings of women, African Americans, Native Americans, and workers because they begin from a different notion of selfhood and a different relationship of the self to the community.

First, Dorothy Smith (1987) and others have shown that "over a lifetime and in the daily routines, women's lives tend to show a loose, episodic structure that reflects the ways in which their lives are organized" (p. 66). Feminist scholars have argued that women's autobiographies do not typically show formal cohesion and completeness but rather use discontinuous, fragmentary forms and circuitous narrative patterns that parallel "the more fragmented, interrupted, and formless nature of [women's] lives" (p. 66). Similarly, in "Transcultural Autobiography: Forms of Life Writing," Rosalia Baena (2005) explores how autobiographies by immigrants and ethnic "minorities" add to an understanding of autobiography seen not in terms of the coherent self but "rather as fragmented, provisional, multiple, in process." She makes the case for studying the ways in which such writers "appropriate and subvert" conventional autobiographical forms (p. 211).

Second, women autobiographers do not typically portray themselves as unique or use the other characters in their lives as part of a landscape of self-discovery; rather, they reveal a consciousness of individual separateness within a shared group identity. In African American autobiography, the self "is not an individual with a private career, but a soldier in a long, historic march towards Canaan" (Selwyn R. Cudjoe, as cited in Fox-Genovese, 1988, p. 70). As in working-class autobiography, the self here is almost a random member of the group; representativeness rather than uniqueness, social struggle rather than personal triumph are seen as foundational to these autobiographies.

For important examples of these approaches to autobiography, see, in addition to the texts cited here, Benstock (1988), Friedman (1988), Fischer (1986), and Ashley *et al.* (1994).

7   For classic statements of feminist standpoint theory, see Harding (2004).

8 See also essays by Mohanty and Moya in Moya and Hames-Garcia (2000).

9 One of the implications of this is that we must revisit a charge that has been used against feminists as well as other post-positivist theories, namely, the charge of relativism, i.e. , the belief that all accounts of the world are equal and that there is no way to determine whether one version of the "truth" is better than another. The challenge posed by feminists and others to the claims that the knowledge-practices of researchers are value-free, objective, and absolute does not mean that some accounts are not more valid than others and more helpful to human purposes of various kinds. The way out of this seeming discrepancy, however, is to distinguish between relativism and a careful accounting of the ways in which knowledge is creative, legitimated, and used. Different social and historical locations lead to different knowledge precisely *because* the world is concrete; knowledge is produced by exploring the material bases of existence, to be sure, but also by human cognitive paradigms, physiological and technological tools of perception, linguistic structures, and social organizations – and by the interaction among them at a given moment of social and intellectual history.

Donna Haraway (1990), whose original academic field was zoology and who has been an important voice for this way of thinking, has little patience for accounts of experience and knowledge that remove the human knower from the dense web of technologies, ideologies, social relationships, and material objects through which the world is both reproduced and known. It is possible and, indeed, necessary to have "*simultaneously* an account of radical historical contingency for all knowledge claims and knowing subjects, a critical practice for recognizing our own 'semiotic technologies' for making meanings, *and* a non-nonsense commitment to faithful accounts of a 'real' world ..." (p. 187).

5

THE BODY IN QUESTION

Eek plato seith, whoso that kan hym rede,
The wordes moote be cosyn to the dede.

[Plato also said, as those who can read him know,
The word must be cousin to the deed.]

Geoffrey Chaucer, *The Canterbury Tales*, I 741–742

In the previous chapter, I explored the ways in which feminist theories of experience and the body speak to the subject matter of adult learning in general and, more specifically, to what Tara Fenwick wonderfully calls the "banished bodies" of experiential learning. In this chapter, I want to further that exploration by examining some of the ways in which the literature on adult learning has begun to engage with the role of the body in learning. In doing so, I will point both to the strengths of some of those approaches and, at the same time, address what I read as a failure to parse our ideas with sufficient attention to their epistemological and political implications. My argument will be that, in spite of the work of such scholars as Stephen Brookfield (2004), Tara Fenwick (2003),[1] and Elizabeth Tisdell (1998), among others, the field of adult learning as a whole remains subject to unexamined assumptions that re-inscribe the disembodied knower and the mind/body dualism, treat embodied experience as the "raw material" for learning, and fail to acknowledge our ideological and political non-neutrality.

In order to offer a close reading and specific examples, I will use *Bodies of Knowledge: Embodied Learning in Adult Education* (Lawrence, 2012a), a recent issue of *New Directions for Adult and Continuing Education*, as an instance of both the strengths and weaknesses of current treatments of the body within the field of adult learning. The authors I will be discussing here are solid practitioners in their disparate fields, which range from dance education and theater to nurse education and management training, and, taken as a whole, the volume provides an important and creative array of learning and teaching strategies. In many ways, *Bodies of Knowledge* is a step in the right direction. It moves the field of adult learning in the direction of a paradigm shift that has been long in coming, and it exemplifies one of the things that is most admirable in adult learning theory, namely, a tenacious insistence on locating the creation of knowledge in grounded human life.

At the same time, much of the volume is troubled by what I see as insufficient attention to the implications of underlying presuppositions. What do we mean by a 'body'? (How) do we understand bodies as natural organisms and/or cultural artifacts? Whose theories of knowledge are we drawing on, and what makes us think they are valid? While I will use this single volume as a case in point, I offer the following in the spirit of collective self-critique and as a means of making a more general point. As I have argued elsewhere in these chapters, not to challenge ourselves seriously intellectually and academically reinforces our professional marginalization, dampens the vitality of adult learning theory, and, in the end, does our students no good.

According to Terry Eagleton's paraphrase, the British economist John M. Keynes once commented that "economists who disliked theory, or claimed to get along better without it, were simply in the grip of an older theory" (1996, p. ix).[2] There is, I think, a similar tendency among adult learning practitioners. We are proud, and rightly so, of our responsiveness to life outside of the sometimes-irritating and often-difficult world of critical theory, and, to our credit, we are relatively free as an academic field of self-importance and pomposity. That said, one of the key insights of critical theory is that there *is* no thinking outside of one theoretical frame or another. When we think that we are free of theory, we are instead subject to conventional understandings that are so ingrained that we hardly know they are there. Given how much we value critical self-reflection, becoming aware of and thinking critically about our thinking is the least we can ask of ourselves.

The title *Bodies of Knowledge: Embodied Learning in Adult Education* plays on a well-seen and clever dual meaning – our physical, sensate *bodies* as bearers of knowledge and, in the more traditional sense, the metaphorical *bodies* of accumulated knowledges that reside in professions, academic disciplines, and other formal knowledge systems. This dual meaning itself raises the question of the relationship between the two meanings of the term. Are "bodies" in these two senses in opposition to each other, as Alisoun of Bath would have it? Does one meaning of the term override the other? Or do the two meanings exist in a more complex tension, feeding into each other so that the opposition is never complete?

Similarly, what assumptions are we inscribing about the relationship of body to mind? Do we code the relationship of mind to body as one of separation and distance, with the perceiving, sensate body as the raw materials for learning? Or do we see the body as itself the bearer of knowledge and the mind as part of our embodiment? Finally, how do we understand the relationship of our bodies to other bodies? Are our bodies atomized units in a world of other such units, or do we understand ourselves as existing in and through interaction with other bodies? What is our responsibility to and for the power-laden social structures within which that interaction occurs?

Whose body? The body and historical specificity

The need to take those questions seriously can be seen as early as the first paragraph in Chapter one, in which editor Randee Lipson Lawrence (2012b) lays out a variety of approaches to the role of the body in knowledge: intuition as "spontaneous, heart-centered, free, adventurous, imaginative, playful, non-sequential, and nonlinear" (p. 5); kinesthetic or somatic learning; holistic forms of knowledge that involve heart, mind, body, and spirit; bodily awareness as a key component of consciousness; and the feminist reclamation of the body as a site of learning and resistance. While the stated goal of the volume, certainly an important one, is to encourage a greater awareness of embodied knowledge and help adult educators think about "how we can reclaim the body as a source of knowing" (p. 12), that goal is compromised from the start.

> Imagine you are walking down a dimly lit street in an unfamiliar neighborhood. It is just before sunset and the streets are fairly deserted. Suddenly you hear a loud noise that might be a car backfiring, or it might even be gunshots. Your heart starts racing, your breathing becomes shallow, and you feel as if you may start to hyperventilate. Some instinct tells you to run and leave the area as quickly as possible. You don't stop to think or reason or figure out what is happening, you just follow your body's cues and move toward safety. You rely on your intuition.
>
> (Lawrence, 2012b, p. 5)

On one level, this imagined scene is simple enough. There is a general, and as I understand it, uncontroversial consensus that human beings share with other species an inborn response to loud noise to which the word "instinct" can accurately be applied. On the other hand, however, it is not clear who the universalized, unmarked "you" is whose instincts induce the urge to flee. The situation is presented in such a way that the particularities of the "you" don't matter – "you" will have the same reactions anyone would in that situation because your body holds the same natural impulses that everybody's does.

The problem is that, by the time any of us is old enough to walk the streets by ourselves, the natural "instincts" of the body have been overwritten in innumerable, complex ways by the hard lessons of a life lived in a quite particular body. What if the body in question can't run because she has been taught that her legs look better in high heels? What if the body in question has had it drummed into his head by loving parents that he should never run while in a white neighborhood because someone will assume he's done something wrong and shoot him? What if the body in question is suffering from traumatic stress injuries, never leaves home without a gun in his pocket, and has an "intuition" that tells him to drop behind the nearest car and shoot anything that moves? Further, what does "unfamiliar neighborhood" imply? What color are the bodies of the people living in that neighborhood, what assumption is being made about that on the part of the reader, and what responsibility does the author have for fostering those implicit assumptions? Thus, Lawrence's opening anecdote re-erases the body at the very moment it tries to render it visible. If the point about bodies is that they carry our knowing histories, then an ungendered, nonracial, nonspecified body, as Susan Bordo (1990) has said in a somewhat different context, is "no body at all" (p. 145).

Lawrence seemingly knows better. She draws in her introduction on work by feminist educators who use embodied performance to help connect students with the pain of their own histories so that "the unsay-able" can be said (Horsfall and Titchen, cited in Lawrence, 2012b, p. 9). But the authors she cites understand learning through the body, not as the "primal" and "preverbal" awareness that babies have naturally and spontaneously (Ibid., p. 7), but as the holding of "historical, cultural, and political memory" (Nieves, 2012, p. 34).

Indeed, two of the chapters in *Bodies of Knowledge*, those by Yolanda Nieves and by Shauna Butterwick and Jan Selman (2012), are exemplary in their understanding of the historically embedded body in which the unspoken effects of oppression, marginalization, and violence are stored. Nieves tells the story of a theater group in which a group of Latina women used movement, embodied performance, and voice to reveal what she significantly calls "undocumented" events (p. 36). Nieves herself is one of the bodies whose history carries meaning, but instead of presenting her twitching facial muscles and trembling lips in terms of universalized instinct, she understands her fear as the product of a personal history that makes visibility dangerous.

One's history – and one's stories about one's history – are not without danger, Nieves tells us; they open one to judgment, carry the risk of further marginalization or cooptation, and raise the specter of exposure and rejection. That the body expresses fear is a function of the ways in which it carries quite specific physical and psychic scars. Nieves notes, further, that the safety to speak what the body knows requires the presences of equally particularized other bodies. The women whose bodies speak their stories trust her because she is one of them, because her body carries the same social markings of gender and ethnicity. The outcome of the women's work together is a performance for which location and audience also matter because place and performance constitute a series of relationships between differently positioned bodies in a space that codes safety for some and not others.

In a second, closely related chapter, Butterwick and Selman introduce the notion of the colonized body to stress the ways in which our bodies become subject to history, sometimes in the form of such brute oppressions as rape or torture, but also through the ways in which we enact on a daily basis the ideological frameworks and power relationships of specifically located members of a society. Butterwick and Selman work with teachers and teachers-in-training, and they point out that teachers, as typically female gendered bodies and as members of a multiply visible profession, are required on a daily basis to perform the particular constructions of gender and professionalism that they have internalized. The authors quote Linda Nicholson to the effect that "the body is a discursive category, a site of struggle ... Pedagogies which are embodied ... involve a more complex understanding of how the body is culturally and socially constructed and experienced" (Butterwick and Selman, 2012, p. 66). De-colonizing the body through dramatizing its story is an act of individual and collective self-revelation that carries the risk of unexpected meanings, surprise, and even re-traumatization. It is a mark of their respect for the power of embodied knowledge that they emphasize the importance of allowing individuals to decide not to participate.

The chapters by Nieves and Butterwick and Selman are powerful because they recognize both the deeply emotional and sensate quality of human experience and the power-laden historicity of the content of embodied memory. Other chapters in this same text, however, pull back from that understanding in one of two directions, both of which re-inscribe the mind/body dualism and deny the body's historicity. On the one hand, claims are made for the body as innocently authentic, as speaking essentialized truths that are blocked by "the tricks [the] mind can pull" (Snowber, 2012, p. 57). On the other hand, experiential learning is channeled back into the conventional mind/body dualism, with embodied experience seen as the raw material for learning that transcends the body and takes place in the mind.

Essentializing the body: The body as "nature" versus "culture"

Celeste Snowber's chapter on "dance as a way of knowing" is evocative and elegantly written. Drawing on Martha Graham's assertion that "movement never lies" (p. 54), Snowber speaks feelingly of our gradual alienation from the body as we move through an education system that forces children to sit still. She argues that, through dance, we can return to kinesthetic forms of learning and recover a "visceral language" that will allow us to understand more deeply "what it means to be human in the world" (pp. 54–5).

Snowber is aware of the body as culturally mediated. She argues that Western culture inevitably distances us from our bodies, teaching us to see them from the outside and attempt to shape them in the image of the culturally valued. At the same time, however, she treats the body as something that somehow survives the markings of culture; we can return to the body in order to access our feelings and, with them, a profound connection to the earth that will lead us to a greater understanding of self and to a sustaining ecological politics. As rhetoric, this is both hopeful and appealing, but casting the body as an unchanging source that we can return to takes the body out of history and relocates it in the realm of the natural in the same way that essentializing notions such as "maternal thinking" do. If we have been taught by Western culture to despise our bodies – and I agree that we have – so that it has stood apart from our conscious understanding until we return to it, where has it been and what has it been doing in the meantime? How has it stayed innocent, as it were, of the all-too-acculturated mind?

That is, I submit, a question it behooves us to consider. Like many people, I have had the experience Snowber describes of being most fully alive when I am most aware of my body and of being taught by the wisdom that seems to live in my heart and my bones. Moreover, I fully take her point that our culture teaches us to experience our bodies from the outside and to worry about how it is perceived by others rather than cultivate awareness of how it feels to 'be' a body from the inside.

But I am also suspicious, *pace* Martha Graham, of this image of the truth-telling body. Indeed, I find myself inclined to believe that the body does sometimes lie. Mine is a strong, healthy, fit female body that has been on this earth for over sixty years, that has tended to be on the wrong side of slender for my culture, that has loved both men and women, that has smoked, that has had cancer, and that is, for anyone conscious of such things, recognizably Jewish. And that body, the body I am, often lies to me, telling me that I am grossly fat, that a cigarette would be just the thing right now, or that I should be able to tame what we used jokingly to call a "Jewfro" into a slick, blond, slightly wavy pony tail that sways with a wiggle when I walk. Is that my culture talking rather than my body? Or is that very distinction the one that needs problematizing? Said differently, which body of mine is the wise one? The one that arrived open to the world and at home in itself, trailing clouds of glory, to quote Wordsworth? Or the one that carries the scars of a contentious professional and political lifetime, of internalized anti-Semitism and homophobia and the rage they trigger in me for myself and others, and of the compassion and the selfishness learned through intimations of mortality?

I am suspicious of claims for the natural wisdom of the body for another reason as well. We are at an historical moment in which other people's gut feelings, as it were, come in truly terrifying versions. It is time in which knowledge claims based on embodied and affective knowledge are not always made in the cause of progressive social possibilities. The newer sections of this book are being written in a decade in which a frightening right wing politic is fed by powerful "gut feelings" concerning the threat posed by a gay man in a bar, a Pakistani on a plane, or, that embodied oxymoron, a Black president in the White House. We grapple as a society with people who know in their bones that God hates fags and whose gut feelings tell them that the world is no longer the fine place it used to be because white men are being displaced by the undeserving and the uppity. In other words, some 'truths' mediated by the body – hate, fear, irrational fundamentalism – can be pathological, and sorting out the implications of what our guts tell us is the important other side of trusting them.

The body as raw material for the mind

Other chapters in *Bodies of Knowledge* reveal a different tendency that still typically frames treatments of adult learning, namely, that of using an embodied pedagogy but continuing to treat the body as a convenient resource for educating a self securely located in the mind. Pamela Meyer's (2012) discussion of embodied learning at work is less about embodied knowledge than it is about using play and playfulness to develop a more committed workforce and a more productive company. She discusses a bank workforce whose morning "motivational moment(s)" (p. 25) range from dodging marshmallows to dancing to the Rolling Stones and a digital media firm whose employees cook together, make beer, and ride bikes. The techniques are such that they reveal the whole person beyond the employee, ease a good bit of the psychic stress of work, and help to develop mutual loyalty between people based on shared experience.

I want to raise two issues concerning this approach to employee relations. First, while the bodies in the workplaces discussed by Meyers are indeed active, the physical activities in which they participate are not intended to engage the body as a source of knowing, but, rather, to use physical activity to develop mental and emotional qualities. That is, the point of these exercises is not to ground knowledge in the body or listen to what the body knows, but to nurture collaborative relations and motivate employees by encouraging the sense that, as one employee of the digital company puts it, "this is not just a job" (p. 27).

The tendency to treat embodied activity as a convenient resource for developing the mind is even clearer in Eric Howden's (2012) essay on outdoor experiential education. Howden's short history of this form of experiential education begins with Kurt Hahn's mid-twentieth-century concern with the decline of such qualities as fitness, initiative, and self-discipline among the youth. Hahn used difficult, physically challenging expeditions to inculcate self-confidence, leadership, initiative, and similar qualities.

Howden notes that Hahn's focus was never the body itself, but the use of physically difficult and frightening experiences to cultivate qualities of mind and character. He notes, further, that contemporary experiential education of this kind includes "a process of exploration that includes reflecting on the experience during and afterward, thereby reorganizing the meaning and directions of the individual's experience" (p. 45). Challenging participants to undergo "moments of great trepidation," face their fears, and "break through physical and mental barriers" (p. 49) through activities such as riding zip lines and climbing ropes results in learning that transcends the physical activity itself: citing Kolb and Lewin, he argues that participants grow in leadership skills, group cohesion, and self-knowledge through undergoing the experience and reflecting on it afterward. Howden quotes Hahn as explaining that such activities "revealed the inner worth of the man, the edge of his temper, the fiber of his stuff, the quality of resistance, the secret truth of his pretenses, not only to himself but to others" and notes that the most significant part of the quotation is that Hahn was focused less on the physical challenge than on the "emotional, social, and psychological" growth thus obtained (p. 46).

Thus, like Meyer's discussion of embodied activity at work, Howden's chapter is not about the body as the bearer of knowledge *per se*. Rather, it re-inscribes the conventional Western understanding of embodied experience as providing the raw

6

MIND AND MATTER

Dewey, Kolb, and embodied knowing

And gladly wolde he lerne and gladly teche.

[And gladly would he learn and gladly teach.]

Geoffrey Chaucer, *The Canterbury Tales*, I 308

In her excellent *Learning through Experience: Troubling Orthodoxies and Intersecting Questions* (2003), Tara Fenwick traces the ways in which, though their own internal frameworks and in dialogue with each other, five contemporary approaches to experience, thought, and cognition productively complicate our understanding of experiential learning in ways that are similar to the points I have been making here. Fenwick points out that the coherent self whose individual consciousness is the origin of meaning has been substantively deconstructed, on the one hand, by psychoanalytic theories that track the complexities of and limits to self-knowledge and, on the other, by theories of situated knowledge that locate learning in the broader environment. Complexity theories, in turn, explore the ways in which thought and environment are mutually creative within a complex ecology, while a wide variety of schools of critical theory reject any view of experience or of knowledge that is not always already mediated by culture, social context, and language.

Fenwick notes that David Kolb's learning cycle is especially problematic because both the learning cycle itself and the individualist model of learning that it represents have continued their hold over the community of adult learning in spite of more rigorous approaches that are now commonplace in other fields. Wilson and Hayes (2002) share the conviction that the ubiquitous presence of Kolb's learning cycle is both troubling and limiting "because it restricts the way we see and understand experience" (p. 173). There are no doubt multiple explanations for the continued faith in this one model of learning, not the least of which is the power of any hegemonic paradigm, and the learning cycle is indeed hegemonic within contemporary adult learning. Kolb's theory also has the apparent advantage of being ideologically friendly and easily understandable – I say apparent because actually using it to capture the dimensions of one's informal experiential learning is enormously difficult. While the learning cycle can be a helpful way to organize a structured learning experience in a classroom or workshop, it is very hard to present informal experiential learning in its terms because it is not an accurate representation of how people generally learn.

Reijo Miettinen (2000) expresses both the attraction and the danger of Kolb's learning cycle thusly:

> Perhaps the idea of experiential learning forms an attractive package for adult educators. It combines spontaneity, feeling, and deep individual insights with the possibility of rational thought and reflection. It maintains the humanistic belief in every individual's capacity to grow and learn, so important for the concept of lifelong learning. It comprises a positive ideology that is evidently important for adult education. However, I fear that the price of this package for adult education research and practice is high. Along with that package, adult education is at risk of remaining a quasi-scientific academic field without connection to the philosophical, anthropological, sociological and psychological studies of learning and thought.
>
> *(Miettinen, 2000, pp. 70–71)*

This chapter, in part, is meant as a contribution to the ongoing critique of Kolb's work.[1] In it, I bring his learning cycle and the assumptions behind it into dialogue with two schools of thought: feminist epistemology and John Dewey's theory of experience and knowledge. Dewey's is a name that is often invoked in discussions of adult and experiential learning, but he is more celebrated than read, more honored than used, and when he is cited, it is often in ways that are more distorted than otherwise. In what follows, I argue that Kolb uses Dewey in a misleading, if not intellectually dishonest fashion, and that his learning cycle represents a return to many of the classic strains in Western epistemology against which Dewey was writing. I then explore the ways in which a number of feminist theorists of knowledge have claimed Dewey as an important precursor. This chapter thus has several interlocking purposes: to introduce Dewey into the discussion, to explore the relationships between Dewey's thought and feminist theories of experiential learning, and to problematize Kolb's claim to have developed his model on Deweyan principles.[2]

Dewey and the isolated knower

I begin with what is perhaps the most visible use of John Dewey in the literature on adult learning, namely, the quotation from *Experience and Nature* with which Kolb opens his influential *Experiential Learning*:

Nor does Dewey view thinking as an individual process in the way that Kolb implies when he takes Dewey's words out of context. To be sure, "there is a private, inchoate moment in which new ideas gestate," but this "does not mean that the self is the source or author of the thought and affection nor its exclusive seat" (p. 233). Sullivan makes the case that Dewey understands bodies as "transactional," that is, as co-constituting each other in dynamic relationship. Organisms live, Dewey argues, "as much in processes across and 'through' skins as in processes 'within' skins" (as cited in Sullivan, 2001, pp. 1–2). "The epidermis is only in the most superficial way an indication of where an organism ends and its environment begins" (as cited in Ibid., p. 2). Neither experience nor knowledge, neither the problems faced by humans nor their solutions is a form of private property. Rather, all are jointly constructed and shared with others.

Finally, Dewey rejects the separation between thought and action and, with it, between mind and body, arguing, as many feminists do, that such a belief is part of the legacy of the ancient Greek class divide that put "a premium … upon the accidental good-fortune of a class that happen[ed] to be furnished by the toil of another class" (p. 50). Dewey uses the term 'body-mind' to indicate that

> thinking, or knowledge-getting, is far from being the armchair thing it is often supposed to be. … Hands and feet, apparatus and appliances of all kinds are as much a part of it as changes in the brain.
>
> *(as cited in Miettinen, 2000, p. 67)*

In this formulation, 'mind' marks meaningful consequences of acts that organisms perform in interaction with the world, while 'body' marks the ongoing interactions and activities through which meaning emerges and changes (Sullivan, 2001; Heldke, 1987).

It should be clear from the above discussion why feminist theorists of knowledge such as Shannon Sullivan, Charlene Haddock Seigfried, and Lisa Heldke see Dewey as deeply relevant to their thinking. Seigfried (2001) notes that both pragmatism and feminism have "challenged the model of disembodied, detached rationality by stressing the importance of concrete experience lived in real bodies and attending to the particulars of embodied experience rather than abstractions" (p. 99). Both pragmatism as represented by Dewey and the schools of feminism I have been drawing on here understand human beings as contiguous with nature and in mutual interaction with it (Sullivan, 2001). Both recognize the value-ladenness of knowledge and understand the knowing self as historically located and socially invested. Finally, both reject "dualisms such as that between sensuous appetite and rational thought, between the particular and universal, between the mechanical and the telic, between experience and science, between matter and mind" (Dewey, 1958, p. 124) Both understand those dualisms as "but the reflections of [a] primary metaphysical dualism" that feminism locates in the gendered dualisms associated with male/female and that Dewey, in a different but parallel fashion, locates in philosophies that posit "a split in Being itself, its division into some things which are inherently defective, changing, relational, and other things which are inherently perfect, permanent, self-possessed" (Ibid.).

Dewey and Kolb

If there is no split between thought and action, and if what we call reflection is simply one more "integration of connections within the environment" (p. 280), what does this do to Kolb's seeming relationship to Dewey? I argued in Chapter two that Kolb's learning cycle reproduces a number of the qualities of conventional Western epistemology: treating experience as immediate and pre-symbolic, staging learning as a two-step process in which unmediated experience is followed by the creation of knowledge through reflection, and gendering epistemological values between loving, communal, emotive apprehension and a form of comprehension that is virtually phallic in its claim to autonomy. I want to continue that analysis here by contrasting Kolb's learning cycle to both the Deweyan and feminist understandings of experiential learning.

Kolb (1984) represents his learning cycle as a circle divided into quadrants, in part because it allows him to connect the cycle with his theory of learning styles.[5] The diagram itself represents the dualist distinctions between the concrete and the abstract, reflection and activity, experience and conceptualization, and observation and experimentation. The series of adjective/noun phrases separate these steps spatially as well as representing them as occurring separately, with the learner moving "in various degrees from actor to observer, and from specific involvement to general analytic detachment" (p. 31). It also creates a series of descriptors that associate each noun with particular characteristics: experience is concrete while conceptualization is abstract; observation is reflective while experimentation is active.

According to both Dewey and feminist theorists of knowledge, however, these definitional and descriptive word pairs are both inaccurate and misguided. On the one hand, experience is not concrete; rather, as we have seen, it is always already mediated by culture, language, and culturally overdetermined presuppositions, none of which Kolb attempts to account for.

> Experience is already overlaid and saturated with the products of the reflection of past generations and by-gone ages. It is filled with interpretations, classifications, due to sophisticated thought, which have become incorporated into what seems to be fresh naïve empirical material. It would take more wisdom than is possessed by the wisest historical scholar to track all of these absorbing borrowings to their source.
>
> *(Dewey, 1958, p. 63)*

It is for this reason that Dewey argued that philosophy has little to gain from a "psychology isolated from a theory of culture" (p. 41).

Nor, in turn, is conceptualization abstract. While abstractions and syllogisms may help us to open "the way to new uses and consequences," new meanings do

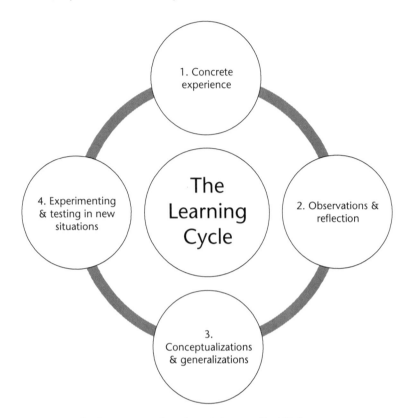

FIGURE 6.1 Kolb's learning cycle (adapted from Kolb, 1984).

not arrive from them as much as from trials, intuitions, wit, and a "sensitive ear" for "harmonies and discords" (p. 195). There is no thinking separate from

> the contextual situation in which thinking occurs… (T)hinking is a continuous process of temporal re-organization within one and the same world of experienced things, not a jump from the latter world into one of objects constituted once for all by thought.
>
> *(Dewey, 1958, pp. 67–8)*

Thus, Dewey rejects any notion of conceptualization or reflection that takes place in temporal isolation from active moments of experience and experimentation because "intelligence is incarnate in overt action, using things as a means to affect other things" (p. 158). What Kolb represents as separate stages are a single unified activity within a world in which human endeavor is both creative and creating, part of what Donna Haraway (1997) has called "the permanent finitude of engaged interpretation" (p. 37). To be sure, Dewey sees experiential learning as taking place within time, but that is because "thought and knowledge are histories" in which human meanings are "not simply states of consciousness or ideas inside the heads of men" (*sic*) but rather moderations in the "public meaning of the world in which men publically act" (p. 156).

This integration of thought and action and of mind and world also challenges the epistemological individualism of Kolb's learning cycle. In "Rethinking Kolb's theory of experiential learning in management education," Holman, Pavlica, and Thorpe (1997) argue that Dewey sees the meditational tools of thought and interpretation as tying us to the world and to others rather than separating us from it because the concepts we use are part of the received structures within which we experience, reflect, and act. Thus, they are shared tools, not individual ones; even when we are thinking on our own, that thinking is mediated through the sociality of language and the social production of meaning. Again, Dewey is aligned with feminist thinking and, indeed, with Bakhtin (1982), in arguing that the language of thought is never individual but is always "overpopulated with the intentions of others" (p. 294).[6] Dewey argues that "when the introspectionist thinks he has withdrawn into a wholly private realm of events disparate in kind from other events, made out of mental stuff, he is only turning his attention to his own soliloquy," which is itself "the product and reflex of converse with others" (p. 170). Language is "a relationship, not a particularity" (p. 185).

Portrait of an experiential learner: The example of Mary

As a way of elucidating how disparate these understandings of experiential learning are, I want to develop a hypothetical example that I have previously used in discussing "the return of the body to experiential learning" (Michelson, 1998, p. 217). Mary has recently been promoted to a position of greater authority at work in which she will be responsible for managing a team of professionals. At the first meeting of her team, she is aware that two of the senior men in the group repeatedly dismiss points made by the less-senior women, only to restate them subsequently as their own. As a new manager, Mary is eager both to comport herself well and to have the team operate effectively, and so she does not address this behavior in any form. She hides her increasing irritation and, by the end of the meeting, is aware that her shoulders are hunched and stiff to the point of physical discomfort. She is still emotionally agitated and in physical pain in the car driving home. When Mary replays the meeting in her thoughts, it occurs to her that she should have found a way to intervene in the two men's conduct. She not only had a general professional responsibility to the team as its manager, but also a political responsibility – and loyalty – to the more vulnerable women in the group. Mary spends the rest of the drive identifying creative options for running the next meeting and beginning to develop strategies.

One of those strategies is to develop her own skills by registering for a course in Leadership. Her instructor, an adult educator who believes in experiential learning, asks each student to relate a learning moment from his or her own experience. Mary tells the story given above. How, then, might Mary's experiential learning be understood?

According to the conventional discourse of experiential learning, what has happened is as follows. While Mary's initial experience included responses that she was not able to process at the time, her subsequent reflections provided a broader perspective in which both the meaning of her emotions and the responsibilities of her position were clarified. As she used her cognitive and analytical powers, she reviewed what she knew about the sexual dynamics of meetings, learned something about professional and social responsibility, and gained insight both into her own values and the responsibilities of leadership. The moment of learning came about when she used her mind to critique her bodily and emotional responses and reflected on her experience from a more distanced perspective. That reflection led to improved decisions about how to behave in the future in her role as manager of her team.

Framed in this way, Mary's learning can be mapped onto Kolb's learning cycle. The cycle begins with the "concrete experience" of the meeting. In the car driving home, Mary engages the next step of the cycle, "reflective observation," by reliving the meeting in her mind, observing in retrospect what transpired, and reflecting on her own actions and those of others. This leads her to a new "abstract conceptualization" of her own value system, the power dynamics of meetings, the role of gender in human interaction, and the roles and obligations of leadership. Her development of strategies based on those new concepts will guide Mary's "active experimentation" with new forms of behavior at subsequent meetings.

What, then, does this version of Mary's learning tell us about Kolb?

First, Mary's story makes both the cognitive individualism and spatial/temporal detachment of Kolb's model particularly visible. There are, in effect, two settings to the story. The first is the meeting room, the "concrete" and "active" world of Mary's workplace. The second setting, read literally, is the car, but it is more meaningfully understood as Mary's reflective inner consciousness. This split in Kolb's learning cycle between self and world is clear if we substitute a diagonal diameter for the horizontal and vertical ones; experience and experimentation take place "out" in the world, while observation and conceptualization take place "in" the mind.

There is, moreover, a curiously one-sided relationship between Mary's mind and the rest of the world. While the world forms the subject matter of Mary's thoughts, it has had no role in shaping her or in molding her thoughts, such that, at the moment of learning, she stands outside the frame within which the events of the world are taking place. This, of course, raises the uncomfortable question of where Mary is if she is not in the world, but it also raises the question of what the world is doing in the meantime. As it is, the "world" is freeze-framed as an entity in Mary's mind to which she can apply something called "conceptualization" but with which she has no ongoing relationship.

Further, let's say that the instructor in Mary's class had asked the students to frame their learning in terms of Kolb's learning cycle, a possibility that, given its ubiquitous nature, is likely enough. Let us say, similarly, that Mary attends a college or university that gives credit for prior learning and that her recounting of this

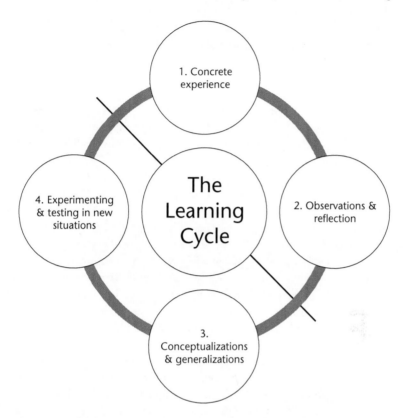

FIGURE 6.2   Kolb's learning cycle – revised (adapted from Kolb, 1984).

learning moment is the stuff of potential credit if she can frame it in acceptably Kolbian terms.[7] In that case, Mary labors under an additional burden. Not only must she articulate what she has learned and locate it within one of a number of possible academic, professional, or sociopolitical frames, which will be required for her to receive credit for her knowledge, but she must also represent her learning process as having happened in a particular series of steps that may well have nothing to do with how she actually experienced it. In effect, she must achieve a double translation. First, she must make explicit and lucid what might originally have been implicit and inchoate, itself a challenge for students whose experiential learning is being assessed. But she must then translate, however artificially, both her learning process and its results into a quite narrow and rigid algorithm. How difficult and artificial this is, is clear from a single example. In my rendition, I placed Mary's 'reflective observation' in Mary's review of the meeting while driving home in her car. But no literal moment of reflective observation ever took place. Mary was not reflective in the usual sense at the meeting – she was getting more and more agitated and uncomfortable. Nor, given that the meeting is now over, is she observing in the usual meaning of the term. Mary is thus put in the position of either having to 'admit' that she has 'missed' one of the stages in the learning process or she has to twist words to make them fit. This verbal juggling has very little to do with the point of Mary's learning, but she runs the risk of having to deal with a Kolbian true believer who thinks that, if the learning cycle hasn't been reproduced, no legitimate experiential learning has taken place.[8]

There is, however, an alternative way to understand this piece of learning, one that tells a different story because it draws on different understandings of the relationships among thought and embodiment, rationality and feeling, and self and world. According to this second view, Mary's moment of learning was at the meeting, not in the car, and was located in her initial emotional and physical response. The understanding that came to Mary on the way home was not a cognitive flash of new learning, but simply the moment in which her mental processes caught up with what her body already knew. This reinterpretation both requires and enables a quite different understanding of the process of learning. First, it posits Mary's emotions and physical responses as the repository of prior experiential learning. Second, it sees her body and her feelings as producers of new knowledge based on events as they are happening. Third, learning is understood as a moment of emotional and physical response, not a moment of dispassionate self-reflection, as the product of an embodied, social selfhood rather than of a disembodied mind. Mary's capacity for insight is a function of a gendered subjectivity, of a social existence lived within a woman's body in which the traces of past angers and hurt feelings, of personal and collective memories reside. Seen in these terms, the production of knowledge is a moment of social self-location, not transcendence, and one that uses all the cognitive, emotional, sensate, and muscular neural faculties.

Clearly, this alternative interpretation changes everything. It constructs a different understanding of the relationship between the personal and the social, refusing the split between a privatized self and a constraining social context. It challenges the assumption that one must transcend emotional and physical responses in order to 'learn,' suggesting, rather, that our bodies and feelings, in this case Mary's aching shoulders, speak truths about the world.[9] Finally, it undermines the conjoining of dialogue, consensus, rationality, and learning that typifies much adult learning, implicitly in Kolb and more explicitly in writers such as Mezirow.[10] Thus, instead of miming the detached rationality of the abstract knower, it tells a story of what Jane Flax (1993) has called "the political genealogies of subjectivity" that connect Mary's gendered partiality to a broader history (p. 96). Rather than being a moment of abstract thought in the privacy of her own unique consciousness, Mary's experiential learning is a product of the complex interactions within which the personal and social meet in a world in which, for better or worse, history runs through us and in which, as feminists have insisted, the personal is political.

In my initial formulation of Mary's experiential learning, from which the above is largely taken, my conclusion was that students such as Mary can learn from their experience, not by detaching from their bodies and feelings, but, rather, by learning to trust them. I stand by that conclusion as far as it goes. To be sure, students must listen to one another, denaturalize their own understandings of the world by learning from the experience of others, and attempt, across different historically located vantage points, to construct fuller and more usable truths. But experiential learning must also be a process of drawing deeper into our own experience, of allowing pain and discomfort to teach us about solidarity, and of letting passion, both of love and anger, ground us in the always marked body of history.

I would now, however, both extend and complicate that conclusion, and I would do so in ways that parallel the developments within feminist epistemology delineated in Chapter four. Specifically, if we are not to fall into the trap of claiming the body as the keeper of an impossible authenticity, we cannot understand Mary's embodied learning as unproblematically insightful. That is, rather than seeing Mary's body in any simplistic sense as the holder of wisdom that her mind would do well to access, we can understand her body as itself holding the tensions and struggles among social and ideological constructions of gender. While her shoulders, for example, may hold the historic rage she shares with others over the intellectual demeaning of women, she may also have been constrained by a tight throat that holds the risks of speaking, if not truth to power, at least clarity and authority to men. In other words, Mary must contend with the contradictory ways in which her body 'speaks' in a variety of ways, none of which is free of the marks of culture and ideology.

Moreover, if Dewey is correct that that our experiences are embedded in the ongoing flow of time (p. 158), then we must take seriously his caution that "choice and the reflective effort involved in it are themselves such contingent events ... bound up with the precarious uncertainty of other events" (p. 52). In other words, Mary needs to understand herself as one of the actors in a complex transaction that does not end at the adjournment of the meeting, or at the surface of her skin. The world has been altered in small degrees by Mary's actions at the meeting, and that world will not hold in place while she exits it in order to reflect. By the time she has settled into her car, the men at the meeting will have noticed or failed to notice that they indulged in some fairly sleazy gender politics. Depending upon how they experienced the meeting, the junior women will have decided that Mary is not to be trusted, or that they are too incompetent to hold their own at professional meetings, or that they need to get together over drinks that night to talk about it, or that they should have ignored the alarm clock that morning and stayed in bed. Decisions taken at the meeting, subsequent actions, and the ongoing life of the organization will be subtly different because of Mary's actions at the meeting, which have contributed to the ongoing transactions among selves, institutions, discourses, and the encompassing environment that constitute the world.

None of what I have been arguing here is in any way to suggest that thinking hard about one's experience and one's behavior is not a good idea. It is, of course, a very good idea. Mary will do well to think hard and long about her location within multiple material, social, and discursive relationships and about what she wants in, from and for herself, her colleagues, and her society. This requires that she see herself within what Tara Fenwick (2006b) has called "the multiple fluctuations in complex systems" that frame experiential learning as occurring "within action, within and among bodies" (2006b, p. 47).

In her classic essay, "The promise of monsters: a regenerative politics for inappropriate/d others," Donna Haraway (2004b) posits an optical device that *diffracts* rather reflects. Rather than reproducing 'the same' displaced, which is what reflection and refraction do, "diffraction is a mapping of interference" (p. 70). Diffraction maps, not sameness, but difference or, rather, the *effects* of the difference, the patterns of interference that are our actions in the world. Haraway is not talking about reflection here in the cognitive sense, but her point is deeply suggestive of how we might understand how our human experience diffuses and is diffused by a world that produces us, not as essentialized cognitive beings, but as embodied, historical ones.

If one word sufficed to sum up Dewey's understanding of how we learn "in-from-to" experience (Wilson and Hayes, 2002, p. 173), that word might well be 'complexity.' Dewey offers a complex view of a world in which "everything that exists in as far as it is known and knowable is in interaction with other things" (p. 174) and in which "things interacting in certain ways *are* experience" (p. 4a: italics in original). Intersection, interaction, change, inseparability, and mutuality are the stuff of learning because they are the stuff of the world in which humanity has its being and out of which the human capacity to learn evolved.

This understanding of experiential learning is beginning to reassert itself, importantly through Fenwick's (2006b) use of complexity theory. Focusing on "the flows across bodies, rather than the boundaries between them," Fenwick contrasts her view of experience as fluid interaction from a "mentalist" formulation. This, Fenwick argues, represents "a crucial conceptual shift ... from a learning subject to the larger collective, to the systems of culture, history, social relations and nature in which everyday bodies, subjectivities and lives are enacted" (p. 46).

This same understanding is given additional support by scholars who draw on cultural-historical activity theory and related schools of thought that draw on Vygotskian theories of learning and Marxian theories of social interaction. Scholars such as Yrjo Engeström and Peter Sawchuk hold that learning is grounded, not in cognitive isolation, but in the cultural and material practices of daily life and in activity systems through which material artifacts, symbolic systems of meaning, epistemic and social standpoints are mediated (Sawchuk, 2005).[11]

As Patricia Williams has wonderfully said, "that life is complicated is of great analytic importance" (cited in Gordon, 2008, p. 3). John Dewey would have agreed entirely.

Notes

1 For an extremely helpful summary of the multiple critiques of Kolb, see Roger Greenaway's website, http://reviewing.co.uk/research/experiential.learning.htm#2.
2 In my discussion, I have drawn largely on *Experience and Nature*, Dewey's extended exploration of human experience as an aspect of complex interactions among entities in nature and how multiple Western philosophies have misunderstood the relationship

of the human mind to nature. Other key texts in Dewey's theory of mind include *How We Think* and *Knowing and the Known*. Miettinen (2000) argues that one of the reasons Kolb can claim to base his work on Dewey is that he drew his quotations from *Experience and Education*, a series of lectures Dewey gave on the subject of school pedagogy in which his focus was on how to structure effective learning experiences for children, not on the ways in which human beings learn in less structured environments.

3 For a related overview of Dewey's view of the historical emergence of the isolated knower, see Seigfried (2001).

4 One ongoing critique of Kolb concerns his use of multiple sources taken out of context and treated superficially. Seaman (2008), for example, argues that Kolb's learning cycle is not the result of a rigorous, internally consistent theory of either social or cognitive processes but a grouping of ideas taking from a variety of disparate writers and schools of thought. "Today, this framework has evolved from a set of practice-driven models with historically specific purposes into a broader belief system underwritten more by liberal-humanist ideology, folk psychology, and administrative interests than by a scientific or epistemological foundation for learning. It has also received considerable criticism in various disciplines such as education, psychology, and philosophy" (p. 9). Similarly, Miettinen (2000) claims that Kolb extracts multiple terms and contexts, which in their own original contexts have different meanings, often in contradiction to each other, and uses them to support his own purpose. One cannot help concluding that Kolb's motive is not critical evaluation or interdisciplinarity but an attempt to construct an attractive collection of ideas that can be advocated as a solution to the social problems of our time (p. 56).

5 Miettinen (2000) points out that Kolb's learning styles inventory was created before the writing of *Experiential Learning*, with the book as a kind of elaboration and promotion of the model. It is thus essentially an example of the genre that Miettinen calls "consultancy literature" (p. 55), which explains in part its lack of academic rigor and careful referencing of source material.

6 See Holman, Pavlica, and Thorpe (1997) on related points concerning Dewey and Bakhtin's understanding of language.

7 Again, the expectation that students frame their prior learning in terms of Kolb's model is common in Anglophone institutions. For an example, see Murphy (2007).

8 Holman *et al.* argued in 1997 that Kolb's influence had been so great that when managers are seen by educators to fail to learn, they are thought to have failed in one or another step in the learning cycle. It would be interesting to know if that would still be the case today.

9 See Boud, Cohen and Walker (1993, p. 8) and Mezirow, (1991, p. 1) for examples of this thinking.

10 See Michelson (1998) and Hart (1998) on the ways in which expectations concerning rational consensus can enforce unequal power relationships.

11 For excellent introductions to this important work, see Fenwick, Edwards, and Sawchuk (2011) and Engström, Miettinen, and Punamäki (1999).

PART III

Power and the assessment of experiential learning

7

CONSERVATISM AND TRANSGRESSION IN THE ASSESSMENT OF EXPERIENTIAL LEARNING

And lete auctoritees, on Goddes name,
To prechyng and to schole eek of clergye.

[In God's name, leave preaching to the authorities
And also scholarship to the clergy.]

Geoffrey Chaucer, *The Canterbury Tales*, III 1276–7

In the fourteenth century, the assessment of the Wife of Bath's experiential learning would have been the work of a moment. The friar who responds to Alisoun in *The Canterbury Tales* articulates what would have been the collective academic judgment: leave preaching to the authorities and scholarship to the clergy. The friar himself is a lecher and a drunk who fusses with his wardrobe, curries favor with the wealthy, and swaps absolutions for money, but as a member of the clergy he feels entitled to chide her for addressing difficult "schole-matere" [scholastic matters] rather than attempting to entertain the company (III 1272).

Contemporary daughters of Alisoun have a better opportunity to have their experiential learning assessed by academic authority. What is variously called prior learning assessment (in the US), prior learning assessment and recognition (in Canada), the recognition of prior learning (in Australia and South Africa), and the assessment of prior experiential learning (in the UK) allows adult learners to gain credit for learning acquired outside of formal education. What I will here call the assessment of prior experiential learning (APEL)[1] is used variously for access into educational programs, for advanced standing within them, and for professional and vocational qualifications, but in each case it allows adult learners to be recognized as knowledgeable authorities in their own right.

In what follows, I take the position of a critical proponent of APEL who has spent many years as an APEL trainer, advocate, and scholar. APEL is enormously helpful to adults, in some cases the central enabling device for those who attempt to gain academic or professional credentials, and at their best, APEL practices contribute to a vital engagement with the multiple sources of knowledge and expertise. APEL is one of the few institutionalized practices anywhere that wrestles with the difficult communication across communities of knowledge and that allows for the recognition of materially situated knowledge claims. It is thus one of the few sites currently available for bringing the insights of feminist epistemology and related schools of thought to bear directly on the life of the academy.

I also believe, however, that the conventional association of APEL with a progressive social and educational vision cannot be taken for granted. The process through which knowledge is judged and quantified is of necessity a contentious, power-laden activity. The valuing of experiential learning takes place through concrete social practices in which specific knowledge – and, therefore, specific knowers – is publicly and institutionally valued and in which questions of epistemological authority explicitly confront questions of social inequality. APEL relies on the power of the academy to determine what kind of knowledge can be accredited and translates epistemological legitimacy into currencies – credits, degrees, professional credentials – that lead to social status and material rewards. Its adjudication of knowledge therefore has direct consequences that are anything but hypothetical.

The American origins of the assessment of prior experiential learning

The assessment for academic credit of students' experiential learning was originally the product of developments within American higher education. First utilized as a way of responding to the academic and professional needs of returning veterans following World Wars I and II, the practice gained traction in the context of the self-directed and student-centered educational movements of the late 1960s and early 1970s. It is the product of a time in which new student populations were both cause and effect of structural and curricular innovations, including programs for individualized and distance education and what, in American English, were known as 'universities without walls.' Supported by influential funders such as the Ford Foundation, the Educational Testing Service, and the US Department of Education, a series of practices were introduced that allowed students' 'college-equivalent' [2] knowledge to be identified and quantified: standardized testing; generic evaluations of non-university-sponsored training programs; and extensively documented narrative submissions, often called portfolios.

A number of social trends came together in the development of APEL. As both the professional need for credentialing and the pursuit of meaningful leisure drove adults back to higher education, the presence in the student body of skilled professionals and knowledgeable amateurs posed problems of both fairness and formal structure, and it did so at a time in which fairness was seen to matter and formal structures were seen as fluid and relatively open to change. In US higher education, the period was characterized by a push for both relevance and access, for shared power and shared inquiry among students and faculty, and for the relaxing of disciplinary, social, and institutional boundaries. It seemed self-evident that broad-minded approaches to education would include a respect for the ability of people to learn in a variety of places and styles and that the willingness of colleges and universities to recognize such learning was a mark of openness and flexibility. It seemed equally obvious that APEL itself was an important progressive innovation, consistent with the meritocratic belief that educational access was the key to both personal transformation and social equity.

Indeed, viewed with a broader historical lens, what becomes clear about the early development of APEL is how very American a phenomenon it was. Higher education in the US has long been characterized by comparatively greater fluidity among courses and programs than is the case in other countries, greater portability among different forms of post-secondary education, and a greater commitment to non-elite communities, be they urban immigrants served by large public universities, African Americans served by historically Black colleges, or rural youth served by Midwestern land-grant universities. Related to these institutions – and, again, in a sense both their cause and effect – is a widely held belief in the role of higher education in Americanization and upward mobility. John Dewey's belief in the educative value of experience, his insistence on the relationship of learning to 'real life,' and his faith in the fundamentally democratic nature of education are themselves deeply American. APEL's first iterations were meritocratic in a particularly American way, reflecting the belief that it doesn't matter where one comes from; rather, justice requires the recognition of individual achievement in the multiple locations in which knowledge, energy, initiative, and good old American know-how thrive. There was something deeply optimistic in the initial assessments of experiential learning and the expansion of higher education of which it was a part. If first-generation APEL had been a fictional character, Gene Kelly would have played it in the movie.

> In 1972 the Commonwealth of Massachusetts gave the vote for president to George McGovern and its university gave the green light to a number of campus-based liberal experiments. One of these, the University Without Walls, was charged to open the doors of the university to those who were eager to learn but who had been excluded because of discrimination, logistics, or other reasons. ... We sought students who were intelligent and skilled and whose accomplishments we respected, but who were outsiders. ... At the same time we sought to stretch the boundaries of the campus to include new places to learn: work, home, the artist's studio, the streets. ... As part of our mandate, we started designing a process for crediting what our "outsider" students had learned from the world of work.
>
> *(Hall, 1990, pp. 88–89)*

Institutional policy and academic knowledge: a case in point

As a way of entering into this exploration, let us posit the following circumstances for one of Alisoun's daughters. Dorothy is a forty-five year old African-American with twenty years of experience as a delivery-room nurse, ten of them spent as a union shop steward and five as head obstetrical nurse in an inner-city hospital. She and her husband have three children, two of whom are still living at home. She has come back to formal education because new hospital policies require a bachelor's degree for supervisory positions, and she has only her original training as a registered nurse in the way of formal credentials. Because the delivery unit she works in serves Latinas among others, she has taken continuing education courses in medical Spanish. She has been trained in grievance handling and arbitration by her union. In her leisure time, she continues a tradition of quilting that she learned from her Southern-born mother and grandmother, for whom quilting was both a creative outlet and a way of keeping their family warm. Dorothy's plan is to get a bachelor's degree in Health Care Management, and she is considering a master's degree.

In what follows, I use Dorothy as an example of the ways in which both institutional policy and belief systems concerning knowledge determine the extent to which experiential learning can be recognized through APEL. I point first to the ways in which the particular practices of a given institution may significantly narrow or expand the possibilities for credit, but I want to pay greater attention to the ways in which APEL currently conforms to the ways in which knowledge is organized in the academy, concretely in the sense of disciplines and departments and, more fundamentally, in the privileging of what I have echoed Susan Bordo in calling abstract masculinity.

As currently practiced – and this is no small improvement over older academic practices – APEL procedures will allow Dorothy to apply for credit for her knowledge of nursing science, labor relations, and health care management. That knowledge will be accredited to the extent that it both overlaps generally with academic subject matter and meets the particular policy requirements of her institution and degree. Those requirements differ from campus to campus. Some institutions define APEL quite narrowly and only accredit knowledge that was gained in structured settings, in which case only Dorothy's RN diploma will apply. Other institutions may also allow her to take standardized exams – a national exam in Supervision, for example, or the final exam in a Spanish course given by the university. If she passes them, she will be granted further credit.

Institutions with a yet more open APEL policy will allow Dorothy to examine the course catalogue to identify courses the content of which aligns with her experiential learning. She will then be asked to submit a written portfolio in which she articulates the knowledge she has gained, narrates the experience through which she gained it, and makes connections between her experiential learning and the course curriculum. Given the difficulty of mapping experiential learning onto an academic syllabus, the fit will rarely be easy. Still, Dorothy will likely be helped to make that fit through a course or workshop in portfolio-development. If she is lucky, the institution will have open course titles such as "Practicum in Health Care Management" or "Studies in Industrial Labor Relations," which can serve as shells into which her learning can be poured.

Dorothy's best option will be to attend an institution that takes a still more fluid approach to APEL. In that case, rather than assessing the overlap between her experiential learning and the content of particular courses, the assessor will focus on more holistic overlaps between her learning and the general attributes of academic knowledge: its intellectual level; its meaningfulness for others; its particular way of utilizing ideas and information in the exercise of professional, artistic, or organizational expertise. In this case, Dorothy will avoid having to find a fit with the content of specific academic courses, but the process of developing a portfolio will in some ways be more challenging; it will require her to think more deeply about how to name and categorize her knowledge, how it has taken shape in the course of her professional, creative, and organizational life, and how it relates to the way in which knowledge is organized academically.

These differences in institutional policy, generally referred to as standardized versus individualized and course-match versus non-course-match assessment, are only some of the policies that will determine what of Dorothy's experiential learning can be accredited. Some institutions, for example, accredit experiential learning only in the student's major field of study. In this case, the question arises as to whether Dorothy's training and experience as a nurse and as a union representative are applicable to a degree in health care administration, a connection that may seem obvious but may not be so to an inflexible department chair. Other institutions accredit learning only in fields in which they offer degrees; in that case, Dorothy may not be given credit for her knowledge of nursing if the institution does not offer a nursing degree. Finally, some institutions accredit experiential learning only at the introductory level but consider "medical Spanish" advanced. In that case, Dorothy's knowledge of Spanish may not be accreditable.

On the simplest level, then, the amount and shape of the credit that Dorothy receives is a question of institutional policy. At another level, however, the question of Dorothy's experiential learning points more broadly to the particular way in which knowledge is organized in the academy and the logic within which curriculum is developed. Academic curricula move from the general to the specific and from the theoretical to the applied, a logic that makes sense for eighteen-year-olds who are truly beginners, but does not match that of the often deep but focused expertise gained experientially by adults. Dorothy is less likely to be able to parse the uses of *por* versus *para* than to guide a laboring mother in workable Spanish, less likely to be able to provide an overview of something called Industrial Labor Relations than to understand the particular demands of representing or supervising a 24/7 workforce, less familiar with the principles of hospital design than with the particular safety and health challenges of operating room personnel.

Similarly, an epistemological framework organized by disciplines and academic departments does not easily manage the proverbial interdisciplinarity of experiential learning. Life is messy, and negotiating it requires multiple frameworks of investigation and interpretation rather than the distinct foci and methods of disciplinary inquiry. What Dorothy knows about nursing, labor relations, and supervision meld into each other in multiple ways that enrich her effectiveness as both a clinician and a supervisor, a more-than-the-sum-of-its parts expertise that may well lose its potency when separated into segments that individual disciplinary academics can assess.

Thirdly, academic disciplines and departments are not innocent of a history that has privileged some kinds of knowledge and skill and marginalized others, often, as we have seen, in ways that parallel social hierarchies of other kinds. As a quilter, Dorothy is heir to a long tradition that has flourished outside of the cultural mainstream. Historically, quilting has been carried on by women, often women of color, poor women, and women of remote rural communities. It is a form both of memory and of bricolage, the recycling of materials in a world of material poverty that at the same time expresses an aesthetic vision and preserves family history. Both functional and imaginative, quilting jostles the ways in art is seen and categorized in conventional art departments and the ways in which various creative artifacts are differently valued. Is quilting an art or a craft? What is the difference, and why does it matter? If it is an art, is it 'primitive' or 'modern' art? Does the meaning and value of a quilt shift when we either lay it on a bed or hang it on a wall?[8] Academic departments, moreover, are more than seats of disciplinary inquiry. They also serve as administrative units, ways of allocating faculty lines and institutional resources, and the specific studies offered within them are often a product, not of age-old intellectual precepts, but of particular contours of student demand or of professorial interest or expertise.

Finally, though, the deepest challenge posed by Dorothy's experiential learning is to the nature of academic knowledge itself, specifically its presumptions concerning abstract masculinity. In making the case for the credit-worthiness of their experiential learning, students are required to frame it in terms of the conventional epistemological dualisms – the abstract over the concrete, theory over practice, and the propositional over the procedural – and make the case that their knowledge is sufficiently detached from the everyday practices of work life, home life, and community. In Chapter two, I used the association of midwifery with empathy and human corporality as an example of the privileging of masculinist detachment. That same binary thinking will shape the ways in which Dorothy will be asked to distinguish between experience and learning. She will not, for example, be encouraged to discuss how her own visceral memories of labor and birth contribute to her academically accreditable knowledge. She will not be rewarded for her kindness to patients or her loyalty to her co-workers. Such things will be considered experience, not learning, feeling, not thought, and the formula through which her learning will be accredited will reproduce the dualisms that associate experience with the body and learning with the mind.

A qualification is in order here. The distinction between experience and learning, which is central to current forms of portfolio-mediated APEL, has been fostered by an important concern on the part of advocates of APEL, namely, the need for quality assurance in a practice open both to continued opposition and real possibilities for abuse. Precisely because APEL locates the source of knowledge in practical human activity, it has been vulnerable to the charge that credit is being awarded for experience alone rather than for the learning thus generated, for simple presence in the learning environment (hours on the job or hours asleep in an on-the-job seminar) rather than for any active acquisition of skills, information, and ideas. Because, as Urban Whitaker puts it, "it is easier to quantify experience than it is to measure learning," and because "unfortunately there is no guarantee that 'x' amount of experience will yield 'y' amount of learning," quality assurance in APEL is viewed as requiring a rigid distinction between the two (1989, p. 10).

The alternative to current APEL practices, however, is not a blithe inattention to the presence or absence of knowledge. Rather, it is to attend to its presence more carefully and grapple with it more deeply, to view the practice of APEL through the lens of alternative epistemologies, and to revisit the social relationships within which knowledge is legitimated. Whitaker continues, "[E]xperience is an *input* and learning is an *outcome*. ... The first and most important standard for quality assurance is that credit should be awarded ... only for *learning*, and not for *experience*" (Ibid., p. 10, italics in original). But if experience is not simply an input, if, as I argued in Part II, experience and learning are the mutually determined products of complex human interactions, then we must approach the distinction between experience and learning with greater nuance. Whatever its usefulness for quality assurance, the way in which the distinction is currently constructed separates the abstract act of knowing from the concrete act of doing and the content of learning from its context. Thus, it contradicts APEL's implicit deconstruction of idealist dualities and reinstates the privileging of abstract masculinity.

The epistemology of current APEL practice

Academic knowledge, described by Bernstein as "uncommon knowledge ... freed from the particular, the local" (as cited by Breier, 2003, p. 50), defines itself by what it excludes, namely, the everyday knowledge that obtains in specific sites of practice among embodied human beings. As we have seen, academics draw on such dualisms as theory/practice, abstract/concrete, propositional/procedural, and explicit/tacit to distinguish their more rarified knowledge from the kinds of knowledge available through ordinary experience. Various twentieth-century theorists extended this list of binary distinctions to include vertical and horizontal knowledge [Bernstein], context-independent and context-dependent knowledge [Vygotsky], Mode 1 and Mode 2 [Gibbons *et al.*], and, perhaps most tellingly, sacred and profane [Durkheim].[9] These continuing habits of categorization both bear out Bourdieu's (1988) characterization of *homo academicus* as a "supreme classifier among classifiers" (p. xi) and connect practices such as APEL to broader epistemological debates.

Specifically, most current APEL practice and institutional policies require students to replicate the universalized knowledge and detachment from context that are the hallmark of abstract masculinity. This detachment is of at least two kinds.

First, the two questions conventionally asked of APEL candidates – What did you do? What did you learn? – require the student to distinguish sharply between experience and learning, with experience happening first and learning a function of subsequent reflection. As the student is guided to move from exploring a first-order phenomenon called 'experience' to identifying and articulating a separate, second-order phenomenon called 'learning,' the experiential context falls away, so that the knowledge can be treated as if independent of any historically or socially specific human life. Thus, while the experience that led to the learning may be seen as situated, the learning itself is accreditable only to the degree that it can be made to look like that of anyone else or, rather, like that of the faceless, disembodied agent of abstract masculinity.

The second erasure of context is contained in the often-repeated justification for APEL on the grounds that 'it doesn't matter where you learned it; it matters what you know.' Compelling as it is as a way to challenge the insularity of academic practice, the slogan again seems to free the learner from the specificity of context and thus belies an equally important point, namely, that it *does* matter where one has learned something because knowledge is part and parcel of the material and social contexts within which it is created, used, and judged. That is, while the intent behind the claim is to affirm non-academic locations as sites of knowledge-production, the slogan ironically reproduces the presumption that the university is somehow not itself a site of material practice, framed by its own geographical and cultural location. For all its radical implications about the sites from which academically valid knowledge can be generated, APEL replicates the irony at the heart of Enlightenment theories of knowledge: while the experiential origins of knowledge are acknowledged and, indeed, extolled, knowledge is credited only to the degree that experience has been transcended, so that both the site of its production and the particularities of the self have been excised.

Thirdly, the requirement that knowledge be 'transferable,' as the usual term has it, enacts a detachment of its own. There is certainly a case to be made for the insistence that, to be accreditable in an academic setting, knowledge must have a clear relationship to that which is taught and produced in the academy. As I will argue in the next two chapters, however, that relationship could take many different forms. As currently practiced, the idea of transferability is based on two sets of assumptions that are in some ways mutually contradictory. On one hand is the assumption that academic knowledge is abstract and decontextualized, freed of the particularities of more situated forms of knowledge, and therefore able to offer broad forms of knowledge with multiple applications. Again, there is a case to be made. At its best, academic ways of knowing have qualities of sustained inquiry and depth that have allowed for the growth and dissemination of vital knowledge in many fields. Standards of evidence, the logic of argumentation, the ethics of research, and peer review support principles of validity and trustworthiness that are not easily abandoned, nor should they be.

On the other hand, however, it is understood that academic curricula are organized in particular ways and for particular purposes and that the knowledge being disseminated is as context-specific as any other kind. Joseph Glick (1995) points out that, however problematically, general knowledge held in abstract principles makes a particular kind of sense in pedagogical contexts. Schools are, by definition, transitional institutions; because school is a place that young people leave, and because the end-use of the knowledge they gain is unknown, it makes sense to stress general knowledge that will "travel well" (p. 367). The difference is not always obvious to academics whose workplace, after all, *is* the academy, but most people don't end up in workplaces in which abstract knowledge structures are privileged.

Even the use of such terms as 'standard,' 'ethics,' and 'peer,' moreover, makes it clear that academic criteria are both a moving target and a highly contentious one. To the degree that APEL treats such descriptors as 'college-level' and 'college-equivalent' as timeless and unproblematized norms, it fails to engage with outsider knowledge as a corrective to knowledge practices that become reified because they are shared by a homogeneous community of insiders. The university is very much in and of the world as a workplace, a site of material practice, and an interested participant in struggles for power and influence.[10] Today's standard practice is tomorrow's unconscionable ethical failing or blinkered vision, as the history of both the sciences and the social sciences makes clear.

The contours of Dorothy's command of Spanish are an example of the ways in which the seemingly more universal nature of academic knowledge can better be understood as the knowledge particular to a specific location with its own particular needs. There are, of course, linguistic structures that underlie all human languages, and language is abstract in the sense that the rules of formal grammar are the same whether one is talking about contemporary Latin American fiction or last night's football game. That said, it is not the case that the Spanish learned in school is less conditioned by situational requirements than the Spanish of the delivery room. It must be taught in a way that can be easily tested, to people whose learning styles vary and who will use it in a variety of contexts, few of which can be foreseen. One might argue that there is no such thing as "Spanish," only a series of Spanishes that vary according, not only to situation and activity, but to country, region, class, generation, level of education, and a difficult, complicated politico-linguistic history. All of these Spanishes are indigenous to a particular social location, one of which is the classroom.

Thus, what APEL promises in the way of opening the academy to other tonalities of experience and knowledge rarely happens in practice. Rather, experiential learning is brought under the authority of academic ways of knowing and legitimated only for its similarity to the structures of academic discourse and thought. Indeed, among the justifications for APEL is the claim that it is consistent with the normal structures of assessment and judgment that characterize formal education. In the following two chapters, I will engage with schools of thought that frame the meeting grounds between communities of knowledge in terms of difference as well as sameness. Those two chapters will draw on quite different approaches, one taking a page out of queer theory and the other a page out of contemporary socio-material and socio-cultural research on workplace knowledge.

Different as they are, both chapters attempt to stretch the boundaries of current thinking concerning APEL. I will first use my somewhat playful treatment of queer theory to reach beyond the boundaries of dualistic thinking and then draw on various versions of practice studies and workplace studies to suggest an alternative assessment methodology.

Notes

1 In spite of the fact that my own assessment work has been done largely in the US and South Africa, I am using the British term because, unlike "prior learning assessment" or "recognition of prior learning," it makes experiential learning explicit.

2 Definitions of "college-level learning" and "college-equivalent learning" are notoriously tautological, often simply saying that, as my institution would have it, "the learning should be equivalent to college-level work in terms of quality" (http://www.esc.edu/degree-planning-academic-review/prior-learning-assessment/credit-for-learning). Other criteria generally state that "the learning should be theoretical as well as practical" in the sense that the student "should be able to identify the principles involved" in undertaking various tasks and that the knowledge and skills involved should be transferable to other venues and sites of practice. Examples given by my institution of college-level learning include the knowledge of office administration, supervision, and office technology gained by an experienced office manager or the knowledge of retailing, early American furniture, and/or small business management gained by the owner of an antique shop. Examples of "commonplace, non-college level learning" that would not lead to a credit award "include maintaining the family budget, putting up bookshelves, buying a house or surviving a serious illness" (Ibid.).

3 See Rydell's (2004) discussion of Metropolitan State University in Minnesota for an example of this shift.

4 For a further discussion of the points raised here, see the "Introduction: Portfolio Development in Historic Context" in Michelson and Mandell (2004).

5 For a helpful survey of developments internationally, see Evans (2000). For a discussion of APEL in the UK, Canada, Australia, and South Africa, see essays by Peters, Pokorny, and Johnson; Hill; Solomon and Gustavs; and Osman, respectively, in Michelson and Mandell (2004). For discussions of APEL in the European context, see Michelson (2012) and Werquin (2012).

6 For an example of what is now an extensive critique of neoliberal notions of selfhood, see Harvey (2007). For examples of the critique of the neoliberalist ideology of lifelong learning, see Garrick and Solomon (2001), Plumb, Leverman, and McGray (2007), and Olssen (2006). For a challenge to the ways in which even this critique marginalizes women, see Gouthro (2009).

7 For interesting exceptions to that general rule, see Hill (2004) and Bofelo *et al.* (2013).

8 For evocative challenges concerning these issues, see Alice Walker's (1973) short story, "Everyday Use" and the documentary "The Quilts of Gee's Bend" (n.d.) produced and directed by Vanessa Vadim and Matthew Arnett. For a classic essay on the power-laden relationship between 'primitive' and 'modern' art, see Clifford (1988).

9 See Bernstein (2000), Vygotsky (1978), Gibbons *et al.* (1994), and Durkheim (2008). The use of epistemological dualisms to argue against APEL is most widely evident in the South African debate on the subject. In other Anglophone countries, these epistemological dualisms tend to be taken for granted and built into APEL policies and procedures, often in unexamined ways and often at the expense of students. See Breier (2003) on this point.

10 This brief discussion in no way does justice to the complex debate concerning the unique efficacy of academic forms of knowledge. For an example of that debate in action, see Muller (2000) and my response (Michelson, 2004).

8

QUEERING THE ASSESSMENT OF EXPERIENTIAL LEARNING

And shortly, turned was al up so doun
Bothe habit and eek disposicioun.

[And shortly, all was turned upside down
Both in costume/customary behavior and temperament.][1]

Geoffrey Chaucer, *The Canterbury Tales*, I 4054

In 2003, as part of my work helping to promote adult learning in South Africa, I attended a conference in Johannesburg on the role of APEL in broadening access to higher education.[2] At that conference, Professor Kathy Munro gave a paper detailing her efforts to introduce a more flexible, adult-friendly curriculum at the University of the Witwatersrand, one of the country's two most prestigious historically white, Anglophone universities. Munro spoke of her attempt to challenge some of the disciplinary boundaries within which knowledge at the university was structured and to help academics think more broadly about how different cultures of knowledge might be brought together. Most specifically, she talked about the role that the 'recognition of prior learning,' as APEL is called in South Africa, might play in fostering that dialogue. She had, she said, been consistently hindered by traditional academic views concerning the presumed incommensurability of academic and experiential knowledge. She concluded by saying: "I feel stonewalled."

As a New Yorker and a lesbian, I couldn't help but hear 'stonewalled' as a vivid and suggestive metaphor for defending the boundary between academic and experiential learning. The Stonewall Inn, of course, was the gay bar in Greenwich Village in which, on an evening in 1969, the contemporary American movement for lesbian and gay equality was born. The police, as was their habit, had raided the bar and started making arrests. This time, the patrons fought back. The first punch was thrown by a New Orleans lesbian of mixed racial parentage and aimed at a policeman who was roughing up a young drag queen. The lesbian was wearing trousers. The drag queen was wearing an evening gown (Coleman, 2000).

The metaphor is particularly suggestive, for reasons that I hope will become clear, because the excuse the police used for their raids of gay bars was a law that made cross-dressing illegal. At the end of the 1960s, a decade noteworthy for the extravagance of its sartorial counterculture, anyone not wearing at least three articles of clothing conventionally associated with his or her anatomical sex was still subject to arrest and prosecution. Thus, the 'crime' that prompted the raid was not homosexuality as such, which was not illegal in New York, but the transgressing of the binary categories through which gender was publicly enacted. Men were men, and women were women, and their public presentation had to be consistent with that gender binary.

The notion of transgression is etymologically embedded in the word 'queer' itself. As the late queer theorist Eve Kosofsky Sedgwick (1993) pointed out, the word shares the Indo-European root *twerkw* with the German *quer* (to transverse), the Latin *torquere* (to twist), and the English 'to thwart.' Cross-dressing in particular is disconcerting because it turns categories on their heads: women wear trousers, men wear evening gowns. But beyond that, and even more frightening to some, it undermines the notion of category altogether and makes it more difficult to maintain clear, ordered distinctions (Garber, 1997). The Stonewall Inn was a liminal space, a space for in-between-ness. That made it dangerous.

As Warner (1993) among others has said, queer theory is less a theory about queers than it is a way of queering conventional academic inquiry. Using the challenge to conventional gender binaries as a paradigmatic case in point, queer theory explores the ways in which both internalized and socially mandated regimes delimit acceptable behaviors, regulated identities, and social classifications. The 'insider' category that queer theory posits is not the 'heterosexual,' but the 'normal,' and this, as Warner points out, includes "the normal business of the academy" (p. xxvi). "For academics, being interested in queer theory is a way to mess up the desexualized spaces of the academy, exude some rut, reimagine the publics from and for which academic intellectuals write, dress, and perform" (Ibid.).

In this chapter, I will use queer theory in general, and the notion of boundary transgression in particular, to offer a queer reading of APEL. I will suggest that APEL continues to be resisted by many because accrediting the experiential learning gained through ordinary human activity breeches the rigid boundary between categories of knowledge. I will argue, in other words, that APEL is disturbing to some because it is a form of epistemological cross-dressing.

I will, however, also continue my argument that as conventionally practiced, APEL may appear to challenge conventional categories of knowledge but in the end reaffirms them. I will suggest how that happens, but then I want to explore the possibility that, rather than merely accepting that academically creditable learning can be gained through experiential means, a queer understanding of APEL might help us challenge the categories of academic and experiential themselves. In some ways, this chapter is more a meditation than a concrete proposal because I will take advantage of the permission granted by queer theory to be a little bit tentative, to roll ideas out past where I can ground them securely, and begin to sketch out a more radical role for APEL practitioners as 'queer' academics, whatever their sexual and gender identity. Let me say up front that I do not know the answers to many of the questions I will raise here. This chapter is better understood as an invitation to think together than as a game plan or a map.

Inside/out

The original version of this chapter appeared in the first issue of *PLA Inside Out*, a new journal that focuses on the scholarship of APEL. In so titling the journal, co-editor Nan Travers sought to further the practice of assessing experiential learning by "turning the concepts inside out" through disciplinary and interdisciplinary research in human development, the science of cognition, the sociology of knowledge, neurobiology, social theory, and other related fields. If, as Travers maintains, "it is time for PLA to be 'out of the closet' and out of the basements of institutions," we need a venue that will allow us to be "direct, open, and honest about what we understand ourselves to be doing" (personal communication, August 14, 2011).

To my mind, this is all to the good.

Inside/out, however, is an interesting turn of phrase. On the one hand, the meaning relies on a clear distinction between 'inside' and 'outside,' a distinction that has both spatial and social meanings. The two words refer to relative positionality, not only of physical placement, but to a location in a social world that permits of two kinds of people: 'insiders' who have membership in a variety of normalized categories and 'outsiders' who are excluded from those norms. The terms 'inside' and 'outside,' in other words, not only align with the taxonomy of dualisms, but presuppose a world in which binary distinctions have social effects, in which relative worth is adjudicated through a system of categorization, and in which, as Diane Fuss (1991) argues, things and people can be distinguished from each other through a logic of borders and boundaries.

At the same time, however, and very much like the Chaucerian 'up-sodoun' [upside-down], the term 'inside/out' challenges the very categories it names by reversing them, by turning them into each other, by bringing what was inside out and what was outside, in. In doing so, the term begs the important question of how such categories are formed in the first place, what material, social, and cultural effects they have, and what alternative meanings might be produced by reversing the criteria through which inside and outside are defined. This points to the possibility of collapsing such boundaries or, at the very least, making it more difficult to take them for granted.

The term 'inside/out' has special resonance among queer theorists, not only because the word 'out' has particular meanings to lesbians and gay men, but because queer theory as a whole attempts to challenge the social and ideological structures through which categorizations such as 'inside' and 'outside' are made. It calls attention to the social constructedness of taxonomies of 'in' and 'out,' points to the ways in which the privileged first term is dependent on the rejection of all that is associated with the second, and notes how claims concerning the distinction take on a heightened sense of urgency when the boundaries between categories are seen to be at risk.

Making visible: positioning the inside and outside

As we have seen, APEL has a complex relationship to the insider status of academic knowledge. On the one hand, APEL challenges the exclusivity of the university as the site at which knowledge is produced, valued, and disseminated. In legitimating the knowledge created in the workplace and community, in acknowledging non-academics as the creators of that knowledge, and in giving that knowledge the status of a credit award, APEL alters the relationship that students have to disciplinary knowledge and nurtures dialogue and interaction between different knowledge communities. Indeed, opponents of APEL correctly maintain that APEL moves the academy in the direction of more fluid and open epistemic boundaries and destabilizes the logic of disciplines and curricula.[3] By acknowledging non-academics as the bearers of academically accreditable knowledge, APEL breaches the stone wall, as it were, between the knowledge practices of the academy and those of other sites of human interaction and activity.

At the same time, however, both the process and the criteria for awarding credit reinstate the 'insider' status of academic knowledge as the norm and academics as the judges of the value of knowledge. In this chapter, I want to trouble the terms under which APEL brings 'out'sider knowledge 'in.' As the student is guided to move from exploring something called 'experience' to identifying and articulating a separate entity called 'learning,' the experiential context falls away, so that the knowledge can be treated as if independent of any historically or socially specific human life. Thus, while the experience that led to the learning can be that of the outsider, the learning itself is accreditable only to the degree that it looks like that of an already-insider, or, rather, like that of the faceless, disembodied, and sexless agent of knowledge in the academy.

In a wonderful send-up of the staid academic conference, Scott Long suggests that his audience think of a paper he is presenting as being delivered "by a small, mustachioed man wearing a gold lamé cocktail dress, black pumps with three-inch stiletto heels, a raven wig, and a beaded cloche with peacock feathers" (as cited in Honeychurch, 1996, p. 348). The image not only challenges the conventions both of gender representation and academic conferences, but insists that the audience recognize that, underneath the conventionally bland and serious academic presenter, *there is someone there*. By destabilizing cultural norms, Long highlights the presence of real human actors whose enactments – of gender, of professional bearing, of social and epistemological legitimation – have, like their knowledge, to be accounted for and explained. In what follows, I focus on three aspects of this concrete human presence that make the power-ladenness of APEL practices visible: the issue of social bias, the presumptive right to judgment, and the shifting of the student from the subject to the object of knowledge.

APEL and social bias

Like any value judgment, the quantification of students' knowledge can't help but be subject to the inequalities and biases present in society generally and specifically in the ways in which epistemological authority lines up with social power of other kinds. Recognizing that the APEL candidate is a specific human being allows us to acknowledge that APEL is subject to the systematic unequal valuing of knowledge that plays out across lines of class, race, and gender. We should expect, for example, that credit awards reflect the under-valuing of women's work and unpaid labor and the under-estimating of the knowledge required of non-professional job categories; although much quantitative research remains to be done, evidence suggests that the woman volunteer doing the same job for which a man gets paid may well receive a lower credit recommendation, as may the person of color with a paraprofessional job title doing the same work and having the same knowledge as a white professional. The metaphors of both equal and comparable worth apply.

This is not, unfortunately, merely a question of the biases of individual faculty, although assumptions made on grounds of gender, race, age, and class are surely often present, and faculty must be encouraged to be both fair-minded and self-critical. First, APEL centers overwhelmingly on knowledge gained in the public sphere; skills such as parenting and family management are unlikely to be accredited, although some sporadic attempts to do so have been made. It is suspicious of learning gained through the social support systems of poor communities and the organizations – churches, community centers – that function outside of the watchful authority of professions such as social work. Second, generic evaluations for noncollegiate forms of training bear the marks of gender bias; my own institution is typical, for example, in awarding an equal amount of credit for the initial training of a registered nurse and licensed journey electricians, although the college-equivalent knowledge required to graduate from nursing school is arguably more extensive than that gained through an electrical apprenticeship. The feminist insistence that knowledge is differently valued when produced by women and men can be applied concretely across the full range of current assessment activities, up to and including the awarding of the credit itself.

The presumptive right to judgment

At the same time, even practices that guard against social bias will continue to cast the university as sole arbiter of epistemological merit if the single criterion is correspondence to academic knowledge and if professors are thought to have cornered the market on academically valuable expertise. Elizabeth Minnich (2004) makes a point about curricula that is equally relevant to APEL and that, like the above example of nursing, will directly affect the credit awarded to Dorothy, the nurse and quilter discussed in Chapter seven:

> There may be no, or few, art critics trained and practicing in the Academy who know enough about quilts to be able to judge them, but many quilters can do so. Academic training is not the only kind of training, nor are academic standards the only standards in the world. The problem of including new kinds of works in the curriculum is not, then, that there is no way to judge their quality, their significance, their meaning. It is, at least in part, that those who are qualified to judge may not be academics at all.
>
> *(Minnich, 2004, p. 105)*

There is a certain irony in the ways in which most APEL practitioners grapple with this denaturalizing of the academic claim to unilateral judgment; for all the critical self-reflection that we ask of students, we are not encouraged to think of ourselves as actors in a drama awash in judgment, power, or the adjudicating of what is or isn't going to be visible within the academy. A queer understanding of APEL, one that, among other things, makes visible the concrete human networks within which it is practiced, permits us to trace the contours of authority. Tara Fenwick (2006a) and Helen Pokorny (2006), whose analyses I will explore more fully in the following chapter, argue that we need to map the larger institutional structures at work in APEL and the particular discourses that are used to structure judgment and meaning. They suggest that we reconceptualize the assessor, not as the neutral filter through which knowledge is brought from outside to inside, but as an actor positioned in a complex network of procedures, artifacts, relationships, institutional structures, and cultural norms.

All judgments concerning knowledge have social consequences, relationships to power and worldly goods, and they are inevitably expressed within discursive forms that make some things commonplace and others both literally and figuratively unutterable. If, as I have argued throughout this book, taxonomies of knowledge are invariably taxonomies of power, then assessments of knowledge inevitably also position both the knower and the social relationships within which knowledge is created and valued. The student in the encounter is inscribed as female, not only because of the situated nature of her knowledge-claims, but also because she is positioned as supplicant to socially organized knowledge practices, petitioning for acknowledgement from academics whose institutional power is based on epistemic authority. To steal a good line from Simone de Beauvoir, one is not born a student; one becomes one.

Subjects and objects of knowledge

Numerous practitioners of APEL have extolled the ways in which the process of portfolio development builds intellectual self-confidence and leads to personal growth.

In the process of exploring their prior experiential learning, students become more aware of themselves as learners, with the credit award being only one of the mechanisms whereby they achieve an expanded sense of themselves, greater confidence in what they know and can do, and a sense of epistemological and social agency (Mann, 2004; Brown, 2002). There is much evidence, both anecdotal and otherwise, to suggest that this is true.

It is, however, only a partial truth, albeit an important one. The process of assessment, which begins with the student as the subject of her own knowledge, ends, in proper Foucauldian fashion, with the student as the *object* of the knowledge of the assessor. For all of our insistence that we are not judging the worthiness of the student's life but rather making a much smaller valuation of some of that student's knowledge according to one particular cluster of criteria, there is still the moment in which, to be assessed, the student must allow her knowledge to become an object of display, visible and vulnerable to the judgment of the insider.

The history of sexuality provides a parallel. Historically, homosexuals have been treated as the objects of other people's knowledge: categorized in absolute terms and subjected to investigation, in both the scientific and judicial senses of the word. The criteria of judgment and the right to judge were both retained by the insider corps of psychoanalysts, physicians, sexologists, police officers, judges, and legislators whose right to make those judgments was predicated on being positioned in the 'normal' category from which those being judged were excluded. The language used to investigate and judge was the language of the insider group, that of an enforced heteronormativity that had been articulated in the first place around the exclusion of homosexuals. The truth of their lives was to be spoken of by others who had been given the status of knower, with homosexuals as the known (Honeychurch, 1996).

It is no accident that Foucault (1995) used both students and homosexuals as examples of how, with the rise of the social sciences, categories of people became the objects of other people's knowledge. The modern educational system evolved as one of the regulatory social institutions charged with managing categories of people by collecting information about them. The word examination, for example, refers both to the inspection of the physical body on the part of physicians and the procedure whereby the minds of students are ostensibly made visible to educators. In the process of the examination, the student goes from the learner to the one who will be learned about, from knowing (the stated purpose of education) to being known.

APEL, of course, is an examination in that sense whether or not a literal exam is part of the process. Portfolio essays are normative; because they are required to make knowledge claims consistent with the norms of the academy, students must closely examine those norms and at least appear to internalize them. They must familiarize themselves with the contours of academic inquiry and sufficiently grasp academic discourse to make a case for themselves in its terms.[4] In the act of presenting learning to be assessed, the student goes from being the subject of her own knowledge to being the object of the assessor's knowledge; and the language of the student's learning, originally that of the site in which it was gained, is translated into that of the academy in a double move in which students are first asked to indicate that their knowledge can indeed be reproduced as academic discourse and then by the assessor who must name the knowledge in more-or-less conventional disciplinary or interdisciplinary terms. The workaday garb is stripped away to reveal the outlines of an academic robe, the collar – white, blue, or pink as may be – replaced by an academic hood. The conservative opposition to APEL makes sense in this context: workaday garb is perfectly respectable – at the workplace. It should just know its place, not try to be something it isn't, and stay where it belongs.

APEL as epistemological cross-dressing

Which brings us back, of course, to the metaphor of cross-dressing, albeit on a somewhat superficial level that keeps the dualisms intact and just messes them up a bit. On this level, men may dress as women, and vice versa, but it is still clear what it means to 'be' one or the other and to dress appropriately or inappropriately. Indeed, it might be argued that transvestites confirm the most extreme stereotypes of gender: how many 'real' women actually dress as the 1950s vamps that many drag-queens imitate? And how many would want to? There is even a suggestion of pitiable aspiration in this approach to cross-dressing; trapped in the binary of the two conventional genders, the cross-dresser becomes a *manqué*, i.e. wannabe, man or woman, mixing up the categories, but still maintaining the dualism (Garber, 1997). Applied to APEL, this suggests that our claims about students' experiential learning are a bit demeaning all around. We make students play dress-up, as it were. We require them to costume practice, application, and problem-solving, all of which are valid and effective in their own context, in the academic regalia of theory, reflection, and transferability. No wonder some people think the practice second-rate.

On another level, however, cross-dressing poses a more serious challenge to comfortably dualistic categories by calling attention to the permeability of the margin between them. On this level, the transvestite is the avatar of a category crisis, what Garber (1997) calls "the disruptive element" (p. 17) that intervenes, not only in gender categories, but in the possibility of categorization itself. Cross-dressing is powerful, in part, because it challenges the idea that we know exactly what we are looking at and thus opens up the possibility of seeing something else. Butler (1999) describes the confrontation with the cross-dresser as

> the moment in which one's staid and usual cultural perceptions fail, when one cannot with surety read the body that one sees, ... the moment when one is no longer sure whether the body encountered is that of a man or a woman. The vacillation between the categories itself constitutes the experience of the body in question.
>
> *(Butler, 1999, pp. xxii–xxiii)*

Butler goes on to argue that, when gender is denaturalized, it can be seen as "a changeable and revisable reality" that might be understood differently (p. xxiii).

This second understanding of cross-dressing speaks to the power of APEL to make the contentiousness of knowledge-practices visible in the same way that cross-dressing makes gender visible, by jolting the viewer out of taken-for-granted and naturalized categories. APEL has deep potential as a liminal space within which to take another look at such binaries as theory and practice, public and private, and rational and emotional, and to ask if and in what way those categories actually hold.

This means that, rather than justifying APEL by attempting to demonstrate how students' knowledge fits the conventional categories, we might use APEL as a way to revisit them. Garber (1997) has argued that the cross-dresser is neither male nor female, but is rather something else, not a third gender or third term so much as "a mode of articulation, a way of describing a space of possibility" (p. 11) that does not rely on binary thinking at all. Thus, rather than trying to place students' knowledge within the available dualisms (theory and practice being a representative case in point), we might dispense with those categories altogether. It follows that students would not have to make their knowledge resemble academic knowledge; they would instead have to establish the efficacy of particular, effective ways of doing things in particular sites of engagement.

We, as academics, moreover, would have to do the same. Our claims to knowledge would no longer rest on privileged claims to objectivity, universality, or abstract conceptualization, but rather on the efficacy of particular forms of knowledge when applied to particular kinds of inquiry, activity, or circumstance. Our interaction with students would no longer come down to a unidirectional judgment, however user-friendly and supportive, but rather a shared engagement with questions concerning the role of knowledge in sustaining the human world and aspiring toward a better human future. That doesn't mean relativism. It does mean accountability. To whom, is an important question. To what, is another.

A sartorial dilemma

There is a more than a bit of the utopian in the above alternative image of APEL: students and academics collectively flattening the epistemological and institutional hierarchies to engage in mutual critique of the usefulness of different kinds of knowledge for different kinds of purposes. But there is something utterly concrete about it as well. APEL is one of the few spaces in the academic world in which students in relatively non-prestigious institutions are challenged to ask themselves what it means to know something and what the relationships are among work, learning, social agency, and personal identity. That they explore such questions explicitly, in class activities, discussions, and homework assignments, is one of the many virtues of APEL.

There is also much that is dangerous about the flattening of epistemological hierarchies, given the historical moment. At a time at which a serious candidate for US president could proclaim that hurricanes are God's punishment for government spending and in which millions of people worldwide believe that AIDS is caused by witchcraft, perhaps we need to stand behind knowledge practices that, for all their failings, have good old, flat-footed Anglo-Saxon empiricism to recommend them. As Stephan Colbert famously said to George W. Bush, reality has a well-known liberal bias,[5] so perhaps this is a moment to cross-dress into a properly positivist lab coat and stop, at least for now, trying to promote any constructs of knowledge that don't insist on evidence-based research, the scientific method, and the disciplines – in both senses of the word – of the Enlightenment academy.

I am not sure there is any way out of that dilemma, but framing the irresolvable is one of the things that queer theory does best. As one of multiple contemporary theoretical approaches that refuse the modernist pretense of a mind at one with itself, queer theory undermines the conventional academic practice of erasing our ambivalence, side-stepping our worries, and cramming the babble of multiple inner voices into a coherent, if largely fictitious whole. What do you get when you cross a postmodernist with a Tea Party activist? I doubt that anyone knows the answer, but at a moment in which epistemology is politics by other means, and with a vengeance, there is much at stake both for APEL practitioners and for part-time-studying, working (if they're lucky) adults.

What it is that people know, how they know it, and why they think it is true has taken on a new centrality in the current period. While that raises the stakes on practices such as APEL that adjudicate the legitimacy of knowledge claims, it also heightens the importance of doing so, precisely because the social and ideological effects are so serious these days. Challenging the authority of academic knowledge is hard for contemporary academics – not only are many of us properly concerned about the weakening of such traditionally academic values as respectful debate and a concern for truth in favor of demagoguery and irrationality, but we are also threatened by the full range of anti-intellectual strategies for "dumbing down" a population, from the withdrawal of public support for higher education to the corporatization of curriculum. Those of us who work in APEL are also, it seems to me, made cautious by the low status of adult learners and of the faculty and institutions that serve them. But that challenge to academic authority is a necessary one. I want to make the case here that, in spite of – or perhaps because of – our relatively marginal position within academic, social and intellectual ranks, APEL practitioners – advisors, assessors, portfolio-development workshop leaders, scholars – have a choice between being the foot soldiers of forms of learning that are not themselves seen as open to question or coming out of the closet as the epistemological cross-dressers we are.

What that might mean in practice requires a long and difficult conversation, and I make no claims to know the answer. If anything, this chapter is that all-too-tedious artifact: an invitation to a dialogue. It might mean allowing our students to help us revisit our received truths in much the same way we wish to help them revisit theirs. It might mean beginning the hard work of learning another language, one that does not rest on binary categories or privilege the names that academics give to things. It might mean becoming champions of outsider knowledges borne of experience on the margins and at the same time holding both ourselves and our students accountable for the necessarily biased, necessarily partial conceptual frameworks within which we and they decide what is true.

Certainly, it means opening ourselves and our practices to critique and being honest with ourselves, our students, and each other about the stakes we have in those practices. It means exploring and encouraging our students to explore how – and why – the ideological frames of the academy permit of some explanatory frameworks and not others. It means addressing the implications of believing or not believing that corporations are people, or that the earth is billions of years old, or that love is just a four-letter word.

All this would require different readings, assignments, and discussion questions that bring knowledge-practices back down to earth. What does a given form of knowledge enable in the way of human activity? In what contexts is that knowledge effective, and why? What values and whose power does it uphold? What forms of equality or inequality does it further? If some of the current unsupported claims to truth are disturbing – that God hates fags or that there is no global warming – then abandoning our own Archimedean point might allow us to further an understanding among our students that all of us are answerable for what we think is true.

The APEL practitioner as queer academic

In the following chapter, I will endeavor to begin to shape a methodology that retains a respect for the efficacy and accountability of knowledge without falling back on 'straight' dualities. Specifically, I will draw on socio-material and socio-cultural approaches to knowledge that disrupt both categories such as theory and practice and the possibility of categorization itself. For the moment, however, I want to stay in this more exploratory timbre and ask: What might it mean to posit APEL practitioners as queer academics or, rather, to queer the identity of the APEL practitioner in a way that might allow us to understand our roles as non-neutral, potentially 'outlaw' presences within the power structures of the academy? Warner (1993) argues:

> Every person who comes to a queer self-understanding knows in one way or another that her stigmatization is connected with gender, the family, notions of individual freedom, the state, public speech, consumption and desire, nature and culture, maturation, reproductive politics, racial and national fantasy, class identity, truth and trust, censorship, intimate life and social display, terror and violence, health care, and deep cultural norms about the bearing of the body. Being queer means fighting about these issues all the time, locally and piecemeal, but always with consequences. It means being able, more or less articulately, to challenge the common understanding of what (not only) gender difference means, or what the state is for, or what 'health' entails, or what would define fairness, or what a good relation to the planet's environment would be.
>
> *(Warner, 1993, p. xiii)*

Seeing APEL practitioners as queer academics, then, is not only a case of professional identity, much less one of sexual orientation. Rather, it is a perspective on the ways in which our function as epistemological referees spins inward into our own phenomenological lives and outward into the world. This requires us to acknowledge the unstable distinction between many kinds of ins and outs and of inner and outer worlds. It requires us to take seriously our relationship to the ways in which knowledge is deployed in social institutions, the ways in which we negotiate the terms of the social and the political, and the lived effects of how evidence is interpreted and knowledge claims are framed.

As mediators of students' engagement with the knowledge-practices of the academy, APEL practitioners as queer academics are in a position to help them explore what their own outsider and even outlaw experiences have required them to struggle with "all the time, locally and piecemeal, but always with consequences," as Warner suggests (1993, p. viii) . If we are willing to do more than apply the criteria of insider knowledge to our students' experiential learning, we might begin with raising questions about whether the conventional dualisms still suffice and what experience, identity, evidence, and knowledge might look like in a liminal space between smug rationality on the one hand and Obama-is-the-anti-Christ irrationality on the other. A gold lamé cocktail dress and raven wig are not everyone's idea of academic office wear. At the same time, it is worth reminding ourselves that academic convocations are nothing if not medieval costume parties and that the original Mentor of *The Odyssey* was a cross-dressing goddess in disguise.

Notes

1   The usual translation of this passage from the Knight's Tale makes the point that what has changed is emotional temperament, not costume. In Middle English, however, "habit" has the same alternative meaning as in modern English, that of clothing. I am not at all sure that Chaucer means the pun, but it works particularly well for my purposes.
2   2nd JET Conference on the Recognition of Prior Learning. CSIR Conference Centre, Pretoria, SA: July 2003.
3   See, for example, Muller (2000).
4   The requirement that all accreditable knowledge closely resemble academic forms of learning is what Peters, Pokorny, and Johnson (2004) refer to as "cracking the code" (p. 160). APEL has been criticized on these grounds for being fraught with implicit or explicit criteria that students do not understand, so that the process becomes what Shalem and Steinberg (2006) call a "cat and mouse chase" (p. 97).
5   White House Press Corp dinner, August 26, 2007.

9

PRACTICE STUDIES, COMPLEXITY, AND THE ASSESSMENT OF EXPERIENTIAL LEARNING

The gretteste clerkes been noght wisest men.

(The greatest scholars are not the wisest men.)

Geoffrey Chaucer, *The Canterbury Tales*, I 4054

In this chapter, I want to explore the possibilities for an assessment of experiential learning that takes workplace-based knowledge, not codified knowledge, as the norm. By codified knowledge, I mean academic knowledge primarily, although the same argument can be made concerning the codification of vocational knowledge in national qualifications grids, unit standards, learning outcomes, and other recent attempts as systemization that, like academic syllabi, require experiential learning to conform to set, pre-determined forms (Pokorny, 2006). In what follows, I will draw on approaches to knowledge that are variously associated with situated learning theory, workplace studies, and practice studies to look at how knowledge emerges out of human activity in general and work in particular.

Originating in fields as diverse as Soviet psychiatry, technology studies, and feminist epistemology, the approaches I will engage in this chapter are less a unified school of thought than what Fenwick, Edwards, and Sawchuk (2011) call heterodox "arenas" of lively and often contentious debate (p. viii). That is, there is both internal disagreement among scholars within each of these arenas and marked differences among them. For my purposes, however, what is important are the general similarities, specifically a shared understanding of knowledge, not as "disembodied and disembedded rationality," but as "a social process, human and material, aesthetic as well as emotive and ethical" (Gherardi, 2006, pp. xii–xiii). Each of these arenas treats learning, not as "an object possessed by an individual," but as a series of interconnections among humans and non-humans, objects, practices, environments, technologies, and social structures that lead to an expanded range of potential action (Fenwick, 2006a, p. 287). They encourage research into taken for granted, tacit, unspoken activities and routines and the interactions among the constitutive elements through which knowledge is created and performed.

The theoretical foundations of these various approaches to knowledge – complexity theory, cultural-historical activity theory, and actor-network theory, among them – are socio-material and socio-cultural; that is, they see learning as emerging out of activity and adhering in material, textual, symbolic, and embodied forms (Gherardi, 2006, p. 48). To *know* is to be capable of participating competently in a particular network of people, objects, and activities. These approaches bypass – indeed, deconstruct – the binary categories that adhere to abstract masculinity: knowledge is of the body as well as the mind; theory cannot be separated from practice; the knower and the known occupy a shared epistemic plane; and the self and the environment are mutually constituted through situated activity. Helen Pokorny (2006) suggests that such an approach also undermines the binary distinction between "experience" and "learning" because it recognizes that "knowledge is contained within the experience itself" (p. 269).

We have already explored many of the ideas contained in these broad schools of thought. Indeed, Silvia Gherardi explicitly associates them with the work of feminist theorists such as Sandra Harding and Donna Haraway. These approaches are also regularly connected to John Dewey, specifically to Dewey's view of knowledge as emerging out of purposeful interaction among situated entities.[1] What is different, however, is that these approaches bring the tools of qualitative research to bear on what philosophy and critical theory tend to posit theoretically and offer detailed ethnographic investigations of particular workplaces. Thus, the contribution made by these approaches to APEL is to help to fill in the details, as it were, tracing the pathways through which workplace knowledge is made manifest, or, as many of these researchers would say, accomplished or performed. This is important, in part, because workplace learning is not easily mapped, and the proverbial difficulty of pinning it down systematically is often used as an excuse for resisting practices such as APEL.[2]

It is not my purpose in this chapter to detail either the differences among socio-material and socio-cultural approaches to knowledge or the many contestations and debates within them. Rather, I want to use the tools they offer to consider alternative practices for the assessment of experiential learning.[3] Specifically, I want to challenge two oft-repeated assumptions concerning the difficulty of "translating" workplace learning into academic currencies: first, that such learning cannot be assessed because of its tacit and unsystematic nature; and second, that, even if it could be measured, it cannot be accredited because it does not have the complexity, depth, and nuance of academic knowledge. I will argue that, in important ways, much workplace knowledge is *more* complex, conceptually compelling, and sophisticated than many forms of academic knowledge, certainly than the forms of academic knowledge generally expected of the undergraduates to whom APEL candidates are typically compared. I will then explore assessment methodologies that might bring workplace and academic knowledges into mutually respectful dialogue and suggest that what practice studies and workplace studies use as a *research* methodology can also serve as an *assessment* methodology.

Knowing in practice

As the debased second term of the theory/practice dualism, practice is typically understood as manual rather than intellectual, tacit rather than conscious, site-specific rather than generalizable, and concrete rather than abstract. While some uses of the word "practice" gesture toward creativity, professionalism, or spirituality – one practices the piano, medicine, and Buddhism, for example – this labeling as "practice" is, in effect, the exception that proves the rule, re-inscribing the disassociation of the intellect from the domains of heart, hand, and soul.

The new field of practice studies, however, sees practice as consisting of multiple knowledges that are intellectual, discursive, social, aesthetic, and moral as well as "applied." Practice, as Silvia Gherardi (2006) would have it, is a "mode of ordering the world," a task made more difficult because both the world and its ordering are fragile, temporary, and complex (p. 35). Education in practical settings is firstly an education in perception: one must learn how to look, know what one is seeing, see what others in the community of practice see. Secondly, it is an education in discourse: how to name and categorize, how to code something as a salient object or event within a domain of practice, how "to make competent use of the categories and the distinctions constituting that domain" (p. 76). Finally, education in practice is an education in cultural competence: in the style and manner in which things are discussed, the values and meanings attributed to things, and the uses to which technological, human, artifactual, and intellectual resources are put. Understanding the objects of knowledge that make up practice requires knowledge of both the material field of play and the ways in which those objects are framed discursively.

In a similar but less theoretical register, Matthew Crawford (2009) has revisited the cognitive demands of manual compared to mental labor. In *Shop Class as Soulcraft: An Inquiry into the Value of Work*, Crawford argues that the analytics of practice lend themselves to a greater complexity than those of theory. In so doing, he reverses the conventional assumption (in the post-Enlightenment West, at least) that we understand the world best through abstractions, general principles, and rules for categorization and that we think most rigorously by drawing on mental constructs that allow the particulars to drop away.

Crawford, a motorcycle mechanic with a PhD from the University of Chicago, argues that the concrete and often recalcitrant particulars of practice provide multiple cognitive challenges. They require us to wrestle with realities not entirely of our own making, attend to complexities that are not amenable to idealization, and take account of those characteristics of the material world – the friction on a surface, the leak in a tank – that idealized abstractions erase. Rather than operating to reduce the number of factors to a measurable and manageable few, which is what controlled experimentation and logical syllogisms do, practice in many workplaces requires us to begin with the assumption that we cannot know exactly which factors will prove to be relevant. We therefore need the capacity for watchful attention and the ability to grapple simultaneously with numerous factors, any of which may be contributing to a situation in ways that are not immediately clear. Crawford argues, further, that practice requires a kind of holistic thinking that is both cognitive and moral; one must, for example, be able to structure investigation so that one is likely to identify a problem sooner rather than later, balance the desire for thoroughness with fiscal responsibility, learn to live with bafflement and failure, and understand that one shares a world with others who see things differently.

Construction-site managers versus engineers

Silvia Gherardi's account of the complexity of practice likewise troubles conventional views of abstract and situated thinking. Focusing on the discourse concerning accident-prevention on the part of engineers and construction-site managers, she traces the different logics of causality and accountability and the different conceptual frameworks between the two communities of practice. The research on which she draws, based on participant-observation and interviews, found that the engineers tended to hold a largely deterministic view of reality, stressed rules and procedures, and couched explanations in generalizable and codifiable terms, whereas the site managers discussed causality in terms of the synchronicity of events, immediate causes, and the complexities and specificities of the work environment. Engineers, she argues, gave a schema, the site managers a plot.

The differences between the two groups of workers are open to multiple interpretations. As formally educated professionals who work with models of the not-yet-built, the engineers were able to think in abstract systems using codified discourse and mathematical language to pre-determine the factors to be taken into account. They understood safety in terms of norms of good practice, the need for regulation, and the generalizable aspects of the workplace amenable to control. Valerie Walkerdine (1988) suggests that this kind of reasoning is not only central to abstract conceptualizations, but is also a "fantasy of symbolic mastery" on the part of the bourgeois order, a dream of an ordered universe subject to rational control (p. 190).

The site managers, on the other hand, saw accidents as an inevitable aspect of the "on-site complexity" of the worksite (Gherardi, 2006, p. 144). They spoke in terms of temporal interdependence – particular actions at one moment setting the stage for a subsequent occurrence – and spatial interdependence – many things happening at the same time. Here, too, multiple interpretations are possible. One can see the site managers as rooted in the particular, unable to generalize from the specificities of their experience and thus unable to conceive of a worksite in which safety would be a matter of course. It is also possible to see them, however, as having a more nuanced, sophisticated view of the complexity of living systems and the ability to map the interchanges and mutual determinations among activities, human movements, technologies, tools, materials, discourses, and cultural expectations across a shifting field of time and space, something for which what Gherardi calls the "check-list mentality" of the engineers was too crude an instrument (p. 114).

Joseph Glick (1995) suggests that we understand this difference, not in terms of the difference between theory and practice, but in terms of the different functions of theory in the academy and the workplace. In the workplace, theory cannot be separated from practice, or knowledge from activity, because theory reveals itself in what is accomplished; it is never outside of a situated, embodied practice because it incorporates the specificities of context as part of itself. Thus, the issue is never what is hypothetically possible, but rather what can be done under particular circumstances. The knowledge that "counts" at the workplace is not theory per se but the ability "to integrate systems of different levels of construction into a seamless integrated functioning unit" based on "the kind of knowledge integration that makes the system work in a real environment" (p. 376).

Glick uses the example of a Manufacturing Resource Planning computer program that organizes production by planning backward from the finished product. The computer 'knows' when to order each part because it 'knows' what the parts are, when they will be needed, the order in which they are assembled, and how much time is needed for the assembly. That 'knowledge,' however, is an abstract construct, an algorithm that in theory would work for any similar manufacturing site. What it doesn't 'know' are the specific contextualizations that obtain in that particular plant at that particular moment: what the weather report is forecasting, whether a strike is looming, whether the contractor supplying a given part is to be trusted. In other words, as Glick points out, "what it doesn't know is the 'outside' world" (p. 374). Glick's point is that, in the workplace, abstract knowledge that can be generally applied isn't actually very helpful unless you can continually adjust for all of the ways in which the theory cannot account for or anticipate what is actually going to happen.

Lawyers versus shop stewards

In the second half of this chapter, I will explore how these understandings of knowledge as emerging from complex interaction might help us reframe the assessment of experiential learning. Interestingly, however, there is already a fascinating case in point in the South African literature. Mignonne Breier (2004, 2006) has studied the ways in which experiential learning was and was not legitimated in two university-based labor law courses into which adults had gained entry on the basis of their experience. While no formal assessment mechanism took place, Breier closely tracked how experiential learning fared in a classroom in which the law was treated as a set of abstract rules.

The adult learners participating in the two courses included well-educated, predominantly White professionals and predominantly Black trade union activists with relatively little formal education. Breier found that while the professionals, like the course lecturers, argued from general rules and appealed to law in the abstract, the shop stewards focused on the particular and the concrete, using specific incidents and cases to argue against the validity of the general rule. Indeed, the unionists seemed to struggle with the abstract theory, seeming to miss the point of the lectures and the logic of abstract modes of thought. Breier maps the differences between the thinking of the two sets of students onto a series of epistemological dualisms: generalizing/localizing, elaborated/restricted, abstract/concrete, etic/emic, context-independent/context-dependent, explicit/implicit, formal mastery/practical mastery.

Again, we can draw a variety of conclusions. A conservative reading of Breier's findings would point to the lack of 'equivalence' between informally gained experiential learning and formal academic knowledge. The trade unionists' inability to rise above the specificity of their own experience precluded the development of a broader, more conceptual view. However experienced and skilled they were, their knowledge simply wasn't commensurate with that of the academy. One possible conclusion is that their knowledge cannot be granted academic credit and that we must take this as an example of the inadequacy of experiential learning to meet academic requirements. According to this interpretation, the shop stewards' struggles with abstract conceptualization points to the very deficits that, with systematic remediation and support, academic study might begin to overcome.

There is something to be said for this point of view. I am familiar with this group of students, and the lack of readiness for academic study was indeed a factor in the failure of some to succeed in the class. In some cases, the trade unionists did not have the kinds of formal literacy required in higher education and so were not able to use the logic of argumentation, understand the use of the hypothetical, or, in the end, fulfill the expectations for the course. Given the vicious withholding of education under Apartheid and the continuing deep inequities in South African schooling, it is not surprising that some of them struggled with the norms of higher education. There is a compelling case to be made that education in formal literacies will serve them well, both as individuals and as a collective movement.

It is also possible, however, to interpret Breier's data as supporting Glick's suggestion that theory operates differently in the workplace and the classroom. Interpreted in this manner, the shop stewards' insistence on the gap between theory and application was not evidence of a failure of abstract thought but rather an oppositional and hard-earned epistemological politics. The relationship between the law as written in the abstract and as experienced in practice had different implications for the various groups represented in the classroom, with the law appearing more generalizable from some social locations than others. According to one course professor, "your legal academic bases him or herself on the study of hundreds of cases. What happens in your one workplace or ten workplaces … is almost irrelevant" (2003, p. 6). One of the unionists, however, pointed to the irrelevance of the general and the importance of what she called the "small, nitty gritty things" of practice. "If I should go according to rules and regulation guidelines ... , then I'd lose all my cases" (p. 8). Thus, the abstract treatment of the law by the professors was less a case of context-independence than the quite particular context in which "your legal academic" functions. Abstract, yes, in a manner of speaking that brings to mind Anatole France's praise for the majestic equality of French law, forbidding both rich and poor from sleeping under the bridges of Paris.[4]

Accident-prevention in the delivery room

As a way to begin teasing out what this might mean for APEL, let us return to Dorothy, the delivery room nurse, shop steward, mother, and quilter I introduced in Chapter seven. As a way of drawing on the research that Gherardi cites concerning workplace safety, let us focus for the moment on how we might approach the knowledge Dorothy has of accident-prevention in the delivery room. Conventional APEL will allow some of that knowledge to be accredited to the degree that Dorothy can pass an exam or articulate it systematically in a portfolio. If her institution does portfolio-development in a holistic way, this assessment will go beyond a matching up of discrete pieces of knowledge and give Dorothy the opportunity to look back over a career of incremental learning and take deep pride in what she knows. But if Dorothy's assessment conforms to the assumptions of conventional technicist or even liberal humanist approaches to assessment, it will remain an exercise in what David Starr-Glass (2002) has called "mapping and confirming the familiar" (p. 223), aligning her knowledge to organizations of knowledge as they exist in the academy. Some of her learning will not be so easily "captured" and may well disappear through the cracks because to conventional academic eyes her knowledge is too diffuse, too unsystematic, too hard to line up in disciplinary terms.

Alternatively, however, we might begin, not with academic norms but with the idea that Dorothy is embedded in a complex system of networks consisting of material, social, discursive, technological, and organizational relationships. In that case, we can identify aspects of her knowledge of accident-prevention and safety, not by extracting it from the workplace and mapping it onto the academy, but by locating it in terms of her relationships to the other parts of that network: to equipment, and whether or not it is well-maintained; to functional or dysfunctional communicative practices that do or do not allow for accurate labeling and effective hazard warnings; to the chemical and biological agents that are present in the delivery room and the artifacts, adequate or not, that are meant to protect workers and patients from harm. Dorothy's knowledge will adhere in her awareness of the multiple processes that take place simultaneously: the progress of patients through the stages of labor and delivery, the movement of personnel on and off duty, the maintenance of a clean environment, the functioning of mechanical and technological systems, the emergency procedures that usually remain on stand-by, and the awkward and untrained movements of family members present at the birth.

In "Nurses at the 'sharp end' of patient care," Ronda Hughes (2008) lays out the ways in which nurses interface with the multiple systems within which levels of workplace safety are determined. I want to use Hughes' matrix concerning what can go wrong to indicate the ways in which Dorothy's knowledge of safety might be made visible in terms of complex interactions across socio-material and discursive fields. Consider the following series of questions that Dorothy might be asked: Are hospital resources misallocated, leading to inadequate staffing, scheduling problems, lack of needed equipment? How do policies and procedures encourage or discourage safe practice? How does technology shape workforce practices? What communication systems are required that allow for timely and adequate information? Follow-up questions might inquire about the ways in which human actors impact and are impacted by those managerial, technological, and communications systems. Dorothy might be asked further: How do various groups of workers coordinate work and structures of responsibility among themselves and each other? How do work procedures support or complicate the shifting interactions among personnel, tasks, tools and technologies, and material objects in the busy, filled spaces of the delivery room? How do personnel policies and cultural norms encourage or discourage personnel to exercise autonomy, work collaboratively, suggest innovations, and assume responsibility?

These systems, of course, are embedded in larger systems, such as the way in which the "natural" processes of pregnancy and birth relate to the social and the cultural. What is the general health of the community being served? What diseases and conditions are brought into the delivery room? How are protocols affected by cultural expectations, legal mechanisms and insurance policies, financial pressures from corporate entities and the public sector? Finally, through what cultural mediations does the hospital itself organize the multiple systems that impact safety? Are accidents understood in terms of human failure or system failure? Is there a culture of denial? Of blame?

Implications for APEL

I would suggest that questions such as these point to far more than the procedural and local, requiring an understanding of complex interactions like those of which Gherardi, Crawford, Glick, and many others speak. The implications of this for the assessment of Dorothy's experiential learning are many. First, they provide entry into the complexity of Dorothy's conceptual knowledge as it actually emerges in what Tara Fenwick (2006a) calls "the fluid and contradictory rhythms of knowledge-making amidst everyday human turmoil" and about which, she reminds us, we know all too little (p. 285). They provide an alternative to the insistence that Dorothy distinguish between the theoretical and the practical, the abstract and the concrete, or the propositional and the procedural.

Moreover, these questions, and others like them, trouble the assumption that Dorothy's knowledge is 'hers' in the sense posed by individualized cognitive theory. They treat Dorothy's knowledge as residing, not in her head or even in her experienced hands, but in the network of which she is one actor among many, with other knowledges adhering in her colleagues, in the birthing mother, and in the regulations and technologies that determine how babies are delivered in the particular site that is Dorothy's delivery room. This means, in turn, as Fenwick suggests, that questions might be asked that

> encourage people to reflect beyond their own participation as if they were central actors in systems, and ask about the larger dynamics at work in the situation, the expectations and shared behavioural patterns, the histories mobilizing the situation, the participation of others and its effect on their own behaviours.
>
> *(Fenwick, 2006a, p. 296)*

That is, instead of being asked the conventional portfolio-development questions, "What did you do? What did you learn?", Dorothy might be asked questions that require analytic conceptualizations and informed conclusions: "What happened? Why did it happen? What might have prevented it? What combinations of factors were in play? What kinds of complexity are currently being under-attended to?" Dorothy might be asked to trace the complex network of actors that produce particular accidents, unsafe conditions, and dysfunctional practices. She might be asked to trace causality and make a case for where the fault lies according to various perspectives. She might be asked to draw on her knowledge to make a case for what needs to change, what she would do differently, and why.

Finally, Dorothy does not only *work* in a complex network – she *is* one. She participates in the work of the delivery room from a number of subject positions, as a nurse, of course, but also as a union representative responsible to and for other workers, as a woman and a mother with her own memories of labor and birth, and as a member of an historically underserved demographic group with a long and complicated relationship to the mainstream institutions of health care delivery. Being treated as an embodied, socially situated human actor and not a stand-in for the universal knower will make it easier for Dorothy to tap into the knowledge enabled by her various social subjectivities, by what W. E. B. Dubois called her bifurcated consciousness as a woman and African American, or by the particular conjoining of her multiple social roles. This approach to APEL might allow her to consider how she balances what may often be a conflict between the nurse whose responsibility is to the patient and the shop steward responsible for the safety of coworkers. It might allow her to explore what being (seen as) female, or professionally subordinate, or Black as taught her about inequity and power; how the embodied experience she has of pregnancy, birthing, and motherhood has informed her professional expertise; or how her own working life as a woman worker in a power-laden, gendered workplace impacts how she understands and performs her role as a trade unionist.

The point here is not that Dorothy is entitled to credits in women's studies, African American studies, or labor studies simply for being an African American woman worker and trade unionist; such a policy would introduce experiential foundationalism with a vengeance and replicate the most unexamined of claims to authenticity. Rather, a fuller exploration of her subject positions might concern itself not only with the content of her knowledge and its formal academic equivalence but also with its vital and critical character. It might ask how she has made use of her subject positions to create knowledge in interaction with the world, what she has learned, not only at the workplace but about it, how she has attempted to build a framework of analysis – a theory – with which to interrogate her experience, adapt to changes in the social environment, question her own ideological assumptions, learn from history, or change her mind. Thus, Dorothy would not receive credit for being female, working-class, or Black, but might well receive it for critical understandings of the effects of racism and sexism, the interactive taxonomies of medical knowledge and social power, changes in the nature of work and the social contract, or the meanings of symbols to both hegemonic culture and the struggle for identity.

Reconceptualizing APEL

Lea Melandri has observed that "idealism, the oppositions of mind to body, of rationality to matter, originates in a twofold concealment: of the woman's body and of labor power" (as cited in de Lauretis, 1984, p. 30). That double concealment is, of course, particularly resonant with Dorothy's experience, as it speaks expressly to the erasure of the knowledge of both the laboring mother and the delivery room nurse. A form of APEL that refuses that concealment might allow students a far broader opportunity to interrogate their own experience, make claims for the availability of knowledges from the multiple social positions they occupy, and, ultimately, critique the discourses and power structures that privilege some concretely positioned knowers over others in the name of abstract epistemologies.

First, a reconceptualized APEL might broaden the opportunity for students and faculty alike to interrogate their experience, treating it not as unmediated sensory data or as the source material for abstract conceptualization, but as the socially produced subjectivity through which we locate ourselves in the world. The dialogue thus initiated would allow us to inquire what knowledge is born of personal and social history, within bodies marked by class, race, and gender, out of feelings of anger and love. The knowledge thus generated cannot be understood solely as the product of detachment and reason. Such knowledge is felt, embodied, sensed; it remains rooted in experience. It is partial in both senses of the word: partisan and incomplete.

Second, if all knowledge is situated knowledge, then similarity to academic knowledge cannot be the sole criterion for assessment because legitimate paths of inquiry do *not* necessarily lead to congruent truths. APEL can institutionalize the refusal to privilege academic knowledge as less partial and less materially situated than that derived from other workplaces and social locations. It allows us to act on the recognition that the knowledge gained by the professor of sociology, nursing science, or women's studies has been produced not in idealist isolation but by particular material practices – those of a particular academic discipline at a particular historical moment – and that the knowledge available to the delivery-room nurse will be different, not because it is less universal but because it is produced through different practices, by a different subjectivity interacting with a different community of practice that has led to the development of different skills. It encourages us to ask different questions, not "what do you know that is like what we in the academy have recognized as knowledge," but "what do you know that is different, additive, or corrective? What do our students need to know that we don't know that you can teach us?" By substituting dialogue and mutual recognition for what was unidirectional judgment, we destabilize the basis on which validation is given and invite a sharing of epistemological authority.

I am not suggesting that, by itself, APEL can alter the power relationships within which universities operate. The gate-keeping function of the academy is maintained by both honorable scholarship and entrenched social privilege, and many people have a stake in both. APEL policies alone will not reformulate the relationships among cultures of knowing or the social hierarchies they justify; challenges to systems of legitimation must often come from outside those systems and be based in broad political struggles for resources and legitimacy. But at the very least, APEL is a way of making the criteria of judgment visible and, therefore, potentially negotiable: for whose knowledge gets to "count," for who may judge whom, and on what basis, for the procedures whereby knowledge is rewarded, and whose interests those procedures serve.

This, of course, has implications far beyond APEL practices or, for that matter, higher education. Elizabeth Minnich (2004) has argued that

> To help liberate humankind from past prejudices and beliefs that derived from and justified the assignment of physical and daily life maintenance work to lower-caste people, we need to know much more about all that truly makes life possible and humane, from mothering, to community-building, to surviving with imagination and dignity intact in deprivation and poverty, to working with our hands with art and integrity.
>
> *(Minnich, 2004, p. 92)*

If we take Minnich's words seriously, APEL can become a venue for examining how each of us moves back and forth between our own particular stories and the social production that is knowledge and for challenging oppressive taxonomies of knowledge and the power relationships they enact. It can grant visibility to knowledge that is valuable for its divergence from academic ways of knowing, not only its similarity, and affirm the knowledge that is produced outside epistemologically sanctioned locations, through dialogue within (and, when we are lucky, between) historically situated communities.

Notes

1 Other key predecessors include Lev Vygotsky and Michael Polanyi. For representative examples of how activity theory draws on the work of Vygotsky and his colleagues, see Engeström, Miettinen, and Punamäki (1999).
2 See, for example, Osman (2006).
3 For two excellent introductions to this field of inquiry, see two works I have been citing here, Gherardi (2006) and Fenwick, Edwards, and Sawchuk (2011). For related discussions of the potential role of actor-network theory and complexity theory to APEL, see Pokorny (2006) and Fenwick (2006a), respectively.
4 *"La majestueuse égalité des lois, qui interdit au riche comme au pauvre de coucher sous les ponts, de mendier dans les rues et de voler du pain."* (In its majestic equality, the law forbids rich and poor alike to sleep under bridges, beg in the streets and steal loaves of bread.) *Le Lys Rouge* [*The Red Lily*] (1894). Downloaded from http://www.dico-citations.com/la-majestueuse-galit-des-lois-interdit-aux-riches-comme-aux-pauvres-de-coucher-sous-les-ponts-de-france-anatole/

PART IV
Narrating the self

10

AUTOBIOGRAPHY AND ADULT LEARNING

In th' olde dayes of the kyng arthour,
Of which that britons speken greet honour,
Al was this land fulfild of fayerye. ...
I speke of manye hundred yeres ago.
But now kan no man se none elves mo.

[In the olden days of King Arthur
Of which Britons speak with great honor
All this land was filled with fairies.
I speak of many hundreds of years ago.
Now, nobody can see elves anymore.]

Geoffrey Chaucer, *The Canterbury Tales*, III 857–64

At the end of her prologue, famous for its raunchy extolling of hardheaded experience, Alisoun of Bath tells a very different tale, one of romance in King Arthur's Britain. Structurally, the Tale is a classic medieval romance; a knight, whose flawed character and lack of understanding precipitate a crisis, a journey of the proverbial year and a day, and a resolution in which the knight learns his lesson through circumstances both amorous and magical. It is a world of fantasy in two senses of the word, enchantment and, for Alisoun, wish-fulfillment, in which homely old women are made young and beautiful and husbands bow to their wives' control.

As Alisoun is fully aware, this word of romance no longer exists; the temporal reality of calendars and clocks has replaced the dream time of "th' olde dayes," and such workaday realities as cities, towns, barns, ships, and dairies "maketh that ther ben no fayeryes" anymore (III 872). Alisoun's Prologue, in contrast to her tale, is that very modern genre: an autobiography. Unlike the romance, in which conflict is played out across a dream landscape, autobiography requires both realism and interiority, the ability, that is, to render a 'real world' that will be recognizable to others through a perspective that is distinctly individual. Fradenburg (1986) argues that Alisoun's nostalgic awareness of the distance between her own world and the world of romance is one of the things that makes her seem so modern, an avatar of the "new bourgeois reality principle constituted through its opposing itself to the world of romantic enchantment" in the Tale (p. 32; see also Ingham, 2002).

Thus, Alisoun is a prototypical experiential learner, not only because she holds experience to be educative, but because she presents her learning as an autobiographical narrative. In the next several chapters, I will explore the ways in which autobiography functions in adult learning, what work it does pedagogically and ideologically, and what this has to do with the ways in which we ask adult learners to think about experience. I will argue that, because adult learning practices tend to cast epistemological questions as autobiographical ones, and *vice versa*, they cannot help but enact, not only a theory of knowledge, but a theory of the self. The life narrative practices of adult learning, that is, require students to present themselves according to particular cultural and linguistic delineations, thus creating a particular kind of 'self' in Ochs and Capps' (1996) sense of "an unfolding reflective awareness of being-in-the-world, including a sense of one's past and future" (p. 21).

Autobiographical narrative and adult learning

Autobiographical narratives take up a good deal of space both in the adult learning classroom and in the literature on adult learning. In some contexts, including the assessment of experiential learning for college credit, students are required to narrate the events of their lives and articulate the ways in which their experiences have led to knowledge. In other contexts, adult educators use critical incidents from students' pasts to tease out habitual life patterns and suppositions or else to identify and celebrate incidents that led to expanded understandings of self and world. In still other contexts, adults are encouraged to find more genuine ways of living by distinguishing between what they truly want and the roles and values that have been imposed on them by others. Taken together, the writing of autobiographical narratives is seen as encouraging the development of the qualities most valued in adult learning: authenticity, self-confidence, cognitive self-awareness, professional growth, freedom of choice in attitudes and action, respect for pluralism, and the willingness to re-evaluate unexamined assumptions, cultural biases, and received truths.

Indeed, for many adult learning theorists, the revisiting of past experience *is* learning. Whether a particular experience has led to valuable skills and insights or constricting habits and beliefs – and adult learning theory recognizes both – "learning may be defined as the process of making a new or revised interpretation of the meaning of an experience, which guides subsequent understanding, appreciation, and action" (Mezirow, 1990a, p. 1). On the one hand, "experience is the adult learner's living textbook" (Lindeman, quoted in Knowles, 1990,

p. 30); by looking back over their lives, adults come to recognize their own learning and learning processes (Knowles, 1990), understand seemingly disparate life experiences as forming a coherent whole (Rossiter, 1999), and develop a sense of epistemological and social agency (Kegan, 2000). On the other hand, we "recognize how our own experience can be a trap which limits learning" (Boud *et al.*, 1993, p. 127); by tracing how modes of perception and meaning-making have become reified in the course of a life, autobiography becomes a vehicle for fostering critical reflection (Mezirow, 1990a), questioning the given (Kennedy, 1990), and transforming beliefs about knowledge, evidence, authority, and certainty (Kitchener and King, 1990). In either case, by "reflect(ing) critically about the knowledge, the values, and the meaning constructed ... through their life experiences" (Dominicé, 1990, p. 196), adults affirm the value of some of what they have learned, shed forms of learning that no longer serve them well, and, by cultivating the ability to distinguish which is which, approach the future with more discerning practices for making decisions, forging identities, and determining what is true and valuable (Brookfield, 1987).

Arguably, this is a great deal of work for a single educational practice to do.

In this chapter, I want to problematize the use of autobiographical writing in adult learning and in the literature that supports it. More specifically, I want to challenge a number of prevailing notions concerning the power of autobiographical narratives to articulate the self in its own terms and to reveal the unique patterns and themes in a given life. I will argue that our practices rest on the particular kind of human self that I have traced through the Enlightenment and the emergence of capitalist citizenship: coherent, unified, knowable, and able to draw on experiential learning as a form of personal property. I will suggest that what we treat as free expressions of a newly uncovered authenticity are actually reproductions of specific narrative tropes and that, rather than engendering free self-exploration, our practices shape self-representations in quite specific ways. My argument is that, for all our valorizing of individuality and uniqueness, there are only some stories we allow to be told and only some forms of selfhood we allow to emerge in the process of telling them.

I want to begin by making an intentionally provocative claim, namely, that the life histories produced by adult learners in our classrooms are, in important senses, fictions. The provocativeness of this claim depends in part on the everyday meaning of the word 'fiction' – something that is untrue, invented; fiction as opposed to fact – and I will indeed argue that we may not so much be allowing students to discover and express a 'true' self as we are teaching them to invent one. But I also want to look at the fictiveness of these narratives in a more theoretical sense by exploring the narrative construction of experience within the norms imposed by adult learning practices. My purpose is to examine the ideological dimensions of narrative in adult learning and the ways in which we, inadvertently perhaps, delimit the very self-narratives we purport to liberate.

This does not mean that students don't experience moments of personal transformation by recognizing and reclaiming their experiential learning and/or extricating themselves from received roles and values, but it *does* mean that they both do so and tell about it within constraints that are largely unacknowledged. Autobiography is what Foucault called a technology of the self, a way of constructing a particular kind of self out of culturally shared discourses. Self-authorship, in other words, is not the *result* of autobiographical practices; rather, it is the practice itself, an exercise in self-creation by human beings who are as much the products of their own narratives as their referents.

Narrative theory and autobiographical practice

A theoretical and scholarly focus on narrative emerged in both cultural studies and the human sciences during the 1970s and 1980s. This development has multiple origins, including the broad application of literary theory to social phenomena and psychoanalytic and postmodernist challenges to notions of unmediated experience. In many ways, narrative theory is consistent with the privileging of experience that typifies adult learning, but it treats experience as constructed rather than as unmediated, a socially overdetermined effect of the interaction of self, culture, and world. Rather than seeing people as having unfiltered access to experience which they then use language to convey, narrative analysis across multiple disciplines looks at how people tell stories of themselves and how they construct identities in and through the process of telling those stories. As the self comes to be understood, not as an essence that predates anything we might say about it, but as the product of social relations and discursive forms, new attention is being paid to the ways in which narratives, including self-narratives, both reflect and construct particular identities, subjectivities, and experiences. The result, to quote Clifford Geertz, is a focus on how people work at "spinning the webs of significance in which they themselves are suspended" (as cited in Holstein and Gubrium, 2000, p. 101).[1]

Within narrative theory, what has come to be known as narrative psychology posits human beings fundamentally as storytellers who organize their understanding of the world and their own sense of self according to narrative structures.[2] Drawing both on Freudian practices of self-narration and on postmodernist notions of the provisional self, narrative psychology rests on the understanding that the stories through which we construct ourselves are, in some ways, necessary fictions. The function of narrative is to impose a usable structure that does not otherwise exist; meaning adheres in the chronological order of the narrative, in culturally available frames for interpreting experience, and in the semblance of a unified selfhood produced by focusing on specific aspects of experience and memory. "We are always and simultaneously author, narrator, protagonist, and reader of our own life story" (Randall, as cited in Tondreau, 2003, p. 15). In effect, we author ourselves.

The literature on adult learning is filled with metaphors of self-authorship and of "restorying" a life. Kegan's (2000) stress on the efficacy of the "self-authoring mind" (p. 68) is typical, as is Dominicé's (2000) claim that "whatever influences and dependencies characterize their individual journeys, [adult learners] can still become authors of their lives" (pp. 10–11). Underlying the rhetoric of self-authorship in adult learning, however, are both a tension between two notions of selfhood and an obfuscation concerning the degree to which self-narratives are always framed by 'influences and dependencies.'[3]

In his helpful taxonomy, "Transforming Selves" (2005), Mark Tennant identifies five forms of selfhood underlying practices of transformative adult learning: the authentic or real self, the repressed self, the autonomous self, the storied self, and the entangled self. As Tennant points out, the five overlap in numerous ways, and multiple theoretical positions exist within each category, but his categories are extremely helpful in teasing out the contradictions that often go unexamined in our practices.

The authentic or real self draws broadly on Enlightenment and modernist notions of identity, but enters adult learning theory more explicitly through the influence of humanistic psychology. In this version of selfhood, the self retains an essential nature that has been masked or distorted by social forces. Its authentic spirit is always there, open to rediscovery if one can free oneself from a socially imposed set of values and roles and/or learn forms of communication that are free of power-laden constraints.

Opposed to the authentic self is what Tennant has termed the storied self. This self, the self of narrative psychology, lives fully in history, continually under construction and available for reinscription and reinterpretation as different themes and identities develop over the course of a lifetime. To the storied self, we, like our narratives, are multiple and open-ended; we (re)create ourselves through a process of re-evaluation over time.

While virtually all contemporary adult learning theory pays lip service to the self as a cultural and historical product, intimations remain of an authentic self who can be liberated from culture and history. The authentic self and the storied self are not reconcilable, however; the positing of an authenticity waiting to be rediscovered belies the historicity of the storied self and the evolving nature of identity. Viewed pedagogically, moreover, there is an important difference in the function that life writing is presumed to play: between narrative as a site of identity-*formation* for the storied self and, for the authentic self, as a site of identity-*discovery* (Guarino, 2003; see also Ochs and Capps, 1996).

The distinction between the authentic Rogerian self and the socially constructed self of narrative psychology, however, is not always parsed in discussions of adult learning. The assumptions of one, that an authentic Self exists under layers of socialization, for example, are folded, as it were, into the other.

> Adulthood can be seen as a process of finding one's autonomy in relation to family, schooling, and the sociocultural environment, the three contexts of emancipation often described in educational biographies.
>
> *(Dominicé, 2000, p. 81)*

> Whoever authors your story authorizes your actions. We gain personal
> authority and power in the measure that we question the myth that is upheld
> by the 'authorities' and discover and create a personal myth that illuminates
> and informs us.
>
> *(Keen and Valley-Fox, as cited in Rossiter and Clark, 2010, p. 90)*

There is a curious slippage here: from the narrative self that is crafted out of
necessarily overdetermined plots and character types back to the humanistic self
that triumphs over any delimiting psychic and historical past. All life experiences
can be affirmed through what Randall (1996) calls the poetics of learning:

> No trouble, no tale; no pain, no gain – and no learning. To pursue the
> poetics of learning pulls us into a territory ... where learning itself is a lifelong
> adventure: where no incident is 'unusable' in illustrating, indeed building,
> our character (Sarton, 1980): no event inherently meaningless; and no
> situation devoid of some clue to our particular destiny, to our unique
> message, to the 'meaning' of our life.
>
> *(Randall, 1996, p. 247)*

Partly as a result of the eliding of the authentic and the storied self, adult learning
theory has largely failed to grapple with the susceptibility of autobiographical
accounts to cultural, interpersonal, and linguistic influence. Self-narratives are
mediated by multiple external factors, among them the social and ideological
circumstances of the telling, the primary recipient of the narrative, the ways we
have been socialized into particular discursive self-representations, and the strategies
we have learned for negotiating our relationships with others (Bruner, 2004; Ochs
and Capps, 1996). Betty Bergland (1994) argues that we err in reading the
autobiographical self as "an essential individual" who is "the originator of her own
meaning." Rather, we must read that self "as socially and historically constructed
and multiply positioned in complex worlds and discourses" that are themselves
value- and power-laden (p. 131; see also Langellier on this point).

Autobiography thus changes according to shifts in the religious, psychological,
and philosophical formations, the sociocultural milieu, and the institutional
power relationships within which particular stories are told and heard. Far from
expressing an unmediated self, the narrated self is an effect of both personal and
social regulation; while we ourselves may alter our self-narrations as ways of re-
ordering experience or reinterpreting our being in the world, we are also subject
to what Ochs and Capps (1996) refer to as the "institutional master storylines"
that prevail in cultural and organizational settings (p. 33). Indeed, the silencing
of alternative stories is a not-insignificant aspect both of socialization and of
social control.

One of the direct forms of influence over autobiographical accounts is the
situational context within which they are produced. Honoria Guarino (2003)
explores the ways in which the self-narratives of people with HIV-AIDS are

reshaped through the frames provided by AIDS service organizations. Through the normative ideology of the organization, personal narratives are structured in such a way that the HIV diagnosis becomes central to the identity of the individual, and the meaning of AIDS changes from a tragic and terrifying diagnosis to an opportunity for uplift and renewal. Nathan Mizco (2003) makes a similar point concerning the ways in which interviewers influence the self-narratives of those suffering from chronic illness, shaping them around the theme that chronic illness has had a powerful and beneficial impact on the patient's life. Bruner suggests that this susceptibility to the situational context may be the reason why psychotherapeutic encounters, religious conversions, and other interventions in a life can lead to profound changes a person's life narrative.

I would argue that adult learning provides an equivalent institutional and cultural setting, with the return to formal education serving as both the precipitating moment and the thematic core of a newly re-authored self. These narratives are overdetermined by the conditions of story-telling in our classrooms, not least of which are the values and assumptions that underlie our practices, the aspects of self that are called into being by the narratives we elicit, and the *telos* – ending – toward which they are expected to move. Bruner (1990) asks, "By what processes and in reference to what kinds of experience do human beings formulate their own concept of Self, and what kinds of Self do they formulate?" (p. 100). What this means in terms of adult learning is that we must ask ourselves: what stories are our students telling, what plots are they devising out of their lives, and why? Rather than treating student autobiographies, as Dominicé (1990) does, as accounts of "how they became themselves" (p. 197), we need also to ask how students are *becoming* themselves – and what selves they are becoming – in the act of writing.

The fictiveness of autobiographical narrative in adult learning

As a way of entering into these issues, let us consider the following autobiographical essay, one that is handed to students at the start of a portfolio-development course currently being taught in an American institution. The document is in many ways a model of good APEL practice: it comes from a venerable liberal arts college with a long-standing commitment to adult learners; it is used by faculty with an impressive history of critiquing their own practice; and it represents a student-centered institutional approach to both APEL and curriculum.[4]

The essay begins:

> I messed up my life, or at least I thought I did. I never thought that my daily experiences, mundane as they have been for most of my life, mattered. Sometimes I'd be driving down a street thinking about whether or not my life made a difference. ... Then I had the good sense to realize the impact I have had in the world. If I was not here, then who would ... water my flowers, feed my cats, love the people I do ...? ... I have learned that

education is a life long journey. My prior experiences have been significant, yet I've not always recognized the importance of these experiences. My education, both formal and informal, has prepared me for the present and will prepare me for the future.

The essay then focuses on five very different types of learning experiences:

- an early love of reading that broadened both the student's vocabulary and her world view;
- a scheduling snafu in high school that initiated her love and knowledge of art;
- participation on the board of a local organization in which her parenting skills were used for purposes of mediation and conflict-resolution among contentious individuals;
- a college sociology course that led her to insights concerning social marginalization; and
- a church fair in which she developed and used organizational skills to raise money for a good cause.

After acknowledging that life has been "pretty out of control lately" and drawing on her prior learning to prioritize and "put things in order," the writer then concludes:

> Experience will not help me approach the future unless I consciously draw on it. Learning from my mistakes and successes, my informal and formal learning experiences form the foundation of my life as an educated woman. If I am conscious of how each moment in life builds on the past, I know I have a great deal to draw from when I must tackle new challenges. I have not messed up my life; I can use it.

Let me begin by stressing what is admirable about this essay as a model for adult learners exploring their own experience. The piece draws on multiple sources of learning – formal and informal, intentional and serendipitous, public and private. It avoids what I argued in Chapter nine are often seen as the hidden biases of prior learning assessment, in this case the devaluing of child-rearing, unpaid volunteer work, and other typically female sources of knowledge. It stresses the transferability of skills and insights between different facets of life. It posits knowledge as an outcome, not only of systematic thought, but of chagrin, experimentation, and surprise. It is also exemplary in the kinds of experiences that are seen as leading to learning, its celebration of the wisdom that comes from everyday experience, and its marking of the ways in which students can gain confidence and self-awareness though the process of re-entry into higher education.

This is, in other words, a commendable example of a kind of material typically provided in our classrooms. It is intended to represent a real human being and to demonstrate the benefits of journeying into and reclaiming oneself. And yet, whether or not it was written by a student, the essay is fabricated in ways that are both informative and troubling. In what follows, I will explore the fictiveness of the essay as a way of teasing out what we say – and think – we are doing in our autobiographical practices and what constructions of life and selfhood are at work.

On one level, the fictiveness of this document might be said to lie in the veracity of specific statements. I would argue, however, that literal accuracy isn't the point. Rather, the piece is, and I believe is meant to be, an introduction to a particular way of thinking about one's life. What is being modeled here is a particular kind of self-awareness, that of the exemplary adult learner, and a particular narrative structure that is an algorithm for how such self-awareness develops. In other words, the essay is both pedagogical and normative; it anticipates both the process – the self-exploration on which the portfolio-development course will focus – and the product – the resultant understanding of self that the student is meant to achieve.

Which leads to the second way in which the essay is a fiction; it has a plot.

Every narrative has a plot, of course. It is in the nature of narrative to select among events, segment them in particular ways, and establish implicit or explicit causal relationships among them. But not every plot is the same, and thus, it behooves us to ask: what is the plot of this story? What elements help to structure this narrative? Who is the self who speaks?

To begin by stating the obvious, the plot of this essay is one of self-empowerment through a process of thinking back on one's life. Its forward movement rests on self-knowledge as the key to social and cognitive agency, and its turning point is the flash of insight that "I have not messed up my life" after all but rather "have a great deal to draw from when I must tackle new challenges." The apparent missteps of a life are only that – apparent. Looking back, it is clear that nothing is wasted, that all experience is meaningful. Seen in terms of structure, this means that the plot is both teleological and comedic, both a story of psychic integration and a redemption narrative. It moves from chaos to order, from confusion to clarity, from despair to an understanding that, for all its apparent confusion, life has had a shape all along.

Second, this is a particularly American plot, and not only because the author has evidently been watching Frank Capra movies. Its narrator/protagonist is someone who respects the 'know-how' that emerges out of ordinary life, who counts on the world to offer second chances, and who, for all her present-day energy and social enlightenment, is an identifiably Henry Jamesean American – earnest, hopeful, prosperous, willing to confront the future with good will. There is no room in this story for looking back on incidents and years that truly were a waste of time, for mistakes that cannot be harnessed as learning, for a life that has forever, in James' phrase, been "complicated by a regret" (as cited in Wood, 1975, p. 31). The past is not only another country; it is the Old Country of the psyche. The happy ending is the result of good old American optimism and self-confidence, which are represented, not only as virtues, but as life skills, keys to success and psychic upward mobility.[5]

Finally, the plot rests on a subplot that is never explicitly rendered, namely, the processes of adult education that have enabled both the revisiting of experience and the recognition of its order and purpose. "Sometimes I'd be driving down a street thinking about whether or not my life made a difference. … Then I had the good sense to realize the impact I have had in the world." The "then" in that sentence is a moment of insight that was initiated by and situated within the practices of adult learning.

Life narratives and the myth of free self-authorship

One of adult learning theory's favorite conceits is that we allow students to choose their own plots. Pierre Dominicé (1990), for example, contends that giving students the freedom to structure their own narratives allows them to take charge of their lives. Marsha Rossiter (1999) distinguishes between building a story around notions of fixed developmental stages and allowing adults to rework the 'plot' of their own lives. Once we recognize the above essay as containing a particular plot, however, what is striking is how enamored we are of it as a professional community, how often we structure course work to elicit this particular narrative, and how committed we are to ensuring that the maximum number of students end by understanding – or at least writing as if they understood – their lives in these terms. The two-sided narrative of shedding and discovery – shedding false roles and values to discover one's true self; shedding diffidence and self-doubt to discover one's true worth – are repeatedly cited in both the literature written for practitioners and the materials given to students. The pendulum swings between the rejection of the past and the celebration of it, two sides of the same story of (re)discovering a self.

Rossiter (1999), for example, grounds her discussion of "adult development as narrative" on a life narrative written by a student named Anne. Anne's story, Rossiter tells us, is one of "difficulty, delays, uncertainty; it is also a story of discovery and change" (p. 77). Anne begins college when "it finally dawned on me that no one was going to build a life for me that was separate and distinct from the life my parents had led, except me" (p. 80). Now, about to graduate, Anne no longer feels the "constraints" of her parents' lives and is "satisfied that the struggle to redefine my sense of self as separate from my parents has been accomplished" (p. 81).

As Rossiter points out, this is a common enough story of young adulthood. What makes the tale worth citing is that it follows Anne's own experience of her life and her own trajectory of insight rather than an imposed theory of development. While Anne's story is part of a larger familial and societal narrative, "the interpretation that is privileged is that of the person whose development is in question" (p. 80) and the *telos* of the tale lies, not in externally imposed outcomes or ends, but in Anne's discovery of her own authentic life path.

What is missing from this account, however, is not Anne's privileging of her own narrative, but Rossiter's. Of the many student narratives that, one assumes, are at her disposal, she has chosen an example of what David Starr-Glass (personal communication, April 1, 2008) has called the "morality play" of adult learning, with the schematized good (self-knowledge, authentic selfhood, and self-confidence) winning out over the bad (received roles and values, self-doubt, and lack of insight). The fall into the unexamined life is followed by the inevitable redemption.

In her study of the impact of portfolio-development on a diverse group of adult learners, Judith Brown (2002) quotes her research subjects as follows:

> Luther noted with amazement: "It made me realize that I had accomplished much more in life than I realized. It made me more cognizant of my abilities and that I could do different things. That I had so much knowledge. ..."
>
> Churchill was beaming when he said: "It sort of gave me more pep in my step and actually gave me a sense of pride...."
>
> The self-assured Ginger went further. ... Poised on the edge of her chair, she vividly described her feeling: "It really made me stop and think. You know, well, I'm not so bad. I am really a pretty neat person. It reinforced my belief in myself. It made me remember ... certain things that I have done that I haven't thought about in years."
>
> *(Brown, 2002, p. 235)*

Similarly, according to Carolyn Mann (2004):

> Preparing the Life History Paper enabled learners to reflect upon how they have grown and changed. ... As one student reported: "This really helped me find new things or new angles that I had not considered about myself." Another concluded: "I found this to be a very valuable process. Due to my lifestyle and my job, I had never taken the time to reflect on what all had taken place in my life."
>
> *(Mann, 2004, p. 89)*

I am not suggesting that these quotations are either inaccurate or disingenuous. Nor I am denying that life writing exercises often have these positive effects. My point, rather, is that, for all our celebration of the uniqueness of students' stories, we end up with a series of narratives that are suspiciously repetitious and that are as least as much the by-product of particular pedagogical practices as they are of authentic self-inquiry.

Ideology and autobiographical practice in adult learning

What, then, is the nature of this particular story and the self that produces and is produced by it? What values and assumptions about the world are inscribed in these narratives? What ideological work are they are doing?

I want to explore these issues by considering another essay that, like the one discussed above, is provided to students in an institution with a long tradition of serving adults and that is meant to model both the process and result of self-exploration. Early in the essay, the narrator presents a vision of her own death:

In the end, when friends and family speak about me, long after my dust is reunited with the Mother Earth, I want them to be able to say, "She really did make a difference in the world." And I don't mean by writing a prize winning book, creating a cure for cancer, or becoming the first woman President of the United States. I want to make a difference in the lives of children, teenagers. I want to be able to teach. …

She then presents an encapsulated version of her remembered past and anticipated future.

Learning from mistakes is usually one of the best learning tools out there. But then again, maybe what is viewed as a mistake is really just a learning experience in disguise. When I first graduated High School …, I knew I wanted to see the world and to find a way to change it for the better. I began college that fall and after two semesters part-time with average grades, I stopped wasting money and went on a pilgrimage to find myself and my life path. I went to work, I visited museums, I hugged trees, I cleaned up trash from lakes, I listened to my Grandparents' stories, I read to my little cousins, I sang with the winds in the trees and I lay in bed with my Grandmother as she took her last breath. I got married. I got divorced. I held my friend's newborn baby and I saw the world of potential in her eyes. The next day I registered for college to begin my path to becoming a teacher. … Within three years from now, I will have finished my Bachelor's degree and have begun my Master's degree. Five to six years from now I will be embarking on my life's journey to educate others. Ten years from now, I may just be teaching that little newborn I held … and making a difference in her life by expanding her education.

After an extensive and detailed discussion of the educational program she has designed, the narrator concludes:

Over the semester while working on developing my degree plan, I not only learned a lot about [the institution] but I also learned a lot about myself. … The seeds of my education were planted many, many years ago when I first attended college. Today they are in full bloom. … And one day my hard work will come full circle when I am standing in a classroom as a teacher instead of a student.

As Vincent Crapanzano (1992) has pointed out, all narratives rest on particular views concerning desirable qualities in human beings. In that sense, all narratives are ideological documents; they both reveal and further particular notions about how the world works (and should work), what human beings are like (and should be like), and how people understand (and should understand) their relationship to the stories they tell and are told. How then do we understand the relationship between the plot of this narrative and the desirable human qualities that both determine and are determined by the plot?

First, as Janet Miller (1998) has said, this form of autobiographical writing emphasizes the production of "predictable, stable, and normative identities" (p. 302). We know what is coming from the first time the author states her wish to "make a difference," and we know that she will become a teacher from the moment we know she wants to teach. The plot is structured in such a way that intention presumes achievement – this is a person who both knows herself and has the wherewithal to bring an achieved self into being. The "adversity" of a life drops away – the vicissitudes of youth, the failure of love, grief in the face of death – in favor of a successful "journey" into self- knowledge in which there is no such thing as wasted time because "a mistake is really just a learning experience in disguise."

Second, what we might call this student's psychic coherence is both reflected in and created by narrative coherence. The narrative trajectory moves "from indifferent student to successful student" and "full circle" from student to teacher. While multiple experiences are referenced, many of which sound intriguing in their own right, the narrative is structured around a particular incident – the moment of discovering she wants to be a teacher – and a particular *telos* – becoming a teacher and, more broadly, becoming a realized human being who can look back satisfied from the grave. There is no room in this narrative for experiences that cannot be integrated into the student's "journey," no odd moments or ragged corners that might have interrupted the coherence of her current self or added complexity or ambivalence to her view of her life. Good comes of difficulty, and virtue is rewarded. The world and the self make sense.

Third, the two parallel plots of the narrative – the process of living through experiences and the process of remembering them – mean that coherence is a function of memory. It is this that allows the plot to be structured according to a series of events through which the remembering self is the same as the remembered self and also different: more insightful, more mature, indeed, better. What is reproduced in this essay is not the unpredictability of 'real' memory, however, but memory as delimiting meaning and structuring a coherent self (Dames, 2001). The coherence of the plot, coherence as the comedic ending, and coherence as a desirable human quality all reinforce each other and provide the ideological underpinning of the tale. The ability to tell one's story in these terms becomes evidence of a life well lived because, whatever its mistakes, they have led, through self-knowledge, to self-authorship.

A case can be made for claiming that, fictions or not, there is much to be said for helping returning adult students find a more empowered, confident version of self. Markus and Nurius have suggested that human self-awareness includes a multiplicity of "possible selves," aspects of our working self-concepts that are defined by our awareness of what we might become in the future (as cited in Bruner, 1990, p. 42). In those terms, the fortunate outcome at the end of the essays discussed above are less the product of new insights concerning a former self than the narrative construction of a possible self that is confident, courageous, and grounded.

What, then, is wrong with that?

To begin with, there is something that I hope is obviously wrong with imposing an imprint on a life story while believing we give adult learners the freedom to tell their own stories as they choose. It is one thing to wish, with Taylor and Marienau (Taylor, 2000), that our students are helped to become more effectual members of a pluralistic, rapidly changing world. It is another to walk into a classroom unaware that we expect students to set their stories within a particular narrative frame. Modeling a pre-determined narrative of self and then citing successful reproductions of that narrative as exemplifying the authenticity-enhancing nature of our practices is a self-fulfilling prophecy at best. It may also be a form of pedagogical and intellectual obfuscation in which the illusion of self-reflection within the frame of the narrative conceals the lack of self-reflection about it (Crapanzano, 1992).

Moreover, even if we acknowledge our ideological bent and commit ourselves to individual and social change, we need to question the assumption that this narrative aligns naturally with "informed, free human choice and social justice" (Mezirow, 2000, p. xiv). Mezirow's original research, published in 1978, focused on a group of women returning to higher education through reentry programs created in the context of the women's movement. Given the historical moment, it was to be expected that many of these women had been led to rethink their socialization and challenge conventional gender roles. As someone deeply committed to transformative politics and social change, I believe in the power of moments at which human beings are jarred out of acquiescence and can see both their own oppression and the possibilities of a more just world. But it is also clear in today's culturally fraught environment that 'I saw the light' narratives are a two-edged sword.

> My mother was right. As a young woman, I should never have majored in chemistry, joined the Peace Corps, perused art museums, or been nice to the gay couple who moved in next door. None of those things made me happy. Then one day I was watching two cardinals building a nest, and I realized that the problem was that I was challenging the order of nature. Having repented of my presumption, I now see that all my efforts were leading me back to the place I began, this time filled with joy instead of rebellion. I have registered at a fundamentalist dating service, and I'm going to marry the first man who asks me.

> I was devastated when I lost my job in the auto plant. What would become of my family? My grandfather helped found the United Auto Workers, and my father always taught me that a good union job, with a living wage and solid benefits, was the right of every American. Now I understand that unions are only for the weak. Last year, I started a company to manufacture auto parts in Asia, where I only have to pay my workers $1 a day. Now that

I have shed the values imposed by my background and identified my entrepreneurial skills, I can *really* support my family.

Or, while we are drawing on American cultural artifacts,

Why am I trying to become what I don't want to be ... when all I want is out there, waiting for me the minute I say I know who I am! Why can't I say that, Willy? I am a dime a dozen, and so are you! ... I am one dollar an hour, Willy. I tried seven states and couldn't raise it. ... Pop, I'm nothing. I'm just what I am, that's all.

(Miller, 1957, p. 217)

These are, of course, extreme examples. But even student narratives of coming into a more socially open-hearted selfhood are less counter-hegemonic than we like to believe. However personally transforming – and I do not mean to underestimate the importance of that – the selves produced in these narratives are acceptably mainstream and not very threatening to the status quo. Our graduates may participate more actively in an American – or global – meritocracy, or they may find their way into less prosaic lives and selves, but these are all individual solutions, predicated on the idea that the terms of the world allow for personal liberations such as these. Our various notions, whether Maslow's self-actualization or Mezirow's transformative learning, finally posit life narratives as ways of writing the self back into individualism. The theme of freedom from social and psychic constraints, moreover, is arguably as conventional within American culture as the conformity against which it purports to rebel. While the literature on adult learning tends to treat this theme as a new and radical construct, it is at least as old as Hester Prynne and Arthur Dimmesdale in the forest and Huck Finn lighting out for the territory. More recently, American culture has become replete with therapeutic and quasi-therapeutic narratives of individual transformation, from daytime television to the Pulitzer Prize.

Finally, as adult educators regularly admit, not every student succeeds in creating this narrative of self. Such failures are typically explained in terms of students' limitations: the inability to separate learning from experience, an underdeveloped faculty for critical self-reflection, insufficient academic literacy, the inability to shake the influence of family and community, or psychological and moral inflexibility. I want to suggest, however, that there is at times something else at work behind these apparent failures. Some students cannot or choose not to create these narratives because they simply can't find themselves in the plot.

Refusing to grow

In his classic story of "Gladys, who refused to grow," Laurent Daloz (1988) pokes gentle fun at the tendency of adult educators to assume the role of "andragogical missionary" (p. 7). Gladys is a woman in her sixties whose energetic life has been spent as a wife, mother, and self-taught manager of a successful nursing home. She returns to formal education in her retirement, firm in her moral and religious beliefs, but expecting to be told what she should study and with no burning curiosity of her own. Daloz, her assigned advisor, is an adult educator who sees his role as helping students "to think more clearly, to understand a complex world more appropriately, and to risk committing themselves despite genuine doubts and pervasive uncertainty" (p. 4). Gladys, however, has no such doubts. She is not open to Daloz's invitation to "reconceive [her] earlier self and cultivate the growth of a more fitting and well-integrated new one," nor is she interested in an advisor who understands his role as midwife in "the process of [his] students' rebirth" (Ibid.).

Daloz recounts two conversations with the menfolk in Gladys' life. Toward the beginning of her course of study, her son comments that "I don't know what she's doing it for. She can't benefit from a college degree. We keep telling her, 'We love you the way you are'" (p. 5). Two years later, toward the end of her studies, Gladys' husband is still echoing those same sentiments: "I don't see what the hell she wants this damn degree for. It ain't going to do her a damned bit of good" (p. 6).

In the event, Gladys' education is not what Daloz would call a success. She never learns to differentiate between a critique of her writing and a devaluing of her life experience, fails to achieve "distance" (p. 5) or theoretical perspective, and eyes Daloz with skepticism when he suggests she "be willing to question [her] own beliefs … and be prepared to let go of some of them" (p. 6). In the end, it is his beliefs that are shaken, specifically the belief that he has the right "to intrude so deeply into this heroic little woman's life" (Ibid.). His conclusion is that, however much adult educators might wish, "not all students grow from their education" (p. 7). Other pressures are too great; we need to put aside our "teacherly narcissism" (Ibid.) and acknowledge the many other influences in our students' lives. For women especially, change requires a renegotiation with significant others of many kinds, and it is simply easier not to 'grow' in the face of those who, like Gladys' son, "love you the way you are" (p. 5). Daloz ends his story by reporting that, three weeks after her husband died, Gladys "followed him" to the grave (p. 7), implying, through the word 'followed' that Gladys' life was spent to the very end in obedience to male direction and authority.

Daloz's essay about Gladys is both humorous and wise, and it is deservedly often cited in the literature (and graduate student reading lists) of adult learning. Daloz positions himself as the anti-hero of the tale, taking a gently self-mocking view of his own frustration and offering the community of adult educators a valuable "morality tale" (p. 4). Yet there is something in his story of Gladys' "refusal" that re-inscribes the narrative of life transformation even as it undermines it. It keeps the story of epistemic growth and self-awareness as the norm that students embrace or refuse, challenging, not the story, but only our arrogant expectation that all students can achieve it.

I would like to suggest that there is another way of understanding this story, one that is equally plausible but that is hidden by the expectation that adult students are meant to "grow" and that Gladys is refusing to do so. The key to that alternative interpretation lies in the very "fabric of relationships" that Daloz sees as holding adult students back from psychic and intellectual growth (p. 7). Specifically, Gladys has continued her education in the face of two years of united opposition from the important men in her life; rather than seeing her husband and son as a conservative and ultimately paralyzing influence, we might see Gladys' dogged degree completion as a small rebellion against male authority, a rare moment of disobedience in a life spent largely in deference to gendered conventionality. Seen in those terms, Daloz's irritated and reluctant decision to "just let her alone, let her have the damned degree" (p. 6) is the ironic echo of her husband and son's frustration that, at least this once, Gladys refuses to let male authority tell her what to do.

I have no idea if this alterative interpretation is the right one, although I expect it is one of which the Wife of Bath would approve. My point is really a broader one, namely, that our affection for and commitment to a particular narrative closes us off from other stories that are at least as disruptive of power and conformity and, in some versions at least, even more disquieting than the one we continue to tell. I am concerned that such alternative stories go missing, in effect, because they do not conform to the narrative we expect to see and that we recognize as successful "transformations" into more coherent understandings and more deeply self-authored lives.

Notes

1   For an introduction to narrative theory in these terms, see Mumby (1993). For a survey of narrative theory as it applies to adult learning, see Tondreau (2003).
2   For a founding text of this school of thought, see T. R. Sarbin (1986). For important representative texts, see Jerome Bruner (1990); Holstein and Gubrium (2000); and Linde (1993).
3   See also Taylor, Marienau, and Fiddler (2000) and Randall (1996).
4   I am afraid that this chapter bears out Oscar Wilde's observation that no good deed ever goes unpunished. I am very grateful to the colleagues, here unnamed, who shared their materials with me. I am aware of having responded to their generosity with critique. In my defense, I can only say that I drew for this chapter only on institutions that I deeply respect in the belief that we learn most by scrutinizing our best practices.
5   In calling this plot American, I do not mean to limit my discussion to American classrooms or to treatments of adult learning that have been written by Americans. Indeed, in citing Dominicé, a French-speaking European, and Australians Boud, Cohen, and Walker, I am intentionally drawing on international sources. I am, however, suggesting that the plot is constructed around values and beliefs that, albeit a highly successful export, have their origins in and draw their energy from American culture and history.

11

TEXTUALIZING THE SELF

Genre, experience, and adult learning

Unto this day it dooth myn herte boote
That I have had my world as in my tyme.

[Even today it does my heart good
That I have had my world in my time.]

Geoffrey Chaucer, *The Canterbury Tales*, III 472–3

In the previous chapter, I explored the autobiographical narratives that typify both the practice of adult learning and the literature about it and argued that the life histories produced by adult learners in our classrooms are, in important senses, fictions. That is, the narratives that students produce, however much they originate in real events, are multiply overdetermined by the structural and ideological frames within which they are encouraged to write. My point in the chapter was that, for all our valorizing of individuality, there are only some stories we allow our students to tell and only some forms of selfhood we allow to emerge in the process of telling them. In making an argument that drew heavily on narrative psychology, I acknowledged that many students experience moments of personal transformation in the generating of life narratives. For all our celebration of the uniqueness of students' stories, however, our pedagogical practices are such that we encourage one particular narrative form that is then repeatedly extolled in our scholarship.

In this chapter, I want to extend that exploration by returning narrative analysis to its original roots in literary theory and posing a very literary question: if the self is a text, what genre is it?[1] I will argue that the narrative forms we impose on students depend on relationships that are fundamentally novelistic: between structure and meaning, between first person narrators and their own past selves, and between learning and time. I will locate these conventions in a specific genre of the novel that was central to the emergence of the self-aware individual of modernity: the novel of development or, as often called by its German name, the *Bildungsroman*. I will then explore how both the ideological encoding and narrative structures of the *Bildungsroman* align with the life narratives of adult learning. Finally, I will focus briefly on an alternative genre, magical realism, to point to alternative ways for narrating experience.

Narrative structure and adult learning

Only some genres and, indeed, some stories are available within a culture. For a tale to have meaning, the teller must draw on a shared cultural store of motifs, events, stock characters, and expectations and must combine them in a way that is comprehensible to a particular audience. This does not mean that every story is meant to mirror the felt conditions of the world, but it does mean that every narrative constructs a spatial and temporal realm in which objects and people exist in particular causal relationships and in which some things can and do happen, and not others. This is no less the case in autobiographical accounts and other narratives of selfhood. As Jerome Bruner (2004) says, "the ways of telling [life stories] and the ways of conceptualizing that go with them become so habitual that they finally become recipes for structuring experience itself" (p. 707).

The protagonist/narrators who are valorized in the literature on adult learning have a recognizable generic role. They are individuals for whom life has not quite come together. Lack of professional fulfillment, a destabilized domestic life, financial insecurity, or similar factors have led to some form of psychic distress and/or social marginalization. Lack of self-confidence and/or socially imposed norms and values have delimited their life possibilities. These individuals, however, have it within themselves to live more integrated and satisfied lives; they are, as Robert Kegan has put it, "in grave danger of growing" (cited in Taylor, 2000, p. 152). The plot set in motion by these factors is one of self-empowerment through a process of thinking back on one's life.

Kathleen Taylor's examples are typical:

> I am the first woman in my family to get a divorce and the first to pursue a college education – I don't know which is harder for my mother to accept. What I know is I must step outside the boundaries of my culture and learn to make my own way in the world.

> In response to the Vietnam draft my family moved to Canada, where I finished high school. I tried higher education but dropped out because I couldn't conform. I didn't want to listen to some stuffy professor; I wanted to change the world! What I finally realized was I would have to have more education to make the kind of contribution to society that's important to me.

> I was raised in an extremely abusive environment. After high school, I
> worked as a lab technician but developed an increasing addiction to
> alcohol and tried suicide more than once. Then I got pregnant, stopped
> drinking, and realized I had to get serious about bringing some financial
> security and stability into my son's life and mine.
>
> *(Taylor, 2000, p. 151)*

Like Laurent Daloz, whose story of "Gladys, who refused to grow," I discussed in
the previous chapter, Stephen Brookfield has aimed gentle but pointed barbs at our
infatuation with this particular narrative, arguing that "narratives of critical analysis
in which people experience contradictions, are visited by revelations, get better,
and come to fuller self-knowledge are necessary palliatives but essentially false"
(2000a, p. 134).

> I used to teach in an unwittingly oppressive way, perpetuating inequalities of
> race, class, and gender. Now – as a result of a disorienting dilemma that
> caused me to reflect critically on my abuse of power – I have washed my
> practice free of the stains of racism, classism, sexism, and oppression.
>
> I used to live my life according to others' expectations; I didn't know who I
> was or how to live according to my own assumptions and beliefs. Now I've
> discovered who I really am – my core self – through critical reflection, and
> I'm living a more authentic and integrated life.
>
> *(Brookfield, 2000b, pp. 133–4)*

If Brookfield is correct, and I believe he is, it behooves us to explore the nature of
this artifact: how it is shaped, how credibility is established, how the self at the
heart of the narrative is understood. My presenting question – If the self is a text,
what genre is it? – is simply the literary form of the question of where our narratives
originate, what ideological meaning they carry, and what kinds of human
experiences are included and excluded in and by the narrative.

The *Bildungsroman* as a genre

A narrative genre can be defined as a collection of structural elements – character
types, plot lines, tones of narrative voice – that together make up an identifiable
kind of narrative, that are repeatedly drawn upon by the tellers of tales, and that are
recognizable to an audience. Whatever their formal elements, genres are deeply
ideological; as both creations and reflections of specific historical and cultural
moments, they carry elemental messages about structures of causality, available
forms of human selfhood, and the ways in which life can, should, and/or might be
lived.

As a genre, the novel has traditionally been associated with what educators of
adults call experiential learning. Rooted in autobiographical and epistolary narrative

forms, the novel both allows individual experience to serve as the structure for the plot and grants epistemological authority to that experience.[2] As "the novel of human emergence" (Bakhtin, 1986, p. 20), the *Bildungsroman* relates how people learn and grow and how the capacity for cognitive self-awareness, i.e. self-reflection, develops through experience. The typical protagonist is a young person who searches for social and personal integration in an erroneous or misguided way and whose maturation comes through painful self-knowledge. As Nancy Armstrong describes it, the *Bildungsroman* depicts how "a human subject with the restlessness to grow – over time and in successive states – [becomes] both more complete as an individual and more worthy in social terms" (2005, p. 4).

Let us take Charlotte Brontë's *Jane Eyre* as an example.

As a first-person narrator, Jane is the exemplar of an adult learner with the "restlessness to grow." Socially marginalized by poverty and orphanhood, psychically oppressed by cruelty and injustice, Jane at the same time has a restless spirit that refuses to remain unsatisfied. Raised by unloving relatives in a home in which she is "less than a servant, for you do nothing for your keep" (1847 [1997] p. 7), Jane passes through a series of experiences at the aptly named Lowood, Thornfield, and Marsh End, each of which offers a distorted version of love and/or meaningful work. The plot consists of a series of experiences, painful but always educative, through which she grows in self-awareness, learning to temper her fierceness and at the same time affirm a humanity equal to that of others. In the end, she succeeds. Having been poor, she is wealthy. Having been rejected, she is loved. Having been confined, she is free. The ultimate resolution, in which she exchanges "famine for food, expectation for content," establishes a happy balance between love and usefulness to others: "I love you better now," as Jane famously tells Rochester, "when I can be really useful to you" (p. 394). Independent wealth and a proper marriage integrate the psychic and the social and reconcile Jane's inner and outer worlds.

I am simplifying somewhat, of course. There are currents to *Jane Eyre* that are threatening, angry, and rebellious enough to have disturbed some of its first readers, who found it, among other things, "unchristian," "coarse" and "undisciplined."[3] Only a superficial reading ignores the force of rage and desire in the novel, the role of dream, myth, and fantasy, or the burnings, blindings, and castrations, both symbolic and otherwise. Ultimately, however, the price for Jane's reconciliation with society is paid elsewhere – on the Caribbean plantations that are the source of her ultimate wealth and in a secret room in the attic in which Bertha Mason, Rochester's mad first wife, is imprisoned. As the irreconcilable avatar of women's rage, Bertha is everything "intemperate" and "unchaste" that threatens Jane's ability to achieve a satisfactory narrative closure. She must literally and figuratively be burned away, a cautionary tale for a protagonist whose experiential learning has taught her the necessity, as Adrienne Rich (1979) described it, of "curbing her imagination at the limits of what is bearable" (p. 99) in a sexist and classist society. Thus, for all its realism concerning class, gender, and the psychic cost of injustice, *Jane Eyre* is a classic *Bildungsroman*; the plot traces a series of meaningful events in which the confusions and dissatisfactions of youth compel the search for something better and in which experiences are meaningful, aspiration rewarded, and desire satisfied.

I want to problematize this narrative as a model of experiential learning, but before I do so, it will be helpful to engage a second *Bildungsroman* published the same time as *Jane Eyre*. Like *Jane Eyre*, Charles Dickens' *David Copperfield* is the first-person narrative of a friendless orphan whose experiential learning leads to psychic and social reconciliation. *David Copperfield* begins with David's birth, at midnight, in the aptly named town of Blunderstone, and the first-person narrator recounts how his younger self blunders his way through a series of missteps and misjudgments. Plagued both by social marginalization and by failures of discernment, the most serious of his shortcomings is a tendency to misjudge people, a character flaw that has its most telling effects concerning the girls he falls in love with and the boys he befriends. The trajectory of experiential learning in the novel moves from "the first mistaken impulse of my undisciplined heart" (1943 [1850], p. 640) – a disastrous first marriage to the childlike Dora – to the "knowledge [that] came upon me, not quickly, but little by little" (p. 788) of what he really wants. Through a series of sometimes painful but always educative experiences, David comes into his own personally and professionally; by the end of the novel, he is a successful professional writer and a happily married man.

That David becomes a writer is significant in several ways. First, as a self-made professional, he is the iconic product of liberal individualism, self-control, and economic meritocracy (Ruth, 2006). David is a model bourgeois for whom intelligence itself is a form of capital, for whom reward is an outgrowth of intellectual labor and for whom success equates with knowing his own mind.

Second, David's status as a writer helps to keep focus on the narrative as "written memory" (p. 791). Until he writes his way into self-authorship, epistemological authority, such as it is, is in his aunt, Betsy Trotwood, who utters the line that could well be the mantra of theories of experiential learning: "It's in vain to recall the past …, unless it works some influence upon the present" (p. 336). The ability to perceive the meaning of one's experience and to recount it as a coherent story is what demonstrates that the narrator/protagonist has achieved psychic and narrative agency.

Ideology and self-narration

In *The Content of the Form,* Hayden White (1987) argues that narrative forms are not neutral; any life contains a multiplicity of events, but how we plot them and how we relate them to each other is necessarily ideological.[4] Narratives – both in the writing and the reading – are not responses *to* society but, rather, social practices *within* it, practices that impose a particular conception of society and a particular way of constituting the self.

White, among others, argues that the *Bildungsroman* narrates the emergence of a kind of individual who is well-socialized into the conditions of life as a citizen of the modern nation-state, a self-regulating individual whose desire for fulfillment and self-expression can be accommodated within the bounds of liberal capitalism. The existence of such an individual presumes particular kinds of social formations, and it is here that the *Bildungsroman* stakes out a position that is both culturally specific and ideologically conservative. In a fascinating study, Joseph Slaughter (2007) traces the relationship between the *Bildungsroman* and a particular rhetoric of human rights that holds human aspirations and social institutions to be harmonious. By legitimating individual ambition, channeling rebellion into membership in benevolent social institutions, and making the individual both the sole agent and sole beneficiary of experiential learning and personal development, the *Bildungsroman* privileges individualist solutions and portrays social institutions as supportive of the needs of ordinary people. Thus, the *Bildungsroman* is able to depict simultaneously an *un*folding of individual development and the *en*folding of the individual into social institutions and roles.

There is, to be sure, an important value embedded here, namely, the belief that civil society should protect the right to personal development. In his Oxford Amnesty Lecture in 1992, literary critic Wayne Booth echoed adult learning's celebration of 'self-authorship' by connecting the freedom to create one's own narrative with a society in which human rights are honored. Booth describes human rights as the guarantors of the individual's "freedom to pursue a story line, a life plot" (cited in Slaughter, 2007, p. 39).

How, then, is this conservative?

First, change in the *Bildungsroman* is seen as the result of individual effort. Both the world and the self are malleable, and the world is structured to both teach and reward. As in *Jane Eyre* and *David Copperfield*, self-knowledge leads in congenial and normative directions. Success is largely marked by admission into hegemonic social formations: marriage, employment, a rise in economic and/or moral status. Progress is the result of the gradual incorporation of marginalized individuals rather than the result of collective action or large-scale social change.

Second, as Ermarth (1983) has argued, the individualizing of perspective in the *Bildungsroman* rests, not on idiosyncratic perception, but on consensus, that is, on "a unity in human experience which assures us that we all inhabit the same world and that the same meanings are available to everyone" (p. 65). Social legitimation is there for the taking, if one can learn, as George Eliot wrote in *Middlemarch*, "to call things by the same names as other people call them" (2008 [1874], p. 505) and in the process learn to self-manage desire within socially legitimate possibilities (Armstrong, 2005).

The educational biography as *Bildungsroman*

In the previous chapter, I analyzed a number of exemplary autobiographical essays that are given to students and used to model the cognitive self-awareness of the consummate adult learner. These models, I argued, are both pedagogical and normative; they anticipate both the *process* – generally called critical self-reflection

– and the *product* – the resultant understanding of self that the student is meant to achieve. The explicit plot of these narratives is extremely close to what George Eliot described as a conflict "between elemental tendencies and established laws by which the outer life of man [*sic*] is gradually and painfully being brought into harmony with his inward needs" (as cited in Redinger, 1975, p. 325). Irvin Roth (1990) characterizes this same process in adult learning as a cyclical movement "between developing environmental mastery and refining our internal process" (p. 118), while Pierre Dominicé (1990) argues that "in their narratives, most adults tell how they struggled to reconcile the expectations of their social environment with their own desire to lead a unique existence" (p. 207).

It might be argued that the similarities among these quotations are not evidence of a direct relationship between the *Bildungsroman* and the life narratives of adult learning. Rather, the similarities are the effect of a shared notion of human development that is so naturalized in contemporary literate cultures that the story will inevitably be told in multiple forms. In other words, the *Bildungsroman* and the educational biography share narrative conventions because, as products of the same cultural environment, they share assumptions about the lives thus narrativized.

This sharing of assumptions, however, is precisely the point. The life narratives of adult learning carry ideological meaning in the sense discussed above, seeing the self as adaptable, the world as forgiving, and the narrator as able to achieve a more coherent socialization that is at the same time a greater personal authenticity. The protagonist/narrator will have begun as marginalized in some way, by the status of 'adult learner' if not by whichever life circumstances have motivated the return to formal education; by the end, s/he will have arrived at a new understanding and be rewarded with approbation from the social mainstream, with the college or university – I suspect our students are more aware of this than we are – serving as a stand-in for social institutions generally. Thus, the examples of student narratives cited in the previous chapter assume that reconciliation with social institutions ("more education") and individualism ("my own way in the world") are in comfortable balance. A difficult world exists in the examples by Kathleen Taylor cited earlier – a war and a draft, sexism and oppressive gender expectations, domestic violence, substance abuse and suicide – but they are there as background to the main event, the transformation that is initiated by a change in consciousness and achievable through one's own efforts.

Finally, the forms of experience that are valorized in the life narratives of adult learning closely conform to those of the *Bildungsroman*: the experience that "counts" (quite literally in the case of the assessment of prior learning) is experience that can be framed as leading to psychic and cognitive self-awareness. It is not enough to know something; one must know that one knows it and how one came to know it. Epistemological self-knowledge is the means to a variety of ends that include psychic independence and social legitimation, and the ability to tell one's story in these terms becomes evidence of a life well lived because, whatever one's "first mistaken impulse," one has arrived at a knowledge of self that equates with social legitimacy.

Life writing and narrative convention

There is evidence, not all of it anecdotal, to suggest that many adults find this form of self-narration liberatory.[5] The opportunity to write oneself into greater self-awareness aligns with many of the forms of psychic development available to the cultural mainstream, and those already on course toward individual self-exploration and self-fulfillment might well find this practice deeply empowering. It may be that our current practices of self-narration work best with students who already implicitly understand how to frame of their lives in those terms. Thus, a white, middle-class woman returning to formal learning may be primed to discover psychic freedom through this form of self-narrative because she loved *Jane Eyre* as a girl.[6]

One might speculate, similarly, that the cultural background shared by many North American adult educators is one in which Jane Eyre and David Copperfield's stories reverberate. One aspect of the nineteenth-century novel's triumph, as Peter Brooks (1984) points out, was "to plot with a good conscience" (p. 114), confident that the plot lines of the genre corresponded to the real complexities and possibilities of human life. That faith has fallen under a good bit of suspicion, and, as fiction, the naïve tale of social and psychic integration now lives largely in mass cultural genres (Slaughter, 2007). But it retains its power, especially in the US, as the dream of upward mobility through education and effort. It is a robust element of the value system within which American adult education is practiced and, I would argue, pulls that practice in the direction of particular life narratives. While some people's lives can be articulated and even enhanced by these narratives, however, they are only one of many processes through which human beings grow, learn, and change, and they are culturally and psychically restrictive in both narrative and epistemological terms.

To tell their stories in the ways we expect, students have to reproduce a highly complex narrative structure utilizing quite particular conventions that are characteristic of the *Bildungsroman*. These include the use of the past to explain the present, and *vice versa*; memory as a form of psychic coherence; and a double plot that has an echo in a split protagonist. These conventions are difficult enough in the artifact of a fictional narrative in which events and characters can be invented and even harder to do with one's own life as the necessary raw materials. Indeed, the sophistication required may have less to do with advanced cognitive development than with already being familiar with the narrative and having already internalized the plot.

The past as explanation

It may be that, as a variety of schools of recent historiography and philosophy have argued, chronological narrative is something that we impose on events as a way of ordering what would otherwise be the chaos of happenstance.[7] It is a way of insisting that life has the kind of coherence that we expect of a well-made story, or at least of living as if we believe that it does. In *Reading for the Plot*, Brooks (1984) argues that plot is "the logic and syntax of those meanings that develop only through sequence and succession" (p. 113). In this view of things, narrative itself is an explanation: the events of the past are what explain the present, while it is only from the vantage point of the present that the past can be understood (White, 1987).

Memory, psychic coherence, and the double plot

This relationship between past and present explains the centrality of memory both to the structure of the narrative and the evolution of the protagonist. Mistakes in the *Bildungsroman* tend to be a function of insufficient experience of the world, and happy endings are the result of the accumulation of memories of relevant experience. As Nicholas Dames (2001) points out, however, the *Bildungsroman* does not depict memory so much as it portrays the struggle to transform the seeming randomness and disorder of 'real' memory into retrospective order. This, however, requires that one's memories are amenable to psychic integration, that they are appropriately shared among relative strangers, and that they are conducive to cognitive stability and clarity.

Moreover, producing a semblance of retrospective coherence requires that two parallel narratives be told simultaneously: the forward-looking narrative of life incidents and the (sometimes explicit, sometimes implicit) backward-looking narrative of the coming into meaning. Arguably, this quality is even more exaggerated in the narrative practices of adult learning than it is in the *Bildungsroman* because the second narrative is being enacted as curriculum. The (not always unsung) hero of the tale is the educator who poses the question and gives the assignment. No wonder we are so enamored of this plot.

The split protagonist

Although first-person narrators are, by definition, writing about themselves, the two parallel plots of the narrative – the process of living through experiences and the process of remembering them – have what are virtually separate protagonists: the past self versus the present self, the remembered versus the remembering self, and the self that is written about versus the self that writes. These multiple splittings of the self must be lined up, so that the self that is written about is the remembered self of experience, while the self that writes is the self that remembers and reflects. These two selves, in turn, are expected to display a particular kind of personality, or, rather two kinds of personalities. While the remembered self can have all kinds of failures of insight and meaning-making – indeed, the greater the failures, the greater the potential for forward movement – the remembering self must be epistemologically sure-footed and capable of cogent moral and intellectual clarity. S/he must be able to perceive order in what, to the protagonist of the first narrative, was only a random series of events. S/he must be able to articulate, not only what has been learned, but what has been learned about the process of having learned it. And s/he must experience the coming to coherence within the self as a form of liberation that is both social and personal.

It is here, moreover, that students bear the brunt of the ways in which adult learning theory conflates oversimplified cognitive models – Kolb's learning cycle is a good example – for the complexities of how knowledge is gained and used in the world. As I argued in Chapter nine, there is much evidence to suggest, for example, that the actual process of learning from experience is quite different from our favored models, that more expert practitioners are *less* deliberate and systematic about the knowledge they draw from than the inexperienced. Moreover, the association of cognitive clarity with psychic coherence and a rewarding life might, these days, be seen as naïve, if not disturbingly misinformed. And it is certainly arguable that being *less* sure of things than one used to be is the better part of epistemological valor, at least in this current world, if not in any world.

Finally, this narrative treats as universal a human experience that is possible only within quite specific historical circumstances. Self-realization is a social process; one cannot participate in what Slaughter calls "the empancipatory plot-logic of progressive linear improvement" (2007, p. 110) under all historical conditions. The expectation that our students can represent themselves in these terms belies the conditions of life in which most people, many of them our students, live out their lives as social beings. For students whose life experience includes conditions of exile, isolation, terror, or even such 'everyday' oppressions of gender, race, nationality, sexual orientation, appearance, and class, self-representation as a newly coherent, socially integrated being all too often leaves the bulk of one's history on the cutting room floor.

Magical realism as the anti-*Bildungsroman*

Among the genres that took the place of the *Bildungsroman* in the intellectual life of the twentieth century, the novels of magical realism have a particular pride of place. Just as the *Bildungsroman* was the product of emerging capitalist individualism in Europe, magical realism is an expression of the political culture of emerging postcolonial settings. The different points of origin, in turn, are closely related to the kinds of experiences that can be depicted in each genre, the patterns of social inclusion and exclusion, and the ideological tropes for what constitutes cognitive and social agency. The truth claims of conventional realism, as we have seen, rest on the reader's confidence that the world portrayed is recognizable to ordinary human perception. Magical realism subverts this through a deadpan recounting of events that we know couldn't 'really' happen, thus destabilizing our sense of what the world is like (Slemon, 1995; Faris, 2004).

In what follows, therefore, I want to tease out what the shift from the *Bildungsroman* to magical realism might mean for self-narratives in adult learning. I mean the word "tease" in both senses; I am not suggesting a change of genres so much as I am asking for a bit of serious play. To do so, I will briefly explore two works of twentieth-century fiction, one an explicit retelling of *Jane Eyre*, the other an implicit reworking of *David Copperfield*.

Magical realism makes the claim that is what is ordinary in one cultural or historical circumstance is fantastic in another, and *vice versa*, a claim that has both political and epistemological implications. Because it disconnects the novel from philosophical traditions historically associated with the West, magical realism, for all its whimsy, has a clear relationship both to the experiences of marginalized peoples and to the official historical record, It both expresses the experience of those whose worlds have been "fissured, distorted, and made incredible by cultural displacement" (Boehmer, as cited in Hart, 2005, p. 6) and challenges the ways in which languages, ways of seeing, and justificatory truth claims were imposed on indigenous populations in the colonized world and oppressed populations in the West.[8] The inability to separate reality from fantasy has an explicit political meaning in societies in which the official record erases or denies the crimes perpetrated by governments against their own people and/or rewrites history and current events to the advantage of the powerful; one cannot claim to learn from experiences that the official record denies ever happened, or, rather, one cannot do so in social contexts in which the official record has authority.

Like Bertha Mason imprisoned in the attic in *Jane Eyre*, the existence of the colonial world is a troubling undercurrent in the nineteenth and early twentieth-century *Bildungsroman*. In *Wide Sargasso Sea* (1966), white Caribbean novelist Jean Rhys set out to trace that undercurrent by retelling the story of *Jane Eyre*, or, rather, the marriage of Bertha Mason and Rochester, as a first-person narrative told from their two points of view. In Rhys's hands, the story becomes one of Bertha driven mad by the psychosocial dynamics of colonialism and patriarchy and Rochester driven to heartless cruelty by the breakdown of the boundaries through which his life is defined. Bertha (her real name in Rhys's work, Antoinette, is one of the things taken from her by Rochester) is the daughter of a mother who is psychically destroyed by grief, male power, and fine distinctions of rank in the aftermath of slavery. But she is also the product of a world of beauty and sensuality, vividly colored and scented flowers, and racial complexity. To Rochester, that world is fantastic, threatening, because the geographical and psychic landscapes are too "wild and menacing" (p. 63) and the defining dualities of class, gender, and race are insufficiently monitored. On one level, *Wide Sargasso Sea* is the story of social inequality – deeply engrained racism, the economic vulnerability of younger sons, the utter powerlessness of married women whose husbands now control their money and property. On another level, it is the story of the refusal of experience, the inability to open oneself to a world of complexity and beauty in which the defining dualities of White and Black, English and patois, sanity and madness are not firm and in which "there is always another side" (p. 166).

Seen in the terms I have been tracing in this book, *Wide Sargasso Sea* is an anti-*Bildungsroman* in which experience is rejected as insufficiently amenable to control by wealthy European masculine rationality. Rochester declares himself "calm" and "self-possessed" (p. 115) when he is being cold and hateful; having freed himself from "all the mad conflicting emotions," he presents himself as "quiet and composed" (p. 144) when he turns from a vapid fortune-hunter to a monster without a heart. Having closed himself off from nature and the body and embraced the role of the white European master, Rochester locks Bertha away because she "belonged to the magic and the loveliness" (p. 156). He exits the narrative explicitly rejecting the educative truth of experience and looking forward to Bertha being "only a memory to be avoided, locked away, and, like all memories a legend. Or a lie ..." (p. 156).

What, then, might this suggest about the narratives assigned in our classrooms? First, it might give us pause to consider that the narrative values we promote in our practices are unsettlingly close to those of Rochester, valorizing the imposition of order on what is visceral, emotional, and insufficiently subject to control. Second, we might note that Rhys's characters are the denizens of a world whose contradictions and inequities are not resolvable within auto-biographical narrative because closure and coherence require the walling off of memory. Third, we might read *Wide Sargasso Sea* as suggesting that there is no such thing as a 'free' individual, that all of us are the products of a constraining history – in the case of this novel, that of the slave trade and its ending, the colonization of the Americas and its effect on the class and family structure of England, and the evolving legal framework of marriage and gender inequality.

This last point, the relationship between individual experience and history, can be seen more clearly if we engage a second iconic twentieth-century text that has achieved the status of a classic of world literature. Salman Rushdie's (1981) *Midnight's Children* takes its title from the 1,001 Indian children who, we are told, were born between midnight and one AM on August 15, 1947, the first hour of India's independence as a nation. Born at precisely midnight and thus sharing a moment of birth with his country, the narrator/protagonist, Saleem Sinai, is "mysteriously handcuffed to history" (p. 9). He is also inextricably tied to midnight's other children who, as they grow up, begin to meet telepathically in a conference that is convened in Saleem's head. Saleem's relationship to the 1000 other children is further complicated by his having been switched shortly after birth with another infant, so that, from the beginning of his life, he is actually someone else.

Saleem's midnight birth is one of the many tropes in *Midnight's Children* that ties individual destiny to the broader historical context. At the same time, it is worth noting that David Copperfield was also born at midnight. Rushdie's novel is, among other things, a kind of anti-*David Copperfield*, a narrative that dismantles both the world and the self that made Dickens's narrative possible. Rushdie has a field day with all of the conventions that define the *Bildungsroman*: the stability of the self, the centrality of the protagonist, the chronological discovery of pattern and meaning, and the existence of a recognizable world about which consensus is possible.

From the first, Saleem's attempt to construct a coherent individual identity is rendered impossible by circumstance: "If I seem a little bizarre, remember the wild profusion of my inheritance ... perhaps, if one wishes to remain an individual in the midst of the teeming multitudes, one must make oneself grotesque" (p. 109; ellipsis in original). Saleem's attempts to discover meaning and purpose are a send-up of the narrative structure of the *Bildungsroman*, in which events in the world are shaped around the protagonist's need for meaningful experience:

> at the end of 1947, life in Bombay was as teeming, as manifold, as multitudinously shapeless as ever ... except that I had arrived; I was already beginning to take my place at the centre of the universe; and by the time I had finished, I would give meaning to it all.
>
> *(Rushdie, 1981, pp. 126–7; ellipsis in original)*

Rushdie is devastating in lampooning the "aha" moment that is so conventional in narratives of adult learning, the moment of perceiving the pattern and meaning of one's existence:

> I struggled alone, to understand what had happened to me, until at least I saw the shawl of genius fluttering down, like an embroidered butterfly, the mantle of greatness settling upon my shoulders. ... I was gripped by hot fingers of excitement ... because finally ... I could glimpse – shadowy still, undefined, enigmatic – my reason for having been born.
>
> *(Rushdie, 1981, p. 163)*

For all the humor, however, Rushdie offers an important challenge to the concept of individual self-exploration and self-authorship; any attempt to construct an individual life narrative is impossible because we are always too bound up in history, so that "to understand one life, you have to swallow the world" (p. 109).

If Saleem's experience is too tied to that of others to be contained within the individual, it is also too fragmented to provide coherence or wholeness. The Double I of the *Bildungsroman*, which allows the narrator to write about his/her younger self from the point of view of psychic wholeness, gives way to a narrator whose "poor body, ... buffeted by too much history, ... , has started coming apart at the seams" (p. 37). Nor can he impose coherence on a story that refuses to cohere; as he watches the cracks appear in his hands, along his hairline, and between his toes, the older Saleem is condemned "to see my own life – its meanings, its structures – in fragments also" (p. 107).

Telling a coherent story of one's life is, finally, impossible in *Midnight's Children* because the world itself is fractured, most clearly in the Partition of India and Pakistan, but also by a world in which truth has been corrupted by politics: "[I]n a country where the truth is what it is instructed to be, reality quite literally ceases to exist" (p. 326).[9] For all these reasons, Saleem cannot achieve narrative or personal coherence both because "I have been so-many too-many persons" and because, as both victim and master of his times, he will instead "be sucked into the annihilating whirlpool of the multitudes" (p. 463).

Magical realism and experiential learning

While there are aspects of magical realism that would be difficult to reconcile with the adult learning classroom, it seems to me likely that the lives of many of our learners conform more to Saleem's narrative than to David Copperfield's. Cultural and geographic dislocation, economic destabilization, war and violence, the upending of expectations, and many other all-too-common contemporary realities mean that the world often does not allow for, let alone reward, a coherent experience of self.

For most people, it probably never did. The construction of a stable social identity grounded in psychic coherence and rewarded with social legitimacy has always been the artifact of a particular, historically restricted form of meritocratic citizenship. In many cases, it has served as a necessary and even helpful fiction, but only – tautologically – for those whom it helps. My concern is for the many students who 'fail' to complete an autobiographical narrative that conforms to our assumptions, reinscribes our favored narrative, and can be recognized in our terms.

What magical realism posits is not the refusal to learn from experience *per se*, but the insistence that there is something in experience that, in a multifarious and unjust world, cannot be captured by hegemonic, normative, and transparent narratives of self. It allows for the exploration of hybrid ways of being and the depiction of liminal spaces that are not easily captured – and I use the word advisedly – in a narrative of unitary selfhood. To take one example, the socialization of immigrants is a story that can be made to conform to the *Bildungsroman* theme of social demarginalization: "In order to find myself, I had to reject my parents' cultural values and come into my own as a citizen of a new country." Alternatively, "I grew up being encouraged by the broader society to look down on my own language and culture, but I have found a more empowered and authentic self by re-claiming my roots." I have no doubt that there are many such narratives being reproduced in our classrooms, but I also suspect that the truth is more complex. In a world of border crossers of many different kinds, disordered, in-between spaces are the norm, and experience there both teaches careful balancing acts and precipitates free falls and hard landings. There is much to say about and much to be learned within such spaces, but they require a different narrative.

As a way to entertain what those different narratives might look like, we might begin with Rushdie's dual metaphors of fragmentation and engulfment. On the one hand, as I have argued here, our practices presuppose the unified self of the *Bildungsroman* in which the only split is between the past and the present and in which the relationship between older and newer selves is fundamentally pedagogical. Other kinds of life narratives might allow for a more disquieting – or a more playful – exploration of selves that are "as teeming, as manifold, as multitudinously shapeless" (p. 126) as life in Bombay in 1947. On the other hand, if we take seriously the notion that "to understand a single life, you have to devour the world" (p. 109), we might structure assignments that allow for the more contingent and historically determined self of magical realism. Rather than imposing the expectation that life narratives somehow free us from historicity, alternative narratives might explore the ways in which individual lives have been "buffeted by too much history" (p. 37) and shaped by forces that are both global and historical.

We might, for example, ask students to write about an experience that they thought they understood at the time but that has seemed more and more complex and confusing as time has gone by. We might ask them to identify a moment of experiential learning that has not made life more intelligible, more authentic, or more empowered, but that left them, like Saleem, "perplexed by meaning" (p. 153). We might ask them about something that happened once that made them themselves instead of someone else they might have been, not because they were shaped by an undue socialization from which we can now help them liberate themselves, but because they are necessarily creatures of a history that both enables and constrains.

I must admit to offering even these alternatives with reluctance because they again assume that we know what questions to ask to give our students greater range of motion and vision. Lurking just behind that assumption is the conviction that we can help them find a truth that is more insightful, or clear-headed, or democratic, at which point Daloz's andragogical missionary is back in business. At the same time, the broadening of approaches to life narrative beyond the *Bildungsroman* has to begin somewhere, and the "swirling universe" (p. 165) of magical realism might be a place to start.

Notes

1   For a now-classic treatment of the self as text, see Geertz (1985). For a more extended discussion that includes the ways in which experience is textualized, see Bruner (1990).

2   See Webb (1981); Watt (1959); and Ermarth (1983).

3   The felt unseemliness of the narrative voice was among the reasons why many of its first readers refused to believe that *Jane Eyre* had been written by a woman. For the now-classic study of *Jane Eyre* as a study in gendered rage and entrapment, including the relationship between Jane and Bertha Mason, see Gilbert and Gubar (1979). For a discussion of the novel's initial reception, including these citations, see Gilbert and Gubar, pp. 337–8. For a discussion of the debate concerning the gender of the author of *Jane Eyre*, see Levine (2000).

4   There is now an extensive literature on the ideological effects of narrative. For important and representative texts, see Eagleton (2006) and Jameson (1981). For an extensive exploration of the psychic and ideological effects of novels, see Cottom (1987); Armstrong (2005); and Davis (1987).

5   See, for example, Brown (2002); Dominicé (2000); and Randall (1996).

6   For discussions of the effects of such novels on people who grow up reading them, see Brownstein (1994) and Davis (1987).

7   For a helpful introduction to a range of theorists, see White (1987).

8   The ways in which magical realism associate the magical with postcolonial cultures has been challenged in recent years by critics who see this as reinscribing the association of the non-Western Other with the irrational. For discussions of this point, see Faris (2004). For a more general discussion of political debates concerning the term 'magical realism,' see Ouyang (2005).

9   Andrei Codrescu, a Romanian writer who has written multiple autobiographies makes a similar point: "In places where history has been falsified by the authorities, people are hard put to remember their true experiences" (1994, p. 22).

12

THE GHOSTS OF WAR

Trauma, narrative, and adult learning

Out goon the swerdes as the silver brighte;
The helmes they tohewen and toshrede;
Out brest the blood with stierne stremes rede;
With myghty maces the bones they tobreste.
He thurgh the thikkeste of the throng gan threste.

[Out go the swords as bright as silver,
Hewing and shredding the helmets;
Out burst the blood in violent red streams;
They broke bones with mighty maces.
He thrust through the thickest of the throng.]

Geoffrey Chaucer, *The Canterbury Tales*, I 2608–12

In the previous two chapters, I have focused on autobiographical practices in adult learning, taking a critical stance toward what I read as a rather single-minded insistence on learners finding positive interpretations of the events of their lives. I have argued that, however much we stress the uniqueness of our students' narratives, we are wedded as a professional community to one particular plot line, an uplifting trajectory that recounts the retrospective finding of coherence and meaning in what appeared to be the happenstance of life. While I explored narrative versus humanistic psychology to a small degree in Chapter ten, I have thus far drawn largely on literary and narrative theory and spoken in terms of genre, character, and plot.

In what follows, I want to develop that analysis further by returning to particular schools of psychology that have powerfully influenced theories of adult learning. I want to explore the notion of adult learning as therapy and problematize the common belief among adult educators in the therapeutic benefits to adult students of 're-storying' their lives. I will focus on one group of those students, namely, military veterans, who are currently appearing on our campuses and in our virtual classrooms with ever-increasing frequency. In focusing on veterans, I do not mean to privilege their experience over that of other survivors of what Shoshana Felman has justly named a "posttraumatic century" (1995, p. 13), but rather to engage them as a helpful case in point. By problematizing the insistence on coherence, meaning, and (relatively) happy endings and by rendering more explicit the ideological implications of psychological approaches and narrative forms, veterans both raise the stakes and heighten the contradictions in our practices. In so doing, they problematize our assumptions concerning the role of life narrative in psychic healing.

Adult learning as therapy

The influence of psychology on the field of adult learning is a vast topic that awaits sustained attention beyond the scope of this chapter. Various schools of adult learning draw, not only on humanistic and narrative psychology, but also on developmental psychology, ego psychology, cognitive psychology, and a newer, particularly American approach known as positive psychology. Given this range and the ways in which psychological discourse permeates adult learning, it is sometimes difficult to say where adult learning theory ends and psychology begins.

In North America and, to a lesser degree, elsewhere, the most prominent use of psychology in adult learning theory is through the influence of Carl Rogers and Abraham Maslow on the "andragogy" of Malcolm Knowles. Offering a view of the individual as struggling between fearfulness and the desire to grow, humanistic psychology sees learning in adulthood as a process of achieving "the full use of talents, capacities, potentialities" (Maslow, cited in Knowles *et al.*, 2011, p. 14) and thus becoming "fully functional" in Rogers's terms and "self-actualized" in Maslow's (Knowles *et al.*, 2011, p. 47). Adult learning and psychotherapy are seen as closely intertwined; therapy is a "learning process" (Rogers, cited in Knowles *et al.*, 2011, p. 49), while learning is in its essence a psychological quest for meaning. Adults choose to learn that which will help maintain or enhance their sense self and support a growing sense of mastery, self-respect, and self-confidence.

To be sure, the psychic certainties that characterize this approach have been destabilized in the four decades since Knowles' classic work, *The Adult Learner: A Neglected Species* (1973 [1990]), first appeared. The individualism and essentialism in his work, the implicit androcentrism and classism in his notion of the unencumbered individual, and the lack of attention to collective aspiration have all been challenged,[1] and, as we have seen, more recent theorists give at least lip service to the influence of postmodernism and constructivism on our notions of learning.[2] At the same time, the romantic humanistic quest for autonomy and authenticity has survived the intellectual discrediting of the belief that, under layers of socialization, a unitary, singular, heroic Self struggles to break free of its constraints.

In the past several decades, narrative psychology has taken the place of humanistic psychology as a lay adult educator's medium for inserting the therapeutic into the pedagogical. Like humanistic psychology, narrative psychology is an available, relatively jargon-free way of understanding the process of rethinking values and assumptions and affirming the possibility of alternative futures lived with greater intentionality. Unlike humanistic psychology, moreover, narrative psychology is at home with constructivist notions of selfhood. Seeing learning and growth as taking place, "not in the fastness of immediate private consciousness but in a cultural-historical situation" (Bruner, 1990, p. 100), narrative psychology moves beyond overly simplistic humanistic notions that hold that "man [*sic*] always and only learns by himself" (Jourard, cited in Knowles *et al.*, 2011, p. 15) and makes authenticity-enhancing choices "in accordance with his own nature" (Maslow, cited in Knowles *et al.*, p. 48). In positing the self as an historical product that emerges through time and narrative, narrative psychology sees experience as always already mediated by the plot lines, character types, and themes that are available to a culture at a given point in time.

Arguably, then, narrative psychology offers a more finely tuned instrument for understanding adult development and adult learning. First, because it permits a greater appreciation for historicity and sociality, it moderates, not only the entrenched individualism, but what might be called the grandiosity of humanistic psychology. Secondly, while recognizing the possibility of choosing among different life narratives and, with them, alternative possible selves, it draws on traditions of depth psychology that acknowledge the complexity of desire and repression and the limits to self-knowledge. The goal of narrative psychology is thus both more modest and more credible that that of humanistic psychology: to construct "a version of the story that makes change conceivable and attainable" (Shaffer, as cited in Bruner, 1990, p. 113) rather than to discover the "wholeness … and uniqueness of Self" (Maslow, as cited in Knowles *et al.*, 2011, p. 14).

As with humanistic psychology, however, narrative approaches to adult learning conflate the therapeutic with the pedagogical. That adults come back to formal education in times of transition, according to Randall (2004), "lends a therapeutic component to our work" (p. 239). Citing Hillman to the effect that successful therapy is "a revisioning of the story into a more intelligent, more imaginative plot" (Ibid.), Randall represents the roles of therapists and educators as parallel: providing a safe environment, helping learners to revisit their self-narratives and claim authorship of their own stories, and becoming catalysts for new ways of storying the self.

One of the problems with this approach is that the point of the narrative quickly moves from exploring the past to rewriting it. In other words, the story being privileged is not the story of a life *per se*. Rather, it is what Gergen calls an "*a priori* narrative" (2004, p. 210) that tells the story of coming to understand that things are not as bad as they once seemed, that a new spin on events lets one understand the past differently, and that reframing the past makes one freer, happier, more empowered.

> Though the events of the past can clearly not be changed, our perception of them can. The remembered past – the past, not as it happened but as we have internalized it, textualized it, stored it in memory… is anything but fixed. Rather, it admits of endless reworking, endless restorying.
>
> *(Randall, 2010, p. 30)*

The advent of positive psychology

I want to suggest that an eliding of different schools of psychology is at work here, from narrative psychology to positive psychology. Rooted in the post-Calvinist New Thought movement, the capitalist boosterism of popular writers such as Norman Vincent Peale and Dale Carnegie, and the religious thought of individuals as disparate as Mary Baker Eddy and William James (Ehrenreich, 2009), positive psychology promotes the "building blocks" of positive ways of being as "optimism, gratitude, mindfulness, hope, spirituality (Max, 2007).

In recent years, the literature on narrative in adult learning has become replete with the message of positive psychology:

> [I]t is a matter of constructing a narrative for ourselves that enables us to deal with an experience. An example here would be responding to an illness by constructing a narrative of restoration and hope, as opposed to a narrative of victimization, struggle, or loss.
>
> *(Clark and Rossiter, 2008, p. 62)*

> As the arthritis in my knee worsened, my life plot changed. In narrative terms I was in a new story, a disability narrative of apprehension, self-doubt, and an overarching theme of "I can't." Once I fell it became a narrative that enveloped not just my body but also my mind; I was too overwhelmed to ask myself, "What story am I in?" and so wasn't able to consider other possible plots.
>
> *(Clark, 2010, p. 9)*

> Some of us chronically construe our past in a negative light. … (H)indsight is enlisted to marshal evidence that we have always been a victim, a failure, a chump. … Conversely, equipped with a sunnier disposition, or with a personality more open to experience to begin with, we will find a way to redeem past pains and disappointments, to regenerate the negatives of our lives into positives.
>
> *(Randall, 2010, p. 31)*

There is, of course, much to be said for mustering optimism in the face of difficulty. At its best, positive psychology promotes the skills of surviving and thriving: tenacity, courage, and hope. It is, however, easily reducible to the facile notion that we can change our lives simply by changing our stories about them. This, in turn, has political implications; by framing life circumstances as less important to happiness than qualities of temperament and belief, it contributes on the conservative side to debates concerning social supports and level playing fields.[3] That is attractive both to those who want to deny the material realities of inequality and injustice and to those who hold to the particularly American insistence that a good attitude is the cure for most bad things.

Currently, positive psychology is being used as a method of choice for addressing psychic wounds among active duty soldiers. In a program known as Comprehensive Soldier Fitness (CSF), the attempt is being made to teach 'resiliency,' 'posttraumatic growth,' and 'learned optimism' to troops in an attempt to help them interpret their experiences more positively and make more optimistic assessments of their current circumstances and options. Martin Seligman, the founder of positive psychology, argues that our human propensity for psychic dis-ease stems from our genetic inheritance; in our ancestral environment of predator-infested savannahs, the expectation that something bad was about to happen was of evolutionary benefit. Now, however, when the possibility of being attacked by a tiger is less of a problem for most of us, we would do far better to "look at more optimistic and realistic choices, rather than falling into negative thought processes" (CSF director Brigadier General Rhonda Cornum, cited in Coleman, 2009, http://www.alternet.org/world/144343/).

The claim that 'posttraumatic growth' follows combat stress rests on the inspiring but unsurprising observation that some people are changed for the better following traumatic events. Positive psychology transforms that piece of time-honored wisdom into an empirical claim concerning "five domains of growth that trauma survivors may report: renewed appreciation of life, new possibilities, enhanced personal strength, improved relationships with others, and spiritual change" (Tedeschi and McNally, 2011, p. 19). Evidence for the existence of posttraumatic growth includes a study claiming that 61 percent of the American aviators shot down, imprisoned, and tortured by the North Vietnamese reported their experiences as psychologically beneficial because they led to "favorable changes in their personalities" (Ibid., p. 20). Similar benefits are said to accrue in our more recent wars; one of the authors of the above-cited article told the American Enterprise Institute in 2009 that even veterans who had lost limbs or been otherwise devastatingly wounded had found their new lives so much more meaningful that "they were glad the events happened to them" (Tedeschi, cited in Coleman, 2009). CSF is a controversial program for many reasons,[4] one of which is its inappropriateness to some of the situations faced by military personnel. It is at least arguable that a propensity toward watchfulness might actually be of benefit when on patrol in Kandahar Province and that teaching military personnel living in a war zone *not* to assume the worst provides dubious advantages at best.

It is, of course, all too easy to ridicule the more outrageous and/or vacuous aspects of positive psychology, and it is in nobody's interest to sneer at the ways in which the human spirit does sometimes win out over adversity. Two points are worth making, however, in that they relate to patterns already at play in the literature on narrative and adult learning. First, because positive psychology locates the response to trauma in the individual, the tendency to blame those who fail to exhibit 'posttraumatic growth' is difficult to avoid; the long, painful history of the military's search for what has been called the 'bullet-proof mind' is matched by an equally long and painful history of blaming those who fail to develop one (Coleman, 2009). Secondly, positive psychology emphasizes the production of a transformational narrative in which traumatic events provide a "fulcrum" or "turning point" that leads to posttraumatic growth (Tedeschi and McNally, 2011, p. 22). Our own focus on what is variously called the "trigger event" (Mezirow, 1990a, p. 14) or "critical incident" (Brookfield, 1990, p. 177) and our disappointment with students who "refuse to grow" (Daloz, 1988) predispose practitioners of adult learning to view traumatic incidents in a similar way. Irene Karpiak, for example, locates her fascination with narrative as arising in a graduate class in which a fellow student's autobiographical chapter titles included "Before P.O.W." and "After P.O.W." (2010, p. 14).

Karpiak, whose students at the University of Oklahoma include those on military bases, frames autobiography as a "movement toward possibility" (2010, p. 13). Writing in an issue *of New Directions for Adult and Continuing Education* devoted to narratives in adult learning, she argues that the goal of autobiographical writing is "to reassemble the scattered elements of [an] individual life and to regroup them in a comprehensive sketch." In the process, the writer finds new meaning and clarity, "some depth or some possibility that up until now has been unrecognized and unexpressed" (p. 19).

What is interesting about Karpiak's writing is the discrepancy between what she says about her students and the ways in which she represents them theoretically. Karpiak is clearly a gifted educator; she makes it evident that, given encouragement to tell the stories of their lives, students often narrate experiences that are not easily represented in simplistically uplifting ways, and she relates with deep appreciation and compassion student narratives "of deployment, war, and the struggles of family reunification" in addition to those of neglect and abuse, the death of siblings and children, and the ravages of poverty and bigotry (p. 17). Her appreciation for the imperfect lives thus recorded, her love for her students, and her gratitude at their openness come through in ways that, very much to her credit, belie any limited and constraining theoretical frame.

Karpiak's examples of student writing, however, include only those that fit snugly into the narrative of positive psychology. A student named Angela, for example, records her initial despair and terror concerning the realities of Army life, only to continue:

> As I started to warm up to the place things started to work out. I began to realize that [the Fort] was really not a bad place and there were some good things about it. Yes I hated running five days a week but looking on the bright side it kept me in great physical condition. I hated taking orders but the more accepting and less challenging I became military life just got better. I began seeing myself more like a soldier.
>
> *(Karpiak, 2010, p. 19)*

Another woman soldier, Rhonda, frames her autobiography as a story

> about the inner resolve of a learner, a person who never thought she would
> ever be worth anything. A person who believed she was a loser but found
> hope to rise above hopelessness and become a winner.
>
> *(Karpiak, 2010, p. 19)*

The tension between Karpiak's openhanded appreciation for her students' complex lives and the use of examples that belie that complexity suggests a felt need to conform to a set theoretical frame concerning self-reflection, the discovery of meaning, and the bracing effects of autobiographical practice. This is disturbing, especially in the case of students, veterans included, whose experiences may not be amenable to such a frame. To take an admittedly provocative example, Angela and Rhonda are apparently not among the 20 percent or more of servicewomen who have been raped or sexually abused by their fellow soldiers,[5] or, if they were, did not choose to share that experience in a venue in which "looking on the bright side" and "becom(ing) a winner" were prized. Given the statistics concerning posttraumatic stress injuries, military sexual violence, and traumatic brain injuries among contemporary veterans, we need to rethink the image of educators helping veterans write themselves into psychic restoration through 'restorying' the past.

The point is not, or not only, that we too often structure our narrative practices in ways that encourage triumphalist endings. It is also that, in our own retelling of our students' writing, we continually bring a triumphalist interpretation to bear. In a deeply moving but, I think, revealing fashion, Judith Beth Cohen and Deborah Piper (2000) tell the story of Ben, a student in a baccalaureate program for adults that combines autobiographical with academic writing and independent study with regular nine-day residencies. Their program is an impressive one in which students have the space to think, interact with peers and mentors, revisit their lives and interests, and plan individualized degrees. Cohen and Piper frame their discussion in terms of recovering a lost self and "reauthorizing [one's] own narrative" (p. 214). One student says, "I found the voice I never used." Another says, "I tapped into a part of myself that had been asleep for so long" (p. 205).

Ben is a Vietnam veteran whose experience of war is tied up with his feelings about an absentee father and his conflicted, reified beliefs concerning masculinity. His life since Vietnam has included substance abuse, shame about his service in the war, the belief that he cannot speak of his experiences to others, and a sense of being "marked by something I could never shed" (p. 224). Before entering the program, the authors tell us, Ben had "neither examined his experience nor put it in any context. Life seemed like a series of accidents, unconnected fragments without a shape" (p. 220). In the course of the program, Ben finally admits that "things happened that I didn't want to be part of" (p. 220), revisits notions of gender, and integrates his experience in Vietnam within both personal and historical contexts. "Wholeness," the authors tell us, "became a metaphor Ben took away from the residency that gave him an image for connecting the pieces of his own history.

What had seemed like a random series of events now began to take shape, revealing new interpretations" (p. 219). Cohen and Piper acknowledge that old patterns in Ben's life continue to plague him and that no educational experience completely transforms a complex life such as his. In the end, however, the quasi-therapeutic process of self-reconciliation has succeeded in making "the protagonist of his narrative … a softer, more reflective man" (p. 225).

Read aloud, as the authors describe it, "in a darkened room … in a shaky voice," Ben's own narrative is the story of a nineteen-year-old's lost youth and of subsequent alienation in which "the most difficult thing about Vietnam was coming home" (p. 224). Cohen and Piper's interpretation, however, stresses the psychic reconciliation and release of creative energy that come of Ben's "put[ting] the war behind him" (p. 225). Thus, Ben's tale – or, rather, their tale *about* Ben's tale – is transformed into one in which meaning and coherence obtain.

Sadly, in my own life, I am familiar with the narratives of Vietnam veterans who learned the hard way that "the Vietnam War wasn't going to leave [them] just because [they] left it" (Garcia, as cited in Coleman, 2006, p. 61). The ongoing issues that characterize Ben's life – substance abuse, emotional isolation, shame – are typical of such veterans. Theirs are often stories of the end of meaning, the end of coherence, of horrific, visceral memories of which no sense can be made. Any resolution, solace, or historical insight that Ben has achieved is of deep human importance, and any contribution made by the practices of adult learning is something of which to be proud. At the same time, I cannot help but wonder what is gained by framing Ben's story as the achievement of psychic coherence. Or, perhaps more to the point, what is lost? Of course Ben needs in his own life to seek to reconcile himself to history, and the yearning for wholeness may well serve as his metaphor. But we – our professional and human community – need rather to remember that some things can never be made whole.[6]

Trauma, memory, and experiential learning

The psychological literature on narrative and trauma provides a very different analysis of the relationship of experience, narrative, and healing.[7] According to experts such as Robert J. Lifton, Jonathan Shay, Judith Herman, Shoshana Felman, and Dori Laub, trauma destabilizes all of the constituent parts of what we commonly understand as life narrative – experience, chronology, and meaning among them – and creates what Cathy Caruth calls "pathologies of memory" (1995c, p. 152). When that is the case, the 'meaning' of life histories slips inevitably between the cracks of a redemption narrative. The psychic coherence on which such narratives rest is precisely what has been made impossible. "It don't mean nothin'," the legendary response of US soldiers to horrific events in Vietnam, becomes true in a newly literal sense.

Robert J. Lifton (2005), a scholar and psychiatrist who has worked with Vietnam veterans for decades, identifies "all-encompassing absurdity and moral inversion" as the "predominant emotional tone" of his group sessions with veterans (p. 37). "Here in Vietnam," one veteran invokes the present tense as he remembers, they're actually shooting people for no reason. … Any other time you think, it's such an extreme. Here you can go ahead and shoot them for nothing. … As a matter of fact it's even … smiled upon, you know. Good for you. Everything is backwards. That's part of the kind of unreality of the thing.

(Lifton, 2005, p. 36)

According to Lifton, the veterans in his groups

express a sense of the war's total lack of order or structure. … We may say that there was no genuine 'script' or 'scenario' of war that could provide meaning or even sequence or progression, a script within which armies clash, battles are fought, won, or lost, and individual suffering, courage, cowardice, or honor can be evaluated.

(Lifton, 2005, p. 37)

In narrative terms, the very thing that is missing is a coherent plot. Jonathan Shay, like Lifton a scholar and psychiatrist who works extensively with veterans, argues in a similar fashion that "traumatic memory *is not narrative*" (1995, p. 172; my italics) because neither chronology nor coherence obtains.

First, traumatic events are such that they cannot be experienced in the conventional sense of the term. On the one hand, they can be impossible to absorb at the time at which they occur; on the other, they are typically re-experienced in the form of flashback or dreams. Judith Herman (1992) describes the psychic injury of war as characterized by an oscillating emotional rhythm in which the mind attempts to integrate horrific memories in order to achieve psychic equilibrium but at the same time blocks the integration of those memories, setting up a self-protective reflex to keep the intolerable at bay.

Second, the belief in experiential learning that is so central to narrative practice in adult learning presupposes that experience is reliable, that is, that one's perceptions can be trusted. Shay (1995), however, notes that the felt unreliability of perception, and thus the untrustworthiness of experience, is at the heart of combat-related psychic wounds. Drawing on his own work with veterans, he recounts the ways in which camouflage, ambush, and other forms of deception, betrayal, and surprise undermine the ability of the individual to believe what he or she has seen. This distrust becomes intractable when, as all too often happens, the experience in question is subsequently denied by those in military and civil authority whose attempts to cover up unpleasant events serve to erase or deny soldiers' experience. In a fashion oddly parallel to events in many novels of magical realism,[8] soldiers are told "You didn't experience it, it never happened, you don't know what you know" (pp. 171–172).

Finally, trauma interrupts the role of narrative in "arranging … experiences into meaningful units," "making sense," and giving "coherence and order" to events (Polkinghorne, 2004, p. 78). The construction of meaningful life narratives requires the recognition of pattern, the ability to connect new experiences to prior experiences, the placement of individual events within pre-existing mental schemata. Traumatic events are often such that this is rendered impossible because there are no analogous prior experiences that can be brought to bear (van der Kolk and van der Hart, 1995). Even when a pattern is discernible, moreover, participating in or even witnessing traumatic events often defeats our ability to explain or rationalize. Claude Lanzmann, creator of the Holocaust documentary, *Shoah*, maintains that such events constitute an "affront to understanding," so that even the attempt to find pattern and meaning is obscene. In the face of truly inhumane events, what Lanzmann calls "active resistance to the platitudes of knowledge" is itself a creative act (1995c, p. 151–157).

This does not mean that remaining traumatized is more noble or virtuous than struggling to heal, or that bearing witness to events is never possible, but it does suggest that there are multiple ways of bearing witness and that one single narrative genre does not account for all of them. Sometimes, the only choice is silence; at other times, it is what Kurt Vonnegut called in another context "an old soldier's itch for just a little treason" (1999/1961, p. 267). Sometimes, the issue is loyalty to comrades, or the dead. The point is that stories of trauma and its survival are as amenable to a "seam of defiance" (Sagan, 2009, p. 626) as they are to "the construction of healing narratives in the face of personal, moral, and social adversity" (Josselson, cited in Clark, 2010, p. 8). The imposition of life narratives that trace a "shift from a pessimistic perception … to a more hopeful and creative one" (Randall, 2010, p. 26) is subject, and must be allowed to remain subject, to a resistance that is both existential and political.

The ghosts of war

In this context, I want to explore *Ghosts of War* (2009), a memoir of Iraq by a young veteran, Ryan Smithson, who began his book as a writing assignment for a community college composition class and published it while earning his bachelor's degree from the college in which I teach. Smithson's memoire repeatedly rejects many of the component elements of growthful personal narrative as understood in adult learning: experience as the source of learning, the self-reflective coming into meaning, and a conclusion that demonstrates that the narrator has arrived at a more coherent self.

Smithson describes the experience of a vast swirling dust devil inside the cab of an M916 tractor trailer as being "inside Satan's clothes dryer" (p. 176). Those inside the cab are blinded and disoriented, and Smithson uses the trope to undermine the coherence of experience, even in retrospect. All that can be seen inside the blinding dirt is

> how impossibly big the world is and how impossibly small we are. We learn that situations, our reactions to them, and the results that follow are all just micro-level nonsense. We are so insignificant. This country engulfs us. It's so beyond what we can see.

> *(Smithson, 2009, p. 177)*

Even when he does attempt to reflect on experience, all he can find is bafflement. The experience itself is horrific:

> We are stuck in the middle of this armpit of a city. The metallic smell of gunpowder and the dusty smell of broken concrete fill my nose. We are stuck, and people are dying. People have died.
> I want to scream. I want to cry. I want to run.
> Instead, I am watching death rain pieces of children from the sky.
>
> *(Smithson, 2009, p. 101)*

The subsequent reflection comes only as a series of questions that have no answers:

> What was the purpose for the loss of life? Was the loss of eleven Iraqis *my* gain? Does *my* life hold a higher value? Do I pity their calamity or honor their sacrifice? Am I lucky to have survived or unlucky to have witnessed those who didn't? Does my life become troubled with guilt or more meaningful?
>
> *(Smithson, 2009, p. 108; italics in original)*

The one conclusion that follows those questions is a mockery of a conclusion, as bitter as it is inadequate:

"It is my full responsibility to give purpose to myself, to my family, and to your freedom" (Ibid.). Even this question of personal responsibility is loaded with irony and paradox:

> I don't even want to think about Iraq. All I want to do is go home. Yet I know that because I'm in uniform some opinionated jerk-off is going to bombard me with his views like I care – like I had anything to do with the invasion of Iraq.
>
> *(Smithson, 2009, p. 162)*

Smithson knows, of course, that his military service has a great deal to do with the invasion of Iraq. His text, however, resists any neat summary of right and wrong. On the one hand, he never abandons his sense of responsibility and purpose. He breaks the rules to hand out Gatorade to Iraqi children because being kind to "one child at a time" is "the only way we can come out of this mess feeling like it's worth something" (p. 209). The "one true moment of glory" (p. 93) in the book consists of giving a child a bottle of clear water. On the other hand, however,

> We Americans, we're occupying their country. CNN says it's wrong, and on some level, I know it's wrong. MSNBC says the people of Iraq hate us, and on some level I know they hate us. And I know that Josh Miller – an average, redheaded farm boy – will be forced to shoot these children when they start throwing rocks at us. That's the SOP (Standard Operating Procedure).
>
> *(Smithson, 2009, p. 75)*

It is telling, I think, that Smithson's narrative was inspired by a composition teacher who did not encourage a narrative of redemption but rather asked the class to write about a time they saw something destroyed. The phrase sticks out at him "like a knife," and the story pours our through multiple drafts until he realizes that

> I need to show what was really destroyed. Not just the bombs. Not just the death. I need to show what was destroyed within me. I realize that it's the innocence of my childhood that was really lost over there in the vile, churning stomach of Iraq. And it's the soldiers with whom I lost it who really understand.
>
> *(Smithson, 2009, p. 297)*

It is difficult to imagine how Smithson's narrative could have been configured as a narrative of healing. "The hard canvas we paint in Iraq is one of scar tissue. It's a bunch of holes crudely patched with cheap concrete" (p. 191). The scar tissue and the holes are internal as well. Smithson sits at home, missing war and longing for it. He tells us it is a lot like love. War is "terrifying and horribly ugly," but it is also "glorious," "magnificent and perfect," "beautiful" (p. 308). "War is hell, but war is also paradise" (p. 309). "I miss the power, and I miss the vulnerability. I miss the innocence, and I miss the guilt. I miss the death, and I miss the life" (p. 310). Smithson's concluding pages are moving, but terrible, not evidence of healing or growth but themselves symptomatic of the loss of innocence and the difficulty of coming home. Smithson bequeaths us his trauma, as it were. He offers up his pathology as a gift. He makes the reader complicit, and the horror of it ours.

Revisiting the role of narrative

For my generation of Americans, the iconic written narrative of the trauma of war is Tim O'Brien's *The Things They Carried*. In this, his most famous work, O'Brien distinguishes clearly between the importance of telling stories about what has happened and the obscenity of a triumphalist narrative of healing or growth. The novel ends with O'Brien's image of Tim, his present, older self "trying to save Timmy's life with a story" (2009/1990, p. 233), but he famously condemns any effort to 're-story' war into a tale of uplift, acceptance, or reconciliation.

> A true war story ... does not instruct. ... If at the end of a war story you feel uplifted, or if you feel that some small bit of rectitude has been salvaged from the larger waste, then you have been made the victim of a very old and terrible lie.
>
> *(O'Brien, 2009 [1990], p. 65)*

To O'Brien, in other words, the healing power of narrative lies in *the telling itself*, not the retrospective act of finding coherence and meaning. Narrative *of* healing may be impossible, but narrative *as* healing, what Smithson (2009) calls "hanging on for the sake of sharing our story," is a vital and available form of "nobility" (p. 93).

> And this truth is what buries us in frustration. We become consumed with anger. No acceptance, no sympathy. Just pure, boiling anger. The way people don't understand, the way they can't understand – it's like a back alley full of hot metal. The only people who understand are stuck here with us, feeling the same outrage and same fear that we'll die without a chance to share our story.
>
> *(O'Brien, 2009 [1990], p. 94)*

Revisiting the uses of life writing in adult learning and opening ourselves to alternative narratives is a challenge for adult educators. Robert Lifton notes that "it is very hard, for anybody, but all the more so as a therapist or as a researcher, to sit in your office and let the details in" (as cited in Caruth 1995a, p. 144). If this is a problem for experienced therapists, I suggest it is at least as much of a problem for educators. I wonder how much of our impulse to "re-story" our students' histories into more optimistic and positive accounts reflects our own disquiet with those aspects of recent history that are beyond our ability to process or comprehend. The challenge is to listen and react to traumatic stories "in a way that does not lose their impact, that does not reduce them to clichés or turn them all into versions of the same story" (Caruth, 1995e, p. vii). How much more comfortable to restory them into a tale of hope over sorrow, coherence over chaos, and victory over adversity.

Sagan suggests that our narrative practices are one of the ways in which the "anxious regimes" of adult learning are masked by its "discourses of certainty" (2009, p. 615). That is, by constraining narratives in particular ways, we delimit what we understand our students to be saying and keep them within the well-known space of what we think we know. For educators to frame their relationship to veterans in terms of healing through re-authoring their lives codes well-being in individualized terms and thus stakes out a position that we may not intend concerning the always-immediate relationship between the personal and the political. Seen in personal terms, this is an injustice to our individual students. Seen politically, it forecloses a shared responsibility for knowing what any given war was about or what war invariably does.

This is not to say that the role of adult educators is to debate the wars in Iraq and Afghanistan with veterans and other students beyond our – and their – obligation to be responsible participants in civic and public life. Such conversations are neither easy nor self-evidently moral; they require skills, self-awareness, and mindfulness concerning many overlapping hierarchies of power, class, education, and authority, and they raise difficult questions about what constitutes evidence, knowledge, and the right to speak. Nor is it to say that we should avoid assigning life narratives to veterans. The long-standing negative cultural stereotype of the veteran – crazed with flashbacks and hyper-vigilance, angry and violent, emotionally fragile, even psychotic – continues to haunt the veterans of our current wars, whose chances of employment, for example, are demonstrably undermined by employers' fears of emotionally unbalanced veterans out of control. To the degree that we help veterans to see themselves and be seen by others as bearers of legitimate knowledge rather than as unreliable narrators of their own stories (Ehrenhaus, 1993), we engage in important acts of discursive advocacy.

The example of veterans serves to remind us, however, that narrative forms carry a politics of their own. Folding deployment to Iraq and Afghanistan into the meta-narrative of revisiting experience, finding meaning, and thus achieving psychic growth is necessarily an ideologically laden act whether or not we intend it to be. Focusing on the need to heal from psychic wounds is one thing when mental health services and protocols are being debated, but quite another when the question is one of pedagogy and narrative meaning. In that context, defining the problem and the solution as one of individual growth and resilience is an act of political containment that militates against oppositional understandings of war and serves as a form of social control over available meanings.

If a traumatic psychic injury must be understood as a pathology, then, as Caruth claims, it is "not so much a symptom of the unconscious, as it is a symptom of history." Our students' recording of their experiences of horror extends beyond their individual healing and "asks how we in this era can have access to our own historical experience" (1995b, pp. 5–6). The ways in which our students' narratives catch them up in history – and arguably, all life narratives do – behoove us to ask questions of and about that history. What story is being told? Whose story is it? Who is its audience? What possibilities are thus unleashed? As Caruth says of therapists, adult educators must learn not only to respond to individuals moving forward "but to open, in the individual and the community, new possibilities for change, a change that would acknowledge the unthinkable realities to which traumatic experience bears witness" (1995e, p. ix). In *Trauma and Memory*, Herman (1992) reminds us that telling and listening are political and social as much as they are personal, noting that attention to trauma narratives has typically been paid within the context of historical moments – and social movements – that undercut the inclination to deny the experience of the traumatized and affirm the reality of the stories being told.

If we are to do that, we must be open to stories that end in bewilderment, not reconciliation, and stop reifying the successful 're-storying' that allows us to "redeem past pains and disappointments, to regenerate the negatives of our lives into positives" (Randall, 2010, p. 31). In his discussion of his work with groups of veterans, Lifton sums up the quality of "retrospective judgment" – what we would call critical self-reflection on experience – not as a healing uncovering of meaning but in two questions posed by a group member that typify both veterans' language and their continuing bafflement: "What the hell *was* going on? What the fuck *were* we doing?" (2005, p. 37: emphasis in original). That "retrospective judgment" is not the result of a lack of self-reflection, or an inability to learn from experience, or a failure to restory the narrative of a life. It is sometimes, tragically, the only thing left to say.

Notes

1   For a critique of Knowles' individualism, see Tennant (1986). For a gender- and race-sensitive reading of these issues, see Alfred (2000) and Boucovalas (2009).
2   For a helpful review of a variety of such approaches, see Fenwick (2003).
3   Sandlin (2006), for example, offers a qualitative analysis of stories told of successful students in GED programs, finding a similar pattern of overcoming obstacles, making a decision to change one's life, choosing optimism over despair, and succeeding through the virtues of determination and hard work. Sandlin argues that these stories do a number of things: they provide a model of what we expect of ABE students, serve as a way to blame students who don't succeed, perpetuate the American "success" story, reiterate the notion that successful change is possible for everyone and reject the need such help as welfare in favor of having the right attitude, the importance of a strong moral (often religious) character,
4   For an introduction to positive psychology, see Seligman (2012). For a critique of positive psychology, see Ehrenreich (2009). For materials supporting the Comprehensive Soldier Fitness, see the Army website on CSF: http://csf.army.mil/index.html. For a critique of CSF, see Leopold (2011) and Coleman (2009).
5   http://www.washingtonpost.com/national/sundance-documentary-the-invisible-war-examines-rape-in-us-military-lack-of-prosecution/2012/01/25/gIQAdQtk PQ_story.html; http://servicewomen.org/wp-content/uploads/2011/01/SWAN-MST-fact-sheet1.pdf
6   Peter Ehrenhaus (1993) has analyzed the ways in which the public understanding of Vietnam veterans and post-Vietnam America has shifted from memories of ideological conflict and social fragmentation to a tale of personal and collective trauma, healing, and recovery.
7   For important explorations of combat-related traumatic injuries, see Shay (1995), Lifton (2005 [1973]), and Coleman (2006). For an excellent anthology of writings on trauma and memory, see Caruth (1995d). For a classic treatment of the effects of trauma, see Herman (1992).
8   For a rightfully famous example of this theme in magical realism, see the slaughter of the 3000 protesting miners in Gabriel Garcia Marquez's *One Hundred Years of Solitude* (1967 [2006]).

CONCLUSION

He saugh a mayde walkynge hym biforn,
Of which mayde anon, maugree hir heed,
By verray force, he rafte hire maydenhed.

[He saw a maiden walking before him.
In spite of all she could do, he soon,
By sheer force, robbed her of her maidenhead.]

Geoffrey Chaucer, *The Canterbury Tales*, III 886–8

As I noted in Chapter ten, the tale told by Alisoun following her famous Prologue is structured as a classic medieval romance. An ignorant young knight of King Arthur's court rapes an unfortunate young maiden, and the story tells of his subsequent lessons in wisdom and his re-admission into society. In terms of narrative structure, the *Bildungsroman* is a not-so-distant descendent of the medieval romance, the story of the social integration of wayward and ignorant youth. While the victim of the original rape fades from the story, the happy marriage that ends Alisoun's tale, like those that end *Jane Eyre* and *David Copperfield*, is the mark of reconciliation and the accommodation of personal desire with social stability.

Real tales of rape are seldom, if ever, stories of healing and reconciliation; like the maiden in Alisoun's Tale, the survivors disappear into the afterlife of horror while the world continues apace. The act of rape brings together a number of themes that have occupied these chapters. It suggests that, abstract masculinity aside, men's bodies are instruments of social power, that experience is written on the body, and that how we tell the stories of experience matter. Rape is the dream of Bakhtin's carnival turned nightmare, in which the penetrability of the gendered body is the ultimate violation of boundaries.

Alcoff and Gray (1993) have suggested that, for narratives of experience to be meaningful in the contemporary period, what we need "is not to confess, but to witness" (p. 287). Indeed, writer and Holocaust survivor Elie Wiesel has suggested that "if the Greeks invented tragedy, the Romans the epistle, and the Renaissance the sonnet," then testimony concerning horrific events such as rape is the literary genre of our time (as cited in Felman, 1995, p. 17). Wiesel's claim here speaks to the ongoing imperatives of experiential learning. Bearing witness is both a narrative act and an act of epistemological agency, and it reminds us of how contentious claims to have learned from experience still are, how fraught they are in our societies and our classrooms, and how difficult it is for educators to foster self-affirming narrative practices while avoiding re-traumatization on the one hand and vacuous platitudes on the other.

Drawing attention, as I have tried to do, to "the interactions between the clinical and the historical, between the literary and the pedagogical," Shoshana Felman (1995) asks an educator's question: after "a century that has survived unthinkable historical catastrophes, is there anything that we have learned or that we should learn about education that we did not know before?" (p. 13). In what follows, I engage Felman's question by revisiting three specific aspects of my argument in this book. I look first at the ways in which 'experiential learning' continues to be coopted by hegemonic discourses, in this case the discourse on lifelong learning and workforce development. Second, I use a final example of a life narrative to explore the gendered body as the bearer of politics and history. Finally, I conclude by asking how we might think about experience in ways that challenge rather than replicate the conventional dualisms of Western thought.

The return of history

In Part I, I argued that the notion of 'experiential learning' is contradictory, that while it is celebrated as the origin of individual freedom, it is also a mechanism through which social norms are internalized. The concept of experience, I argued, has been drained of association with the communal and sensual life of carnival through the privatization of both the body and the mind and brought into conformity with the social relations of capitalism. Arguably, that is truer now than ever; not only do we sell our experiential learning for whatever a variety of markets will bear, but we consume standardized forms of experience the commodification and management of which have become global industries. To the degree that modern capitalist societies organize, not only production, but leisure, patterns of consumption, and the mass-production of desire, the management of experience has become a way of regulating how people define themselves and construct identities.

David Harvey (1989) has noted that the standardization of experience as labor power is implicit in Marx' view of a money-based economy that links everyone through a standard mechanism of value and valuation. As a glance at one's own *curriculum vitae* suggests, experiential learning is something we own, market, and trade. Current trends in the discourse on adult learning make the field complicit with such uses of experience. Specifically, the relationship of experiential learning to workforce development – in national qualifications grids, for example – turns experience into a standardized commodity open to the fluctuations of supply and demand. In effect, the use of assessment techniques to quantify experience in an environment of high unemployment and competition for jobs and resources reenacts the standardization move of mass-production: Fordism without the job security.

Resistance to this instrumentalist view of experiential learning is on-going within mainstream adult learning theory, but has continued to come largely from Romantic and liberal humanist celebrations of uniqueness and freedom. In Part I, I traced this in terms of Maslow and Rogers' influence on Malcolm Knowles, in the connections made by multiple theorists between the freedom to "chart the course of our own destiny" (Kolb, 1984, p. 109), and, more generally, in the celebration of what Bakhtin (1984) called the "interior infinite" (p. 44). More recent treatments of experiential learning – Celeste Snowber's (2012) celebration of "dance as a way of knowing" (p. 53), for example – frame this as more embodied and holistic terms but still in those of freedom and authenticity.

There is much that is compelling in this coding of subjectivity as an alternative to technicist uses of experiential learning. If we can locate an experience of self outside hegemonic structures and the instrumentalist use of human beings, then experience can indeed be a site for transgressing repressive, overdetermined meanings and creating knowledge – i.e., learning – within a wider play of possibilities.

I have also argued, however, that such claims continue to rely on notions of a private, authentic selfhood that frames us as atomized individuals, a view that has been contested by multiple schools of thought. Marxism and other materialist theories see the privatized self as the historically derived fiction of a society in which rights inhere only in the individual. They offer an alternative understanding of human beings as developing within pre-existing social arrangements and of subjectivity as always social and relational. In a partially overlapping vein, postmodernism challenges the assumption that under all the repression and socialization is a realm of natural and pure experience. In arguing that all subjectivity is socially and linguistically constructed and that all experience is mediated by discursive structures, postmodernism rejects the idea that there is any pre-social self. If we are to develop a new understanding of experiential learning, this leaves us with a central question. How do we disentangle the quest for a substantive and life-affirming experiential realm from the notion of authentic experience unmediated by language, ideology, and structures of power? In other words, once we abandon any naïve beliefs concerning the authentically experiencing self, how do we claim a space in which experience, or something like it, can stake its claim?

Both materialism and postmodernism offer a view of the insurgency of experience that does not rely on an autonomous individual for whom authenticity requires freedom from social forces. Rather, the same social forces that create order create the possibilities for subverting that order. Stable identities, hegemonic meanings, and powerful social institutions are undermined by their own internal contradictions and incongruities. This notion, which draws both on Marxist notions of contradiction and on postmodernist views of epistemological indeterminacy, holds that hegemonic structures are never total. The transgressive possibilities of experience are not outside sociality and history, but within them; just as experience, desire, and identity are ordered within socially available meanings, so transgressive, destabilizing interventions are made possible by counter-hegemonic discourses and resistive social practices.

This suggests that there is an alternative to the autonomous knower of abstract masculinity. That alternative is named in assorted ways in contemporary critical theory −variously called border-crossing, hybridity, and, indeed, carnival − but in all cases, it is a liminal space in which binary categorizations break down. It is a space that cannot be tamed by reason, that is not fully transparent to itself, and that cannot be accounted for through notions of socialization and hegemony. As in carnival, we can welcome the excess of experience and, with it, the contingent qualities of both meaning and identity. But unlike the Romantic internalization of carnival, we can acknowledge, indeed insist on, the sociality of those meanings and identifies. By regrounding knowledge in the embodied and the social, we can dispense with the impossibly autonomous self and recognize the necessary interaction between social history and available subjectivities.

The dream of escape from history is an abiding one in Western cultures; nostalgia for a lost, authentic existence haunts even the Marxist yearning for unalienated labor and true consciousness and, as Plant (1992) has argued, postmodernist notions of molecular desires, pure events and Imaginary and pre-Symbolic realms. Reclaiming the transgressive possibilities of experience, however, overcomes the non-choice between the autonomous and the historically determined in the construction of subjectivity. Rather than postulating an experiencing self gradually freed from 'misconceptions,' 'ideologies,' 'distortions,' 'false consciousness,' 'colonized life-worlds' and other remnants of dependency, it allows us to explore the availability of meanings within our cultures and societies. The construction of meaning requires neither that we close off the boundaries of the self nor deny the experience of our own historically embedded subjectivity. Rather, experiential learning can be an exercise in opening ourselves to the transgressive, the oppositional, the Other within our own discourses and societies.

In his quest for certainty, Descartes made three moves: to withdraw from the world of passion and labor; to deny the body; and to ground both identity and certainty in the indivisibility of the mind. Carnival, that is, the transgressive possibilities of experiential learning, unmakes all three of those moves. Carnival, in this context, means working in opposition to the autonomous self of stable identity, socially authorized experience, and unitary reason. It means exploring, even claiming, subversive knowledges, excluded experience, and impossible identities. It means redefining as 'learning' that which makes us less, rather than more certain of what we know.

The return of the body

The return of the individual to history is concomitant with the return of the body to theories of experiential learning. I use 'the return of the body' in two senses here, both to indicate the need for theories of experience that do not replicate the mind/body dualism and to acknowledge that there is no final separation between one's own body and the broader socio-material world. The self is not, in Descartes' words, "only a thinking thing," but a being of visceral embodiment. Nor is it Rousseau's individualized self in the *vérité* of his uniqueness, but a being defined in and by a complex relationship to other beings and to the material world.

To explore this, I will draw on one final life narrative, Eve Ensler's recent (2013) cancer memoir, significantly named *In the Body of the World*. In this memoir, Ensler engages many of the themes that have woven through these chapters: the fragmenting of the self through trauma, disease, and war; the situatedness of the experiential learner in history; and the body, in Judith Butler's sense, as "not a 'being,' but a variable boundary" (as cited in Smith, 1994, p. 266). What happens to Ensler's own body during the experience of cancer is both the subject of the memoir and a metaphor for a politicized space in which invasion, eruption, and pollution play out on the bodies of women and the ecosphere.

As most famously the author of *The Vagina Monologues*, Ensler is closely associated with the carnal hermeneutics of plain speech, desire, bodily fluids, and the transgression of taboo. Through V-Day, a global movement to end violence against girls and women, Ensler has been active internationally in funding anti-violence organizations, women's shelters, workshops, and conferences. Most recently, she has been working in the Congo, where a thirteen-year war over mineral rights has included the horrific rape and torture of hundreds of thousands of women and girls. The bodies of the women she works with are subject to the carving, sometimes literal, of culture, power, and history: genital mutilation, sex trafficking, and rape, torture, and gynocide as instruments of war.

Midway through her work in the Congo, Ensler is diagnosed with uterine cancer that has spread to her colon and rectum. With "men cutting into it and tubes coming out of it and bags and catheters draining it and needles bruising it and making it bleed," her body is "no longer an abstraction." She is "blood and poop and pee and puss" (2013, p. 7). *In the Body of the World* is shaped around a series of parallels Ensler draws between her experience of cancer and subsequent treatment, the destruction of the ecology of the earth, and the experience of women raped and tortured by the proxy soldiers of military and corporate greed. Terrible ironies abound. A post-operative abscess ruptures her body, "spilling" and "purging" feces and pus on the same day in 2010 that the BP oil rig explodes and begins spilling oil into the Gulf of Mexico. Even more pointed, Ensler's tumor has "fistulated" her rectum, leaving her with the same kind of wound as those of the Congolese women with whom she works (p. 41).

Fistulas, holes between the vagina and the bladder and/or rectum caused by multiple rapes or rapes with objects, make women leak urine and feces continually.

They render the gathered, autonomous self doubly impossible; the body both "leaks" beyond the self-enclosure of the skin and merges with a broader geopolitics. Ensler brings the graphic power of her writing to bear on the demolishing of any sense of a privatized self: "Sometimes the bag just exploded. … My shit and it was out there. There was no more hiding it or keeping it in" (p. 150). But her cancer is itself an indication of the connections among entities whose separateness from each other is illusory and unsustainable: "Suddenly the cancer in me was everywhere. The cancer of cruelty, the cancer of greed, the cancer that gets inside people who live downstream from chemical plants, the cancer in the lungs of coal miners" (p. 7). The connections are not always easy to trace: "I don't know where governments end and corporations begin. I cannot show you exactly how the mining of the coltain that is in your cell phone is linked to Jeanne being raped in her village" (p. 211). But her unity of self is "blown apart" by stories she hears that have "entered" her (p. 41), and the tumor is "a flesh monument inside of me … spun out of the stories of women, made of tears, silent screams, rocking torsos, and the particular loneliness of violence" (p. 27). Hearing a story so vile that it "shattered [her] psyche," she falls through a "fistulated crack in the world" (p. 154).

This is powerful stuff, and yet there are moments of joy and grace in the writing. "Chemo was burning away the wrapper and suddenly I was in my version of life. Thus began the ecstasy – the joy" (p. 166). Ensler, however, explicitly refuses the illness narrative of growth through suffering. Her moments of joy and of personal insight are not framed within a trajectory of coherence, but rather an embrace of the impossibility of coherence, of "the messy, evolving, surprising, out-of-control happening that is life and reckoned with its proximity and relationship to death" (p. 88). The refusal to tell a story of psychic reconciliation is thus anything but a failure to learn from experience; rather, it is the bitter fruit of experience itself.

As we saw in the discussion of genre in Chapter eleven, the *form* of a narrative is part of its content (White, 1987). Like the writers of magical realism, Ensler refuses the illusion of a unitary narrative. Her writing is marked by sentence fragments, bullet points instead of paragraphs, and a resistance to chronology. She writes, not an integrated story line, but a series of what she calls "scans." The reference is not only a nod to the CAT scans of cancer diagnosis, but a narratological necessity: "Scanning is somehow the only way I could tell this story. Being cut open, catheterized, chemofied, drugged, pricked, punctured, probed, and ported made a traditional narrative impossible" (p. 9).

What stands in place of a chronological narrative is a scene that is, in its own way, a version of Bakhtin's carnival, a collective enactment of the breakdown of boundaries of inner and outer, self and others. Bald, incontinent, and weak from chemotherapy, Ensler returns to the Congolese refuge that she has helped to found for raped and traumatized women. The women who live in the community have a daily dancing and drumming ritual that enacts what Bakhtin (1984) called the "material bodily principle" (p. 18) that transgresses boundaries, overflows its own limits, and refuses the crafting of personal identity based on the closing off of the self.

> We do our ritual together with hundreds of the women survivors. We breathe, scream, kick, punch, release, and then there is mad drumming and we dance. … As I dance, I have no control over my bowels, and for the first time I don't care. Before when I was with the women and they were leaking from their fistulas, I could only imagine what it felt like. Now we are one wild mass of drumming, kicking, raging, leaking women.
>
> *(Ensler, 2013, p. 198)*

It is an amazing image, one of joy, certainly, of community as a "sanctuary for healing" (p. 203), and of a commitment to "turn our pain to power, our victimhood to fire, our self-hatred to action, our self-obsession to service, to fire, to wind" (p. 216). But I think that it is important to distinguish Ensler's description from a celebratory narrative denouement. Such moments come, not because this is a story of triumph, but because it is one of the things that human beings create, even in a world in which "the systematic rape, torture, and destruction of women and girls was being employed as a military/corporate tactic to secure minerals" (p. 5). It does not get us off the hook politically, and it should not distance us emotionally, from a world in which unspeakable things happen, from the "swampy pouch of unexpressed feelings" that are our bodies (p. 150), or from the implications of our own complacency.

The return of the carnival

Viewed most optimistically, the promise of experience is the promise of a realm of authentic life – thought and feeling, action and interaction, the construction of usable, sharable truths and imagination and play. It is, in other words, the promise of Bakhtin's carnival, the affirmation of a realm of sensuous, material, and relational activity in which a bracing spontaneity obtains. For all the pseudo-carnivals of a consumer culture – theme parks, shopping centers, package tourism, and the like – our societies are haunted by a hunger for more genuine forms of engagement. If we can locate an experience of self outside hegemonic ideologies and structures, then experience can indeed be a site for transgressing repressive, overdetermined meanings and creating knowledge – i.e., learning – within a wider play of possibilities.

In the Forward to *Tendencies,* her exploration of literature and sexualities, Sedgwick (1993) offers a description of the 1992 Gay Pride parade in New York City:

> [T]here was a handsome, intensely muscular man in full leather regalia, sporting on his distended chest a T-shirt that read, KEEP YOUR LAWS OFF OF MY UTERUS. The two popular READ MY LIPS T-shirts marketed by ACT-UP were also in evidence, and by the thousands. But for the first time, it was largely gay men who were wearing the version of the shirt that features two turn-of-the-century-looking women in a passionate

clutch. Most of the people wearing the version with the osculating male sailors, on the other hand, were lesbians. ... And everywhere at the march, on women and men, there were T-shirts that said simply QUEER.

(Sedgwick, 1993, p. xi)

I want to use Sedgwick's image of the Gay Pride parade, with its cross-dressing, category-defying T-shirts, as one image – there are others, certainly – of a latter-day Bakhtinian carnival. Like the carnival, it carries excess within it, both in the representation of socially unsanctioned identities and in the richness of experience that cannot be contained within technologies of social control. Possibilities for insurgent meanings emerge from the breakdown of gendered duality in which the cognitive cannot be separated from the embodied, the sexual, the parodic, and the defiant. The celebratory is nothing if not serious.

It seems to me as well that many identity regimes are coming under the kind of challenge represented by destabilized gender norms. For many, class structures are in upheaval as rising unemployment and underemployment threaten middle-class identity, and peoples in geographic and cultural flux undermine neat national borders and identities. As in carnival, the hybrid has become the norm. Our search for ourselves in such an environment – which in some ways is what 'experiential learning' means – cannot be a search for an autonomous, unitary self. Rather, we must locate our experience within a confusing historical moment in which, as William Carlos Williams wrote, "the pure products ... go crazy" (as cited in Clifford, 1988, p. 1) and in which instability and transgression alike lay siege to once-entrenched boundaries.

To be sure, many adults return to formal education to help anchor themselves in the storm. Given their wish to bolster their security through various forms of credentialing and re-training, they do not need us to tell them that the world is unstable or that insecurity and flux are on the rise. But this is also a world in which interdependence has taken on an increasingly contentious meaning. The stance one takes towards such a world, and towards the importunate demands of others, is a political issue, not simply a pedagogical one. Old forms of interaction promoted by adult educators – reason, dialogue, dispassionate inquiry – must be combined with a willingness not to wall off the self from the unreasonable, the incoherent, the passionate. Certainly, we must continue to enable students to reason with each other and attend respectfully to each other's voices and experiences. But we must also allow students to live with experiences that are not easily reducible to reason and coherence, in which the incompatible elements and unauthorized identities of Bakhtin's carnival obtain. We must ask, and allow our students to ask, what can be learned from the outrageous and the transgressive, from the wisdom of anger and desire, from the uppity-ness that refuses its place, that refuses to know its place.

I would like to close by rendering explicit a metaphor that is implicit throughout this book: namely, the idea of epistemology as a form of immunology. I have used that metaphor in several ways, first to argue that theories of experiential learning are based, in part, on the isolated knower and, second, to trace the relationship of

Enlightenment theories of knowledge to the fear both of contagion by others and of the Otherness within. As the discovery – some would say the creation – of twentieth-century science, the immune system has become central to the discourse on contagion and permeable boundaries. With its military semantics of defense and invasion (Haraway, 1991b), it has become a major framework for drawing and attempting to maintain the boundaries of the self. Through much of the century, immune system discourse has functioned as a means for negotiating what can count as self versus other, normal versus pathological, protection versus transgression in a world "full of 'difference', replete with non-self" (p. 214).

Yet contemporary immunology, Haraway contends, presents an alternative to a model of disease as an 'invasion' of the autonomous self; the immune system functions rather as testimony to the impossibility of autonomy. The immune system must be understood as negotiating the passage between rather than policing borders; it serves as "chief witness for the irreducible vulnerability, multiplicity, and contingency of every construct of individuality" (p. 220). I would like us to think of experience likewise, as the historically located but always provisional continuity between the self and the non-self. At a moment in which the attempts to ward off Otherness include everything from ethnic cleansing to vigilante border patrols, experience, like the immune system, stands as one more interface between a permeable, unstable selfhood and the multitudinous world.

BIBLIOGRAPHY

Alcoff, L., and Gray, L. (1993). Survivor discourse: Transgression or recuperation? *Signs*, 18 (2): 260–290.

Alfred, M. (2000). The politics of knowledge and theory construction in adult education: A critical analysis from an Afrocentric feminist perspective. *Proceedings of the 41st adult education research conference*. Retrieved on 4/5/2014 from: http://www.adulterc.org/Proceedings/2000/alfredm1-final.PDF

Alicea, M., Holton, D., and Tolliver, D. (2004). All of who we are: Foundations of learning at the School for New Learning, DePaul University. In E. Michelson and A. Mandell, *Portfolio development and the assessment of prior learning* (pp. 194–215). Sterling, VA: Stylus.

Allison, D. (1994). *Skin: Talking about sex, class, and literature*. Ithaca, NY: Firebrand Books.

Allison, D. (1996). *Two or three things I know for sure*. New York, NY: Penguin.

Aptheker, B. (1989). *Tapestries of life: Women's work, women's consciousness, and the meaning of daily experience*. Amherst, MA: University of Massachusetts Press.

Armstrong, N. (2005). *How novels think: The limits of individualism from 1719–1900*. New York, NY: Columbia University Press.

Asante, M. K. (1987). *The Afrocentric idea*. Philadelphia, PA: Temple University Press.

Ashley, K., Gilmore, L., and Peters, G. (Eds.). (1994). *Autobiography & postmodernism*. Amherst, MA: University of Massachusetts Press.

Baena, R. (2005). Transcultural autobiography: Forms of life writing. *Prose Studies*, 27 (3): 211–217.

Bakhtin, M. M. (1982). *The dialogic imagination: Four essays*. (M. Holquist and C. Emerson, Trans.). Austin, TX: University of Texas Press. (Original work published 1975).

Bakhtin, M. M. (1984). *Rabelais and his world*. (Helene Iswolsky, Trans.). Bloomington, IN: Indiana University Press.

Bakhtin, M. M. (1986). The *Bildungsroman* and its significance in the history of realism (toward a historical typology of the novel). In *Speech genres and other late essays*. (V. W. McGee, Trans.). Austin, TX: University of Texas Press. (Original work published 1979).

Belenky, M. F., Clinchy, M. B., Goldberger, N. R., and Tarule, J. M. (1986). *Women's ways of knowing: The development of self, voice, and mind*. New York, NY: Basic Books.

Benhabib, S. (1986). *Critique, norm, and utopia: A student of the foundations of critical theory.* New York, NY: Columbia University Press.

Benstock, S. (1988). Authorizing the autobiographical. In S. Benstock (Ed.), *The private self* (pp. 10–33). Chapel Hill, NC: University of North Carolina Press.

Bergland, B. (1994). Postmodernism and the autobiographical subject. In K. Ashley, L. Gilmore, and G. Peters (Eds.), *Autobiography & postmodernism* (pp. 130–166). Amherst, MA: University of Massachusetts Press.

Bernstein, B. (2000). *Pedagogy, symbolic control and identity: Theory, research, critique.* Revised edition. New York, NY: Rowman & Littlefield.

Blom, R., Parker, B., and Keevy, J. (2007). *The recognition of non-formal and informal learning in South Africa: Country background report prepared for the OECD thematic review on recognition of non-formal and informal learning.* Hatfield, SA: SAQA.

Bofelo, M., Shah, A., Moodley, K., Cooper, L., and Jones, B. (2013). Recognition of prior learning as "radical pedagogy": A case study of the Workers' College in South Africa. *McGill Journal of Education*, 48 (3): 511–530.

Bordo, S. (1986). The Cartesian masculinization of thought. *Signs: Journal of Women in Culture and Society*, 11 (3): 439–456.

Bordo, S. (1990). Feminism, postmodernism, and gender-skepticism. In L. Nicholson (Ed.), *Feminism/postmodernism* (pp. 133–156). New York, NY: Routledge.

Boston Women's Health Book Collective. (1971). *Our bodies, ourselves: A book by and for women.* New York, NY: Touchstone.

Boucouvalas, M. (2009). Revisiting the concept of *self* in self-directed learning. *International Journal of Self-directed Learning*, 6 (1): 1–10.

Boud, D., Cohen, R., and Walker, D. (1993). *Using experience for learning.* Bristol, UK: SRHE and Open University Press.

Boud, D., Keogh, R., and Walker, D. (1985). *Reflection: Turning experience into learning.* New York, NY: Routledge.

Bounous, R. (2001). Teaching as political practice. In V. Sheared and P. Sissel (Eds.), *Making space: Merging theory and practice in adult education* (pp. 195–208). Westport, CN: Bergin & Garvey.

Bourdieu, P. (1988). *Homo academicus.* Palo Alto, CA: Stanford University Press.

Bowers J. M. (2000). Chaucer after Smithfield: From postcolonial writer to imperialist author. In J. J. Cohen (Ed.), *The postcolonial Middle Ages* (pp. 53–66). New York, NY: St. Martin's Press.

Breier, M. (2003). *The recruitment and recognition of prior informal experience in the pedagogy of two university courses in Labour Law.* PhD thesis, University of Cape Town.

Breier, M. (2004). Horizontal discourse in law and labour law. In J. Muller, B. Davies, and A. Morais (Eds.), *Reading Bernstein, researching Bernstein* (pp. 204–217). London, UK: Routledge.

Breier, M. (2006). A disciplinary-specific approach to the recognition of prior informal experience in adult pedagogy: 'rpl' as opposed to 'RPL'. In P. Andersson and J. Harris (Eds.), *Re-theorising the recognition of prior learning* (pp. 77–96). Leicester, UK: NIACE.

Breier, M. and Burness, A. (2003). *The implementation of recognition of prior learning at universities and technikons in South Africa: Draft report.* Cape Town, SA: Centre for the Study of Higher Education, University of the Western Cape Press.

Brontë, C. (1997). *Jane Eyre.* Knoxville, TN: Wordsworth Editions. (Original work published 1847).

Brookfield, S. (1987). *Developing critical thinkers: Challenging adults to explore alternative ways of thinking and acting.* San Francisco, CA: Jossey-Bass.

Brookfield, S. (1990). Using critical incidents to explore learners' assumptions. In J. Mezirow and Associates, *Fostering critical reflection in adulthood: A guide to transformative and emancipatory learning* (pp. 177–193). San Francisco, CA: Jossey-Bass.

Brookfield, S. (1993). Through the lens of learning: How the visceral experience of learning reframes teaching. In D. Bond, R. Cohen, and D. Walker (Eds.), *Using experience for learning (Society for Research into Higher Education)* (pp. 21–33). Buckingham, UK. SRHE and Open University Press..

Brookfield, S. (2000a). Self-directed learning as a political idea. In G. Astraka (Ed.), *Conceptions of self-directed learning: Theoretical and conceptual considerations* (pp. 9–22). New York, NY: Waxmann.

Brookfield, S. (2000b). Transformative learning as ideology critique. In J. Mezirow and Associates, *Learning as transformation: Critical perspectives on a Theory in Progress* (pp. 125–148). San Francisco, CA: Jossey-Bass.

Brookfield, S. (2004). *The power of critical theory: Liberating adult learning and teaching.* San Francisco, CA: Jossey-Bass.

Brooks, P. (1984). *Reading for the plot.* New York, NY: Alfred Knopf.

Brown, A. H. (2001). African-American women of inspiration. In V. Sheared and P. Sissel (Eds.), *Making space: Merging theory and practice in adult education* (pp. 213–226). Westport, CN: Bergin & Garvey.

Brown, J. (2002). Know thyself: The impact of portfolio development on adult learning. *Adult Education Quarterly*, 52 (3): 228–245.

Brownstein, R. (1994). *Becoming a heroine.* New York, NY: Columbia University Press.

Bruner, J. (1990). *Acts of meaning.* Cambridge, MA: Harvard University Press.

Bruner, J. (2004). Life as narrative. *Social Research: An International Quarterly of Social Sciences,* 71(3): 691–710.

Butler, J. (1999). *Gender trouble: Feminism and the subversion of identity.* New York, NY: Routledge.

Butterwick, S., and Selman, J. (2012). Embodied knowledge and decolonization: Walking with theater's powerful and risky pedagogy. *New Directions for Adult and Continuing Education.* Summer. Issue 134: 61–69.

Carruthers, M. (1979). The Wife of Bath and the painting of lions. *PMLA*, 94: 209–222.

Carter, J. (2007). *The heart of whiteness: Normal sexuality and race in America, 1880–1940.* Durham, NC: Duke University Press.

Caruth, C. (1995a). An interview with Robert Jay Lifton. In C. Caruth (Ed.), *Trauma: Explorations in memory* (pp. 128–147). Baltimore, MD: Johns Hopkins University Press.

Caruth, C. (Ed.). (1995b). Introduction to Part I. In C. Caruth (Ed.), *Trauma: Explorations in memory* (pp. 3–12). Baltimore, MD: Johns Hopkins University Press.

Caruth, C. (Ed.). (1995c). Introduction to Part II. In C. Caruth (Ed.), *Trauma: Explorations in memory* (pp. 151–157). Baltimore, MD: Johns Hopkins University Press.

Caruth, C. (1995d). *Trauma: Explorations in memory.* Baltimore, MD: Johns Hopkins University Press.

Caruth, C. (1995e). Preface. In C. Caruth (Ed.), *Trauma: Explorations in memory.* (pp. vii–ix). Baltimore, MD: Johns Hopkins University Press.

Chapple, J. A. V., and Pollard, A. (Eds.). (1966). *The letters of Mrs. Gaskell.* Manchester: Manchester University Press.

Chodorow, N. (1999, original work published 1978). *The reproduction of mothering: Psychoanalysis and the sociology of gender.* Berkeley, CA: University of California Press.

Clark, M. C. (2010). Narrative learning: Its contours and possibilities. *New Directions for Adult and Continuing Education*, 126: 3–11.

Clark, M. C., and Rossiter, M. (2008). Narrative learning in adulthood. *New Directions for Adult and Continuing Education*, 119: 61–70.

Clifford, J. (1988). Histories of the tribal and the modern. In *The predicament of culture: Twentieth-century ethnography, literature, and art* (pp. 189–214). Cambridge, MA: Harvard University Press.

Codrescu, A. (1994). Adding to my life. In K. Ashley, L. Gilmore, and G. Peters (Eds.), *Autobiography & postmodernism* (pp. 22–30). Amherst, MA: University of Massachusetts Press.

Cohen, E. (1991). Who are "we"? Gay "identity" as a political (e)motion (A theoretical rumination). In D. Fuss (Ed.), *Inside/out: Lesbian theories, gay theories* (pp. 71–92). New York, NY: Routledge.

Cohen, J. B., and Piper, D. (2000). Transformation in a residential adult learning community. In J. Mezirow and Associates, *Learning as transformation: Critical perspectives on a Theory in Progress*, (pp. 205–288). San Francisco, CA: Jossey-Bass.

Coleman, P. (2000). *Village elders*. Boston, MA: Beacon.

Coleman, P. (2006). *Flashback: Posttraumatic stress disorder, suicide, and the lessons of war*. Boston, MA: Beacon.

Coleman, P. (2009). Pentagon's advice to traumatized veterans: Think happy thoughts! *AlternNet*. Dec. 9. Available at: http://www.alternet.org/world/144343/

Collins, P. H. (1991). *Black feminist thought: Knowledge, consciousness, and the politics of empowerment*. New York, NY: Routledge, Chapman, and Hall.

Cooper, L. (2006). 'Tools of mediation': An historical-cultural approach to RPL. In P. Andersson and J. Harris (Eds.), *Re-theorising the recognition of prior learning* (pp. 221–240). Leicester, UK: NIACE.

Cottom, D. (1987). *Social figures: George Eliot, social history, and literary representation*. Minneapolis, MN: University of Minnesota Press.

Crapanzano, V. (1992). *Hermes' dilemma and Hamlet's desire: On the epistemology of interpretation*. Cambridge, MA: Harvard University Press.

Crawford, M. (2009). *Shop class as soulcraft: An inquiry into the value of work*. New York, NY: Penguin.

Criticos, C. (1993). Experiential learning and social transformation for a post-apartheid learning future. In D. Boud, R. Cohen, and D. Walker (Eds.), *Using experience for learning* (pp. 157–168). Buckingham, UK: Society for Research into Higher Education/Open University Press.

Cupers, K. (2008). Governing through nature: Camps and youth movements in interwar Germany and the United States. *Cultural Geography*, 15: 173–205.

Dalmiya, V., and Alcoff, L. (1993). Are 'old wives' tales' justified? In L. Alcoff and E. Potter (Eds.), *Feminist epistemologies* (pp. 217–244). New York, NY: Routledge.

Daloz, L. A. (1988). The story of Gladys, who refused to grow: A morality tale for mentors. *Lifelong Learning: An Omnibus of Practice and Research*, 11 (4): 4–7.

Dames, N. (2001). *Amnesiac selves: Nostalgia, forgetting, and British fiction, 1810–1870*. Oxford, UK: Oxford University Press.

Davis, L. J. (1987). *Resisting novels*. New York, NY: Methuen.

Deci, E., and Ryan, R. (2000). What is the self in self-directed learning? Findings from recent motivational research. In G. Astraka (Ed.), *Conceptions of self-directed learning: Theoretical and conceptual considerations* (pp. 75–99). New York, NY: Waxmann.

Descartes, R. (1960). *Discourse on method. The rationalists*. (J. Veitch, Trans.). Garden City, NJ: Doubleday. (Original work published 1637).

Descartes, R. (1985). *The philosophical writings*. Cambridge, UK: Cambridge University Press. (Original work published in 1701).

Dewey, J. (1933). How We Think. Lexington, MA: Heath.

Dewey, J. (1958). *Experience and nature.* New York, NY: Dover. (Original work published 1925).

Dewey, J., and Bentley, A. F. (1949). Knowing and the Known. Boston, MA: Beacon.

Dickens, C. (1943). *David Copperfield.* New York, NY: Dodd, Mead, and Co. (Original work published 1850).

Dickens, C. (1950). *Dombey and son.* New York, NY: Dodd, Mead, and Co. (Original work published 1846–1848).

Dominicé, P. (1990). Composing education biographies: Group reflection through life histories. In J. Mezirow and Associates, *Fostering critical reflection in adulthood: A guide to transformative and emancipatory learning* (pp. 194–212). San Francisco, CA: Jossey-Bass.

Dominicé, P. (2000). *Learning from our lives: Using educational biographies with adults.* San Francisco, CA: Jossey-Bass.

Douglas, M. (1966). *Purity and danger.* New York, NY: Routledge.

Durkheim, E. (2008). *Elemental forms of religious life.* Unabridged US edition. New York, NY: Oxford University Press. (First published 1912).

Dyreson, M. (1999). Sport and visions of the 'American century.' *Peace Review,* 11: 565–571.

Eagleton, T. (1996). *Literary theory: An introduction.* Second edition. Minneapolis, MN: University of Minnesota Press.

Eagleton, T. (2006). *Criticism and ideology: A study in Marxist literary theory.* New York, NY: Verso. (Original work published 1976).

Ehrenhaus, P. (1993). Cultural narratives and the therapeutic motif: The political containment of Vietnam veterans. In D. K. Mumby (Ed.), *Narrative and social control: Critical perspectives* (pp. 77–96). Newbury Park, CA: Sage.

Ehrenreich, B. (2009). *Right-sided: How the relentless promotion of positive thinking has undermined America.* New York, NY: Henry Holt.

Ehrenreich, B., and English, D. (1978). *For her own good: 150 years of the experts' advice to women.* New York, NY: Anchor.

Eliot, George. (2008). *Middlemarch.* Oxford, UK: Oxford University Press. (Original work published 1874).

Engeström, Y., Miettinen, R., and Punamäki, R. L. (Eds.). (1999). *Perspectives on activity theory.* Cambridge, UK: Cambridge University Press.

Ensler, E. (2013). *In the body of the world: A memoir of cancer and connection.* New York, NY: Picador.

Ermarth, E. D. (1983). *Realism and consensus in the English novel.* Princeton, NJ: Princeton University Press.

Evans, N. (2000). *Experiential learning around the world: Employability and the global economy. Higher education policy series, 52.* Philadelphia, PA: Taylor & Francis.

Fabian, J. (1983). *Time and the other: How anthropology makes its object.* New York, NY: Columbia University Press.

Falk, P. (1994). *The consuming body.* Thousand Oaks, CA: Sage.

Faris, W. B. (2004). *Ordinary enchantments.* Nashville, TN: Vanderbilt University Press.

Felman, S. (1995). Education and crisis, or the vicissitudes of teaching. In C. Caruth (Ed.), *Trauma: Explorations in memory* (pp. 13–60). Baltimore, MD: Johns Hopkins University Press.

Fenwick, T. (2000). Expanding conceptions of experiential learning: A review of the five contemporary perspectives on cognition. *Adult Education Quarterly,* 50(4): 243–272.

Fenwick, T. (2003). *Learning through experience: Troubling orthodoxies and intersecting questions.* Malabar, FL: Krieger.

Fenwick, T. (2006a). Reconfiguring RPL and its assumptions: A complexified view. In P. Andersson and J. Harris (Eds.), *Re-theorising the recognition of prior learning* (pp. 284–300). Leicester, UK: NIACE.

Fenwick, T. (2006b). Inside out of experiential learning: Fluid bodies, co-emergent minds. In R. Edwards, J. Gallacher, and S. Whittaker (Eds.), *Learning outside the academy: International research perspectives on lifelong learning* (pp. 42–55). London, UK: Routledge.

Fenwick, T., Edwards, R., and Sawchuk, P. H. (2011). *Emerging approaches to educational research: Tracing the sociomaterial.* New York, NY: Routledge.

Ferre, M. (1980). Working class feminism: A consideration of the consequences of employment. *Sociological Quarterly*, 21 (2): 173–184.

Fischer, M. (1986). Ethnicity and the post-modern arts of memory. In J. Clifford, and G. Marcus (Eds.), *Writing culture: The poetics and politics of ethnography* (pp. 194–233). Berkeley, CA: University of California Press.

Fish, S. (1984). Authors-readers: Ben Jonson's community of the same. *Representations*, 7: 26–58.

Flannery, D. D., and Hayes, E. (2001). Challenging adult learning: A feminist perspective. In V. Sheared and P. Sissel (Eds.), *Making space: Merging theory and practice in adult education* (pp. 29–41). Westport, CN: Bergin & Garvey.

Flax, J. (1993). *Disputed subjects: Essays on psychoanalysis, politics, and philosophy.* New York, NY: Routledge.

Foucault, M. (1979). *Discipline and punish: The birth of the prison.* New York, NY: Vintage.

Foucault, M. (1995). *Discipline and punish: The birth of the prison.* Second edition. (A. Sheridan, Trans.). New York, NY: Vintage.

Fox-Genovese, E. (1988). My statue, myself: Autobiographical writings of Afro-American women. In S. Benstock (Ed.), *The private self* (pp. 63–90). Chapel Hill, NC: University of North Carolina Press.

Fradenburg, L. (1986). "The Wife of Bath's passing fancy." *Studies in the Age of Chaucer*, 8: 31–58.

Freire, P. (1974). *Pedagogy of the oppressed.* New York, NY: Seabury.

Freire, P. (1993). *Pedagogy of the oppressed.* Revised edition. New York, NY: Continuum.

Freud, S. (1989). Fragment of an analysis of a case of hysteria (Dora). In P. Gray (Ed.), *The Freud reader* (pp. 172–238). (Original work published 1905).

Friedman, S. S. (1988). Women's autobiographical selves: Theory and practice. In S. Benstock (Ed.), *The private self* (pp. 34–62). Chapel Hill, NC: University of North Carolina Press.

Fuss, D. (1991). Introduction. In D. Fuss (Ed.), *Inside/out: Lesbian theories, gay theories* (pp. 1–10). New York, NY: Routledge.

Gallagher, C. (1987). *The industrial reformation of English fiction: 1832–1867.* Chicago, IL: University of Chicago Press.

Gallop, J. (1988). *Thinking through the body.* New York, NY: Columbia University Press.

Galloway, A. (1997). Private selves and the intellectual marketplace in late fourteenth-century England: The case of the two Usks. *New Literary History*, 28 (2): 291–318.

Garber, M. (1992). *Vested interests: Cross-dressing and cultural anxiety.* New York, NY: Routledge.

Garber, M. (1997). *Vested interests: Cross-dressing and cultural anxiety.* New York, NY: Routledge.

Garrick, J., and Solomon, N. (2001). Technologies of learning at work: Disciplining the self. In V. Sheared and P. Sissel (Eds.), *Making space: Merging theory and practice in adult education* (pp. 301–313). Westport, CN: Bergin & Garvey.

Gaskell, E. (1997). *Mary Barton.* New York, NY: Penguin. (Originally published in 1848).

Gatens, M. (1988). Towards a feminist philosophy of the body. In B. Caine, E. A. Grosz, and M. M. De Lepervanche (Eds.), *Crossing boundaries: Feminisms and the critique of knowledges* (pp. 50–70). Boston, MA: Allen & Unwin.

Geertz, C. (1985). Blurred genres: The reconfiguration of social thought. In *Local knowledge: Further essays in interpretive anthropology* (pp. 19–35). New York, NY: Basic Books.

Gergen, K. (2004). Beyond life narratives in the therapeutic encounter. In J. Birren (Ed.), *Aging and biography: Explorations in adult development* (pp. 205–223). New York, NY: Springer.

Gherardi, S. (2006). *Organizational knowledge: The texture of workplace learning.* Maldon, MA: Blackwell.

Gibbons, M., Limoges, C. Nowotny, H. and Schwartzman, S. (1994). *The new production of knowledge.* New York, NY: Sage.

Gilbert, S., and Gubar, S. (1979). *The madwoman in the attic: The woman writer and the nineteenth-century literary imagination.* New Haven, CT: Yale University Press.

Gilligan, C. (1982). *In a different voice: Psychological theory and women's development.* Cambridge, MA: Harvard University Press.

Gilmore, L. (1994a). Policing truth: Confession, gender, and autobiographical authority. In K. Ashley, L. Gilmore, and G. Peters (Eds.), *Autobiography & postmodernism* (pp. 54–78). Amherst, MA: University of Massachusetts Press.

Gilmore, L. (1994b). The Mark of autobiography. In K. Ashley, L. Gilmore, and G. Peters (Eds.), *Autobiography & postmodernism* (pp. 3–18). Amherst, MA: University of Massachusetts Press.

Glick, J. (1995). Intellectual and manual labor: Implications for developmental theory. In L. Martin, K. Nelson, and E. Tobach (Eds.), *Sociocultural psychology: Theory and practice of doing and knowing* (pp. 357–382). New York, NY: Cambridge University Press.

Gordon, A. (2008). *Ghostly matters: Haunting and the sociological imagination.* Second edition. Minneapolis, MN: University of Minnesota Press.

Gouthro, P. (2009). Neoliberalism, lifelong learning, and the homeplace: Problematizing the boundaries of 'public' and 'private' to explore women's learning experiences. *Studies in Continuing Education,* 31: 157–172.

Grosz, E. (1993). Bodies and knowledges: Feminism and the crisis of reason. In L. Alcoff and E. Potter (Eds.), *Feminist epistemologies* (pp. 187–215). New York, NY: Routledge.

Grosz, E. (1994). *Volatile bodies: Toward a corporeal feminism.* Bloomington, IN: Indiana University Press.

Grudin, M. P. (2000). Credulity and the rhetoric of heterodoxy: From Averroes to Chaucer. *Chaucer Review,* 35: 204–222.

Guarino, H. (2003). AIDS and identity-construction: The use of narratives of self-transformation among clients in AIDS service organizations. Unpublished doctoral dissertation, University of Arizona.

Hall, G. (1990). The University of Massachusetts–Amherst. In A. Mandell and E. Michelson (Eds.), *Portfolio development and adult learning: Contexts and strategies* (pp. 88–98). Chicago, IL: CAEL.

Haraway, D. (1989). *Primate visions: Gender, race, and nature in the world of modern science.* New York, NY: Routledge.

Haraway, D. (1990). *Primate visions.* New York, NY: Routledge.

Haraway, D. (1991a). Situated knowledges: The science question in feminism and the privilege of partial perspective. In *Simians, cyborgs, and women: The reinvention of nature* (pp. 183–202). New York, NY: Routledge.

Haraway, D. (1991b). *Simians, cyborgs, and women: The reinvention of nature*. New York, NY: Routledge.

Haraway, D. (1997). *Modest_witness@second_millennium.FemaleMan_meets_OncoMouse™: Feminism and technoscience*. New York, NY: Routledge.

Haraway, D. (2004a). Introduction: A kinship of feminist figurations. In *The Haraway reader* (pp. 1–6). New York, NY: Routledge.

Haraway, D. (2004b). The promises of monsters: A regenerative politics for inappropriate/d others. In *The Haraway reader* (pp. 63–124). New York, NY: Routledge.

Haraway, D. (2004c). Ecce homo, ain't (ar'n't) I a woman, and inappropriate/d others: The human in a post-humanist landscape. In *The Haraway reader* (pp. 47–61). New York, NY: Routledge.

Harding, S. (1991). *Whose science? Whose knowledge? Thinking from women's lives*. Ithaca, NY: Cornell University Press.

Harding, S. (1993). Rethinking standpoint epistemology: What is 'strong objectivity'?, In L. Alcoff and E. Potter (Eds.), *Feminist epistemologies* (pp. 49–82). New York, NY: Routledge.

Harding, S. (Ed.). (2004). *The feminist standpoint theory reader: Intellectual and political controversies*. East Sussex, UK: Psychology Press.

Hart, M. (1990a). Critical theory and beyond: Further perspectives on emancipatory education. *Adult Education Quarterly*, 40: 125–138.

Hart, M. (1990b). Liberation through consciousness raising. In J. Mezirow and Associates, *Fostering critical reflection in adulthood: A guide to transformative and emancipatory learning* (pp. 47–73). San Francisco, CA: Jossey-Bass.

Hart, M. (1998). The experience of living and learning in different worlds. *Studies in Continuing Education*, 20 (2): 187–200.

Hart, S. M. (2005). Magical realism: Style and substance. In S. M. Hart and W. Ouyang (Eds.), *A companion to magical realism* (pp. 1–12). Rochester, NY: Tamesis.

Harvey, D. (1989). *The condition of postmodernity: An enquiry into the origins of cultural change*. Cambridge, MA: Basil Blackwell.

Harvey, D. (2007). *A brief history of neoliberalism*. New York, NY: Oxford University Press.

Heldke, L. (1987). John Dewey and Evelyn Fox Keller: A shared epistemological tradition. *Hypatia*, 2: 129–140.

Heldke, L., and Kellert, S. (1995). Objectivity as responsibility. *Metaphilosophy*, 26: 360–378.

Herman, J. (1992). *Trauma and recovery*. New York, NY: Basic Books.

Hiemstra, R. (2000). Self-directed learning: The personal responsibility model. In G. Astraka (Ed.), *Conceptions of self-directed learning: Theoretical and conceptual considerations* (pp. 93–108). New York, NY: Waxmann.

Hiemstra, R. (2003). More than three decades of self-directed learning: From whence have we come? *Adult Learning*, 14 (4): 5–8.

Hill, D. (2004). The wholeness of life: A Native North American approach to portfolio development at First Nations Technical Institute. In E. Michelson and A. Mandell, *Portfolio development and the assessment of prior learning* (pp. 135–159). Sterling, VA: Stylus.

Holman, D., Pavlica, K., and Thorpe, R. (1997). Rethinking Kolb's theory of experiential learning in management education: The contribution of social constructionism and activity theory. *Management Learning*, 28: 135–148.

Holstein, J. A., and Gubrium, J. F. (2000). *The self we live by: Narrative identity in a postmodern world*. Oxford, UK: Oxford University Press.

Honeychurch, K. G. (1996). Researching dissident subjectivities: Queering the grounds of theory and practice. *Harvard Educational Review*, 66: 339–355.

hooks, b. (1981). Racism and feminism: The issue of accountability. In *Ain't I a woman: Black women and feminism* (pp. 119–158). Boston, MA: South End Press.

hooks, b. (1984). Black women: Shaping feminist theory. In *Feminist theory: From margin to center* (pp. 1–15). Boston, MA: South End Press.

hooks, b. (1990). *Yearning: Race, gender, and cultural politics*. Boston, MA: South End Press.

Howden, E. (2012). Outdoor experiential education: Learning through the body. *New Directions for Adult and Continuing Education*. Summer. Issue 134: 43–51.

Hughes, R. (2008). Nurses at the 'sharp end' of patient care. In R. G. Hughes (Ed.), *Patient safety and quality: An evidence-based handbook for nurses* (pp. I-7–I-36). Rockville, MD: Agency for Healthcare Research and Quality.

Huppe, B. (1964). *A reading of The Canterbury Tales*. New York, NY: SUNY Press.

Ingham, P. (2002). Pastoral histories: Utopia, conquest, and the Wife of Bath's tale. *Texas Studies in Literature and Language*, 44 (1): 34–46.

Intemann, K. (2010). 25 years of feminist empiricism and standpoint theory: Where are we now? *Hypatia*, 25: 778–796.

Jaggar, A. (1989). Love and knowledge: Emotion in feminist epistemology. In A. Jaggar and S. Bordo (Eds.), *Gender/body/knowledge: Feminist reconstructions of being and knowing* (pp. 145–171). New Brunswick, NJ: Rutgers University Press.

Jaggar A., and Bordo, S. (1989). Introduction. In A. Jaggar and S. Bordo (Eds.), *Gender/body/knowledge: Feminist reconstructions of being and knowing* (pp. 1–12). New Brunswick, NJ: Rutgers University Press.

Jameson, F. (1981). *The political unconscious: Narrative as a socially symbolic act*. Ithaca, NY: Cornell University Press.

Jansen, J. D. (1991). Introduction. In J. D. Jansen (Ed.), *Knowledge and power in South Africa: Critical perspectives across the disciplines* (pp. 3–16). Johannesburg: Skotaville.

Jarvis, P. (1987). *Adult learning in the social context*. London, UK: Croom Helm.

Jennings, C., and Wargnier, J. (2010). Experiential learning – A way to develop agile minds in the knowledge economy? *Development and Learning in Organizations*, 24 (3): 14–16.

Johnson-Bailey, J., and Alfred, M. V. (2006). Transformational teaching and the practices of black women adult educators. *New Directions for Adult and Continuing Education*, 109: 49–58.

Justman, S. (1994). Trade as pudendum: Chaucer's Wife of Bath. *The Chaucer Review*, 28: 344–352.

Karpiak, I. (2010). Summoning the past: Autobiography as a 'movement toward possibility.' *New Directions for Adult and Continuing Education*, 126: 13–24.

Kegan, R. (2000). What 'form' transforms? A constructive-developmental perspective on transformational learning. In J. Mezirow and Associates, *Learning as transformation: Critical perspectives on a theory in progress* (pp. 35–69). San Francisco, CA: Jossey-Bass.

Kennedy, W. B. (1990). Integrating personal and social ideologies. In J. Mezirow and Associates, *Fostering critical reflection in adulthood: A guide to transformative and emancipatory learning* (pp. 99–115). San Francisco, CA: Jossey-Bass.

Kerka, S. (1994). Self-directed learning: Myths and realities. ERIC Clearinghouse on Adult, Career, and Vocational Education 3. Available at: http://eds.a.ebscohost.com.library.esc.edu/ehost/detail/detail?vid=2&sid=9b18d35e-11aa-4c0a-beb0-2cc74b06f6ab%40sessionmgr4003&hid=4110&bdata=JnNpdGU9ZWhvc3QtbGl2ZQ%3d%3d#db=eric&AN=ED365818

Kitchener, K. S., and King, P. M. (1990). The reflective judgment model: Transforming assumptions about knowing. In J. Mezirow and Associates, *Fostering critical reflection in adulthood: A guide to transformative and emancipatory learning* (pp. 159–176). San Francisco, CA: Jossey-Bass.

Knapp, P. (1990). *Chaucer and the social contest.* New York, NY: Routledge.

Knowles, M. (1990). *The adult learner: A neglected species.* Revised edition. Houston, TX: Gulf Publishing. (Original work published 1973).

Knowles, M., Holton, E., and Swanson, B. (2011). The Adult Learner: The Definitive Classic in Adult Education and Human Resource Development, 7th Edition. London: Taylor & Francis.

Kolb, D. (1984). *Experiential learning: Experience as the source of learning and development.* Englewood Cliffs, NJ: Prentice-Hall.

Langellier, K. M. (1999). Personal narrative, performance, performativity: Two or three things I know for sure. *Text and Performance Quarterly,* 19: 125–144.

Lanzmann, C. (1995). The obscenity of understanding: An evening with Claude Lanzmann. In C. Caruth (Ed.), *Trauma: Explorations in memory* (pp. 200–220). Baltimore, MD: Johns Hopkins University Press.

Larsen, H. H. (2004). Experiential learning as management development: Theoretical perspectives and empirical illustrations. *Advances in Developing Human Resources,* 6 (4): 486–503.

de Lauretis, T. (1984). *Alice doesn't: Feminism, semiotics, cinema.* Bloomington, IN: Indiana University Press.

de Lauretis, T. (1986). Feminist studies/critical studies: Issues, terms, and contexts. In T. De Lauretis (Ed), *Feminist studies, critical studies.* Vol. 8. Bloomington, IN: Indiana University Press.

Lawrence, R. (Ed.). (2012a). *Bodies of knowledge: Embodied learning in adult education. New Directions for Adult and Continuing Education.* Summer. Issue 134.

Lawrence, R. (2012b). Intuitive knowing and embodied consciousness. *New Directions for Adult and Continuing Education.* Summer. Issue 134: 5–13.

Lawrence, R. (2012c). Coming full circle: Reclaiming the body. *New Directions for Adult and Continuing Education.* Summer. Issue 134: 71–78.

Lawson, K. (1991). Philosophical foundations. In J. M. Peters (Ed.), *Adult education: Evolution and achievements in a developing field of study* (pp. 282–300). San Francisco, CA: Jossey-Bass.

Leicester, H. M. (1990). *The disenchanted self: Representing the subject in The Canterbury Tales.* Berkeley, CA: University of California Press.

Leopold, J. (2011). Army's 'spiritual fitness' test comes under fire. *Truthout.* Jan 5. Available at: http://www.truth-out.org/armys-fitness-test-designed-psychologist-who-inspired-cias-torture-program-under-fire66577

Levine, C. (2000). Harmless pleasure: Gender, suspense, and *Jane Eyre. Victorian Literature and Culture,* 28: 275–286.

Levy, A. (1991). *Other women: The writing of class, race, and gender: 1832–1898.* Princeton, NJ: Princeton University Press.

Lifton, R. (2005 [1973]). *Home from the war: Learning from Vietnam veterans.* New York, NY: Other Press.

Linde, C. (1993). *Life stories: The creation of coherence.* Oxford, UK: Oxford University Press.

Livingstone, D. W., and Sawchuk, P. H. (2005). Hidden knowledge: Working-class capacity in the 'knowledge-based economy'. *Studies in the Education of Adults,* 37: 110–122.

Locke, J. (1964). *An essay concerning human understanding.* New York, NY: Meriden. (Originally published 1689).

Longino, H. (2010). Feminist epistemology at Hypatia's 25th anniversary. *Hypatia,* 25: 733–741.

Lugg, R., Mabitla, A., Louw, G., and Angelis, D. (1998). Workers' experiences of RPL in South Africa: Some implications for redress, equity and transformation. *Studies in Continuing Education,* 20: 201–216.

Luke, C. (1992). Feminist politics in radical pedagogy. In C. Luke and J. Gore (Eds.), *Feminisms and critical pedagogy* (pp. 25–33). New York, NY: Routledge.

MacKinnon, C. (1989). *Towards a feminist theory of the state.* Cambridge, MA: Harvard University Press.

Mann, C. (2004). Learning from our experience. In E. Michelson and A. Mandell, *Portfolio development and the assessment of prior learning* (pp. 85–99). Sterling, VA: Stylus.

Marquez, G. G. (2006). *One hundred years of solitude* (Gregory Rabassa, Trans.). New York, NY: Harper. (Work first published in 1967).

Masolo, D. A. (1994). *African philosophy in search of identity.* Bloomington, IN: Indiana University Press.

Max, D. T. (2007). Happiness 101. *New York Times Magazine.* January 7. Available at: http://www.nytimes.com/2007/01/07/magazine/07happiness.t.html?ex= 1325826000&en=2e27ba2144dae290&ei=5090&partner=rssuserland&emc=rss

Maynes, M. J. (1989). Gender and narrative form in French and German working-class autobiographies. In The Personal Narratives Group (Eds.), *Interpreting women's lives: Feminist theory and personal narratives* (pp. 103–117). Bloomington, IN: Indiana University Press.

Merchant, C. (1980). *The death of nature: Women, ecology, and the scientific revolution.* New York, NY: Harper & Row.

Merchant, C. (2008). The violence of impediments. *Isis,* 99: 731–760.

Merriam, S. B. (2001). Andragogy and self-directed learning: Pillars of adult learning theory. *New Directions for Adult and Continuing Education,* 89: 3–13.

Merriam, S. B., Caffarella, R. S., and Baumgartner, L. M. (2007). *Learning in adulthood: A comprehensive guide.* San Francisco, CA: Jossey-Bass.

Meyer, P. (2012). Embodied learning at work: Making the mind-set shift from workplace to playspace. *New Directions for Adult and Continuing Education.* Summer. Issue 134: 25–32.

Mezirow, J. (1990a). How critical reflection triggers transformative learning. In J. Mezirow and Associates, *Fostering critical reflection in adulthood: A guide to transformative and emancipatory learning* (pp. 1–20). San Francisco, CA: Jossey-Bass.

Mezirow, J. (1990b). Conclusion: Toward Transformative Learning and Emancipatory Education. In J. Mezirow & Associates, *Fostering critical reflection in adulthood: A guide to transformative and emancipatory learning* (pp. 354–376). San Francisco, CA: Jossey-Bass.

Mezirow, J. (1991). *Transformative dimensions of adult learning.* San Francisco, CA: Jossey-Bass.

Mezirow, J. (2000). Learning to think like an adult. In J. Mezirow and Associates, *Learning as transformation: Critical perspectives on a theory in progress* (pp. 3–33). San Francisco, CA: Jossey-Bass.

Michelson, E. (1998). Re-membering: The return of the body to experiential learning. *Studies in Continuing Education,* 20: 217–234.

Michelson, E. (1999). Social transformation and the recognition of prior learning: Lessons for and from South Africa. *South African Journal of Higher Education,* 13: 99–102.

Michelson, E. (1997). The politics of memory. In S. Walters (Ed.), *Globalisation: Rethinking adult education and training* (pp. 141–153). London, UK: Zed Books.

Michelson, E. (2004). On trust, desire, and the sacred: A response to Johann Muller's Reclaiming Knowledge. *Journal of Education*, 32: 7–30.

Michelson, E. (2012). Report and recommendations to the South African Qualifications Authority based on international models of the recognition of prior learning. *SAQA Bulletin*, 12 (3): 11–34.

Michelson, E., and Mandell, A. (2004). Introduction. In *Portfolio development and the assessment of prior learning* (pp. 1–20). Sterling, VA: Stylus.

Miettinen, R. (2000). The concept of experiential learning and John Dewey's theory of reflective thought and action. *International Journal of Lifelong Education*, 19: 54–72.

Miller, A. (1957). *Death of a salesman*. In *Collected plays*. New York, NY: Viking. (Original work published 1949).

Miller, J. L. (1998). Autobiography as a queer curriculum practice. In W. F. Pinar (Ed.), *Queer theory in education* (pp. 301–308). Mahwah, NJ: Lawrence Erlbaum Associates.

Minnich, E. K. (2004). *Transforming knowledge*. Second edition. Philadelphia, PA: Temple University Press.

Mizco, N. (2003). Beyond the fetishism of words: Considerations on the use of the interview to gather chronic illness narratives. *Qualitative Health Research*, 13: 469–490.

Mohanty, C. T. (1988). Under Western eyes: Feminist scholarship and colonial discourses. *Feminist Review*, 30: 61–88.

Mohanty, C. T. (1992). Feminist encounters: Locating the politics of experience. In M. Barrett and A. Phillips (Eds.), *Destabilizing theory: Contemporary feminist debates* (pp. 74–92). Palo Alto, CA: Stanford University Press.

Mohanty, C. (2003). 'Under Western Eyes' revisited: Feminist solidarity through anticapitalist struggles. *Signs*, 28 (2): 499–535.

Mohanty, S. (2000). The epistemic status of cultural identity: On beloved and the postcolonial condition. In P. Maya and M. Hames-Garcia (Eds.), Reclaiming identity: Realist theory and the predicament of postmodernism (pp. 29–66). Berkeley, CA: University of California Press.

Moya, P. (2000). Postmodernism, 'realism', and the politics of identity: Cherríe Moraga and Chicana feminism. In P. Moya and M. Hames-García (Eds.), *Reclaiming identity: Realist theory and the predicament of postmodernism* (pp. 67–101). Telangana, India: Orient Blackswan.

Mudimbe, V. Y. (1988). *The invention of Africa: Gnosis, philosophy, and the order of knowledge*. Bloomington, IN: Indiana University Press.

Muller, J. (2000). *Reclaiming knowledge: Social theory, curriculum, and education policy*. New York, NY: Routledge.

Mumby, D. (1993). Introduction. In *Narrative and social control: Critical Perspectives* (pp. 1–14). Newbury Park, CA: Sage.

Murphy, E. J. (2007). A review of Bloom's taxonomy and Kolb's theory of experiential learning: Practical uses for prior learning assessment. *Journal of Continuing Higher Education*, 55 (3): 64–66.

Myers, M. (1988). Pedagogy as self-expression in Mary Wollstonecraft. In S. Benstock (Ed.), *The private self* (pp. 192–210). Chapel Hill, NC: University of North Carolina Press.

Nead, L. (1992). *The female nude: Art, obscenity and sexuality*. New York, NY: Routledge.

Nieves, Y. (2012). Embodying women's stories for community awareness and social action. *New Directions for Adult and Continuing Education*. Summer. Issue 134: 33–42.

Noble, D. (1992). *A world without women: The Christian clerical culture of Western science*. New York, NY: Oxford University Press.

O'Brien, T. (1990/2009). *The things they carried*. New York, NY: Houghton Mifflin Harcourt.

Ochs, E., and Capps, L. (1996). Narrating the self. *Annual Review of Anthropology*, 25: 19–43.

Oksala, J. (2004). Anarchic bodies: Foucault and the feminist question of experience. *Hypatia*, 19 (4): 97–119.

Olssen, M. (2006). Understanding the mechanism of neoliberal control: Lifelong learning, flexibility and knowledge capitalism. *International Journal of Lifelong Education*, 25: 213–230.

O'Reilly, D. (1989). On being an educational fantasy engineer: Incoherence, 'the individual' and independent study. In S. W. Weil and I. McGill (Eds.), *Making sense of experiential learning: Diversity in theory and practice* (pp. 94–100). Milton Keynes, UK: Society for Research into Higher Education/Open University Press.

Osman, R. (2004). After apartheid: The recognition of prior learning at the College of Education, University of the Witwatersrand. In E. Michelson and A. Mandell, *Portfolio development and the assessment of prior learning* (pp. 255–269). Sterling, VA: Stylus.

Osman, R. (2006). RPL: An emerging and contested practice in South Africa. In P. Andersson and J. Harris (Eds.), *Re-theorising the recognition of prior learning* (pp. 205–220). Leicester, UK: NIACE.

Ouyang, W. (2005). Magical realism and beyond: Ideology of fantasy. In S. M. Hart and W. Ouyang (Eds.), *A companion to magical realism* (pp. 13–19). Rochester, NY: Tamesis.

Oxford English Dictionary. (1971). Oxford, UK: Oxford University Press.

Park, K. (1984). Bacon's 'enchanted glass'. *Isis*, 75: 290–303.

Pateman, C. (1988). *The sexual contract*. Palo Alto, CA: Stanford University Press.

Patterson, L. (1983). For the wyves love of Bathe: Feminine rhetoric and poetic resolution in the *Roman de la Rose* and the *Canterbury Tales*. *Speculum*, 58: 656–695.

Peters, H., Pokorny, H., and Johnson, L. (2004). Cracking the code: The assessment of prior experiential learning at London Metropolitan University. In E. Michelson and A. Mandell, *Portfolio development and the assessment of prior learning* (pp. 160–179). Sterling, VA: Stylus.

Plant, S. (1992). *The most radical gesture: The situationist international in a postmodern age*. New York, NY: Routledge.

Plumb, D., Leverman, A., and McGray, R. (2007). The learning city in a 'planet of slums'. *Studies in Continuing Education*, 29: 37–50.

Pokorny, H. (2006). Recognising prior learning: What do we know? In P. Andersson and J. Harris (Eds.), *Re-theorising the recognition of prior learning* (pp. 261–281). Leicester, UK: NIACE.

Polanyi, M. (1958). *Personal knowledge*. Chicago, IL: University of Chicago.

Polkinghorne, D. (2004). Narrative knowing and the study of lives. In J. Birren (Ed.), *Aging and biography: Explorations in adult development* (pp. 77–99). New York, NY: Springer.

Poovey, M. (1988). *Uneven developments: The ideological work of gender in mid-Victorian England*. Chicago, IL: University of Chicago Press.

Pratt, M. (1986). Fieldwork in common places. In J. Clifford and G. E. Marcus (Eds.), *Writing culture: The poetics and politics of ethnography* (pp. 27–50). Berkeley, CA: University of California Press.

Pratt, M. K. (1991). Arts of the contract zone. *Profession*, 91: 33–40.

Putney, C. (2001). *Muscular Christianity: Manhood and sports in Protestant America, 1880–1920.* Cambridge, MA: Harvard University Press.

Randall, W. (1996). Restorying a life: Adult education and transformative learning. In J. E. Birren, G. Kenyon, J.-E. Ruth, and J. J. F. Schroots (Eds.), *Aging and biography: Explorations in adult development* (pp. 224–247). New York, NY: Springer.

Randall, W. (2004). Restorying a life: Adult education and transformative learning. In J. Birren (Ed.), *Aging and biography: Explorations in adult development* (pp. 224–247). New York, NY: Springer.

Randall, W. (2010). Storywork: Autobiographical learning in later life. *New Directions for Adult and Continuing Education,* 126: 25–36.

Redinger, R. V. (1975). *George Eliot: The emergent self.* Colchester, UK: Bodley Head.

Reeves, E. (1999). Old wives' tales and the New World system: Gilbert, Galileo, and Kepler. *Configuations,* 7 (3): 301–354.

Rhys, J. (1982). *Wide Sargasso Sea.* New York, NY: Norton. (Original work published 1966).

Rich, A. (1979). Jane Eyre: The temptations of a motherless woman. *On lies, secrets, and silence: Selected prose 1966–1978* (pp. 89–106). New York, NY: Norton.

Rich, A. (1986). *Of woman born: Motherhood as experience and institution.* New York, NY: Norton.

Robertson, D. W. Jr. (1962). *A preface to Chaucer: Studies in medieval perspectives.* Princeton, NJ: Princeton University Press.

Robertson, K. (2000). Common language and common profit. In J. J. Cohen (Ed.), *The Postcolonial Middle Ages* (pp. 209–228). New York, NY: Palgrave Macmillan.

Robinson, F. N. (Ed.). (1957). *The works of Geoffrey Chaucer* Second edition. Cambridge, MA: Houghton Mifflin.

Root, J. (1994). 'Space to speke': The Wife of Bath and the discourse of confession. *Chaucer Review,* 28: 252–274.

Rossiter, M. (1999). Understanding adult development as narrative. *New Directions for Adult and Continuing Education,* 84: 77–85.

Rossiter, M., and Clark, M. C. (2010). Editors' conclusion. *New Directions for Adult and Continuing Education,* 126: 89–91.

Roth, I. (1990). Challenging habits of expectation. In J. Mezirow and Associates, *Fostering critical reflection in adulthood: A guide to transformative and emancipatory learning* (pp. 116–133). San Francisco, CA: Jossey-Bass.

Rousseau, J.-J. (2003). *Emile, or on education* (W. H. Payne, Trans.). Amherst, NY: Prometheus. (Originally published in 1762).

Ruddick, S. (1989). *Maternal thinking: Toward a politics of peace.* Boston, MA: Beacon.

Rushdie, S. (1981). *Midnight's children.* London, UK: Picador.

Ruth, J. (2006). *Novel professions: Interested disinterest and the making of the professional in the Victorian novel.* Columbus, OH: The Ohio State University Press.

Rydell, S. (2004). Building on the past, moving toward the future: Prior learning assessment in a changing institution at Metropolitan State University. In E. Michelson and A. Mandell (Eds.), *Portfolio development and the assessment of prior learning* (pp. 180–193). Sterling, VA: Stylus.

Sagan, O. (2009). Anxious provision and discourses of certainty: The sutured subject of mentally ill adult learners. *International Journal of Lifelong Education,* 28 (5): 615–629.

Said, E. (1978). *Orientalism.* New York, NY: Pantheon.

Said, E. (1994). *Culture and imperialism.* New York, NY: Vintage.

Sandlin, J. (2006). Horatio Alger and the GED diploma: Narratives of success in adult literacy education. *Literacy & Numeracy Studies,* 15 (1): 79–96.

Sarbin, T. R. (Ed.). (1986). *Narrative psychology: The storied nature of human conduct.* Cambridge, MA: Harvard.

Sawchuk, P. H. (2005). Activity and power: Everyday life and development of working-class groups. In P. H. Sawchuk, N. Duarte, and M. Elhammoumi (Eds.), *Critical perspectives on activity: Explorations across education, work, and everyday life* (pp. 245–269). New York, NY: Cambridge University Press.

Scott, J. W. (1991). The evidence of experience. *Critical Inquiry*, 17: 773–799.

Seaman, J. (2008). Experience, reflect, critique: The end of the 'learning cycles' era. *Journal of Experiential Education*, 31: 3–18.

Sedgwick, E. K. (1993). Foreword. In *Tendencies* (pp. xi–xvi). Durham, NC: Duke University Press.

Seigfried, C. H. (2001). Beyond epistemology: From a pragmatist feminist experiential standpoint. In N. Tuana and S. Morgen (Eds.), *Engendering rationalities* (pp. 99–121). Albany, NY: SUNY Press.

Seligman, M. (2012). *Flourish: A visionary new understanding of happiness and well-being.* Reprint edition. New York, NY: Free Press.

Shalem, Y., and Steinberg, C. (2006). Portfolio-based assessment of prior learning: A cat and mouse chase after invisible criteria. In P. Andersson and J. Harris (Eds.), *Retheorising the recognition of prior learning* (pp. 97–116). Leicester, UK: NIACE.

Shapin, S. (1994). *A social history of truth: Civility and science in seventeenth century England.* Chicago, IL: University of Chicago Press.

Shay, J. (1995). *Achilles in Vietnam: Combat trauma and the undoing of character.* New York, NY: Touchstone.

Shied, F. (2001). Struggling to learn, learning to struggle: Workers, workplace learning, and the emergence of human resource development. In V. Sheared and P. Sissel (Eds.), *Making space: Merging theory and practice in adult education* (pp. 124–137). Westport, CN: Bergin & Garvey.

Shotwell, A. (2011). *Knowing otherwise: Race, gender, and implicit understanding.* University Park, PA: Pennsylvania State University Press.

Sitas, A. (2011). Why are we so disabled? Higher Education and the RPL challenge. In *Proceedings, National RPL Conference: Bridging and expanding existing islands of excellent practice* (pp. 14–19). Pretoria, SA: SAQA.

Slaughter, J. R. (2007). *Human rights, inc.: The world novel, narrative form, and international law.* New York, NY: Fordham University Press.

Slemon, S. (1995). Magic realism as postcolonial discourse. In L. P. Zamora and W. B. Faris (Eds.), *Magical realism: Theory, history, community* (pp. 407–426). Durham, NC: Duke University Press.

Smith, D. (1987). *The everyday world as problematic: A feminist sociology.* Boston, MA: University of Massachusetts Press.

Smith, S. (1994). Identity's body. In K. Ashley, L. Gilmore, and G. Peters (Eds.), *Auto-biography and postmodernism* (pp. 266–292). Amherst, MA: University of Massachusetts Press.

Smithson, R. (2009). *Ghosts of war: The true story of a 19-year-old GI.* New York, NY: Harper-Collins.

Snowber, C. (2012). Dance as a way of knowing. *New Directions for Adult and Continuing Education*. Summer. Issue 134: 53–60.

Solomon, N., and Gustavs, G. (2004). Corporatizing knowledge: Work-based learning at the University of Technology, Sydney. In E. Michelson and A. Mandell, *Portfolio development and the assessment of prior learning* (pp. 255–269). Sterling, VA: Stylus.

Spivak, G. (1985). Three women's texts and a critique of imperialism. *Critical Inquiry*, 12: 243–261.

Spivak, G. (1988a). French feminism in an international frame. In *In other worlds: Essays in cultural politics* (pp. 134–153). New York, NY: Routledge.

Spivak, G. (1988b). Can the subaltern speak? In C. Nelson and L. Grossman (Eds.), *Marxism and the interpretation of culture* (pp. 271–313). New York, NY: Macmillan.

Stallybrass, P., and White, A. (1986). *The politics and poetics of trangression*. Ithaca, NY: Cornell University Press.

Stanley, L. (1992). Is there a lesbian epistemology? *Feminist Praxis* monograph no. 34, University of Manchester.

Starr-Glass, D. (2002). Metaphor and totem: Exploring and evaluating prior experiential learning. *Assessment and Evaluation in Higher Education*, 27: 221–231.

Stephan, L. (2011). *The English utilitarians*. Vol. I. Cambridge: Cambridge University Press. (Originally published in 1900).

Stevens, M. E. (2011). Trauma's essential bodies. In M. J. Casper and P. Currah (Eds.), *Corpus: An interdisciplinary reader on bodies and knowledge* (pp. 171–186). New York, NY: Macmillan.

Stone-Mediatore, S. (1998). Chandra Mohanty and the Revaluing of 'Experience'. *Hypatia*, 13: 116–133.

Sullivan, S. (2001). *Living across and through skins: Transactional bodies, pragmatism, and feminism*. Bloomington, IN: Indiana University Press.

Swartz, A. (2012). Patient education: From nurses' self-awareness to patient self-caring. *New Directions for Adult and Continuing Education*. Summer. Issue 134: 15–24.

Tate, P. (1993). Foreword. In B. G. Sheckley, L. Lamdin, and M. T. Keeton (Eds.), *Employability in a high performance economy* (pp. xv–xviii). Chicago, IL: CAEL.

Taylor, K. (2000). Teaching with developmental intention. In J. Mezirow and Associates, *Learning as transformation: Critical perspectives on a theory in progress* (pp. 151–180). San Francisco, CA: Jossey-Bass.

Taylor, K., Marienau, C., and Fiddler, M. (2000). *Developing adult learners*. San Francisco, CA: Jossey-Bass.

Tedeschi, R., and McNally, R. (2011). Can we facilitate posttraumatic growth in combat veterans? *American Psychologist*, 66 (1): 19–24.

Tennant, M. (1986). An evaluation of Knowles' theory of adult learning. *International Journal of Lifelong Education*, 5 (2): 113–122.

Tennant, M. (2005). Transforming selves. *Journal of Transformative Education*, 3: 102–115.

Tinkle, T. (2010). Contested authority: Jerome and the Wife of Bath on 1 Timothy W. The Chaucer Review 44 (3): 268–293.

Tisdell, E. (1998). Poststructuralist feminist pedagogies: The possibilities and limitations of feminist emancipatory adult learning theory. *Adult Education Quarterly*, 48: 139–156.

Tondreau, D. M. (2003). Weaving storylines in adult education: The narrative construction of self, society, and structures of knowledge. (Unpublished doctoral dissertation). Union Institute and University.

Torgovnick, M. (1990). *Gone primitive: Savage intellects, modern lives*. Chicago, IL: University of Chicago Press.

Toulmin, S., and Goodfield, J. (1999). *The fabric of the heavens: The development of astronomy and dynamics*. Chicago, IL: University of Chicago Press.

Tuana, N. (2001). Introduction. In N. Tuana and A. Morgen (Eds.), *Engendering rationalities* (pp. 1–20). Albany, NY: SUNY Press.

Usher, R., and Solomon, N. (1999). Experiential learning and the shaping of subjectivity in the workplace. *Studies in the Education of Adults*, 31: 155–163.

Vadim, V., and Arnett, M. (Directors and Producers). (nd). *The quilts of Gee's Bend*. United States: Tinwood.

van der Kolk, B., and van der Hart, O. (1995). The intrusive past: The flexibility of memory and the engraving of trauma. In C. Caruth (Ed.), *Trauma: Explorations in memory* (pp. 158–182). Baltimore, MD: Johns Hopkins University Press.

Vicinus, M. (1974). *The industrial muse*. London, UK: Croom Helm.

Vonnegut, K. (1999/1961). *Mother night*. Reissue edition. New York, NY: Dial.

Vygotsky, L. (1978). *Mind in society: The development of higher psychological processes*. M. Cole, V. John-Steiner, S. Scribner, and E. Souberman (Eds.). Cambridge: MA: Harvard University Press.

Walker, A. (1973). Everyday use. *In love and trouble: Stories of black women* (pp. 47–59). San Diego, CA: Harcourt.

Walkerdine, V. (1988). *The mastery of reason: Cognitive development and the production of rationality*. New York, NY: Routledge.

Warner, M. (1993). Introduction. In M. Warner (Ed.), *Fear of a queer planet: Queer politics and social theory* (pp. vi–xxxi). Minneapolis, MN: University of Minnesota Press.

Watt, I. (1959). *The rise of the novel: Studies in Defoe, Richardson, and Fielding*. Berkeley, CA: University of California Press.

Webb, I. (1981). *From custom to capital: The English novel and the Industrial Revolution*. Ithaca, NY: Cornell University Press.

Weiler, K. (1991). Freire and a feminist pedagogy of difference. *Harvard Education Review*, 61: 449–474.

Weintraub, K. (1978). Value of the individual: Self and circumstance in autobiography. In K. Joachim and K. Weintraub (Eds.), *The value of the individual: Self and circumstance in autobiography*. Chicago, IL: University of Chicago Press.

Werquin, P. (2012). Enabling recognition of non-formal and informal learning outcomes in France: The VAE legislation. *SAQA Bulletin*, 12 (3): 55–117.

Whitaker, U. (1989). *Assessing learning: Standards, principles, and procedures*. Chicago, IL: CAEL.

White, H. (1987). *The content of the form*. Baltimore, MD: Johns Hopkins University Press.

Wildemeersch, D., and Jansen, T. (Eds.). (1992). *Adult education, experiential learning and social change: The postmodern challenge*. Driebergen: Vuga.

Wilson, A., and Hayes, E. (2002). From the editors: The problem of (learning in-from-to) experience. *Adult Education Quarterly*, 52 (3): 173–175.

Winterson, J. (1993). *Written on the body*. New York, NY: Vintage.

Wollstonecraft, M. (2008). *A vindication of the rights of woman with strictures on political and moral subjects*. New York, NY: Cosimo Classics. (Work first published in 1792).

Wood, M. (1975). *America in the Movies: Or 'Santa Maria, it had slipped my mind.'* New York, NY: Basic Books.

Wood, M. (2005). *Literature and the taste of knowledge*. Cambridge: Cambridge University Press.

INDEX